INSTITUTIONAL ETHNOGRAPHY AS PRACTICE

INSTITUTIONAL ETHNOGRAPHY AS PRACTICE

Edited by
Dorothy E. Smith

ROWMAN & LITTLEFIELD PUBLISHERS, INC.
Lanham • Boulder • New York • Toronto • Oxford

ROWMAN & LITTLEFIELD PUBLISHERS, INC.

Published in the United States of America
by Rowman & Littlefield Publishers, Inc.
A wholly owned subsidiary of The Rowman & Littlefield Publishing Group, Inc.
4501 Forbes Boulevard, Suite 200, Lanham, Maryland 20706
www.rowmanlittlefield.com

PO Box 317
Oxford
OX2 9RU, UK

British Library Cataloguing in Publication Information Available

Library of Congress Cataloging-in-Publication Data

Institutional ethnography as practice / edited by Dorothy E. Smith.
p. cm.
Includes bibliographical references and index.
ISBN-13: 978-0-7425-4676-9 (cloth : alk. paper)
ISBN-10: 0-7425-4676-4 (cloth : alk. paper)
ISBN-13: 978-0-7425-4677-6 (pbk. : alk. paper)
ISBN-10: 0-7425-4677-2 (pbk. : alk. paper)
1. Ethnology—Methodology. 2. Ethnology—Research. 3. Feminist anthropology. 4. Applied anthropology. I. Smith, Dorothy E., 1926–
GN345.I377 2006
305.8'001—dc22 2005034034

Printed in the United States of America

Contents

Figures

Acknowledgments

WE ACKNOWLEDGE WITH thanks and appreciation permission to reprint received from the publishers of two papers that appear in this book.

Thanks to Sage Publications for permission to reprint Marjorie L. DeVault and Liza McCoy's "Institutional Ethnography: Using Interviews to Investigate Ruling Relations," which appeared originally in Gubrium, J. F., and Holstein, J. A., eds. *Handbook of Interviewing Research: Context and Method,* Thousand Oaks, CA: Sage Publications (2002), pp. 751–775.

Thanks also to Kluwer Academic/Plenum Publishers for permission to reprint Marie Campbell's "Institutional Ethnography and Experience as Data," originally appearing as an article in *Qualitative Sociology* vol. 21, no.1 (1998), pp. 55–73.

I, the editor, also want to add special thanks to Alison Griffith without whom I'd not have survived getting the manuscript to the publisher on time.

1
Introduction

Dorothy E. Smith

THIS BOOK IS NOT A MANUAL; it is not a "how-to-do-it" collection that will give you all the answers, tell you exactly how to produce a piece of research that others can recognize as institutional ethnography, solve all the problems you run into in doing and writing up your ethnographic research, or otherwise provide you with models with which you can bring your work into conformity. It is not intended to confine, discipline, or subordinate your own experience of institutional ethnographic work. Though there are certainly some definite principles of procedure, there are also many ways of realizing them in practice. This must be so. Institutional ethnography is committed to exploration and discovery. It takes for granted that the social happens and is happening and that we can know it in much the same way as it is known among those who are right in there doing it. With this major difference: institutional ethnography is committed to discovering *beyond any one individual's experience* including the researcher's own and putting into words supplemented in some instances by diagrams or maps what she or he discovers about how people's activities are coordinated.

It is important that institutional ethnography not become a sect, a group of insiders who know how to talk and write it, and insist on a kind of orthodoxy in its practice which puts in hazard its fundamental commitment to inquiry and discovery. Institutional ethnography is distinctive among sociologies in its commitment to *discovering* "how things are actually put together," "how it works." The colloquialisms leave what "things" are or what "it" is undefined but establish the ideas of encountering the actualities of people's everyday lives, of research that discovers the social as the ongoing coordinating of people's activities, and of the researcher as being changed in the dialogic of research. Hence although there is theory formulating how institutional ethnography might be thought as a sociology with such a commitment, although there is excellent practical advice about how to go about it, and although, in this volume, there are examples, models, technical notions, and other sources based on the experience of practitioners, none of these are intended to impose an orthodoxy.

Inquiry, discovery, learning, as central to the institutional ethnographic project means orienting toward effective research practices rather than methodological dogma. Practitioners engaged in different areas are confronted with different research exigencies; different research strategies are evolved as researchers work through the engagement of their own research inclinations—and people differ greatly in terms of what interests them, what they are responsive to, and what they attend to—with the actualities of the social in the region they have chosen to explore.

At the same time, and ambiguously, there is something to get hold of without which what is claimed as institutional ethnography falls on its face or never gets going at all. I'm not sure if I can formulate it adequately. It's to do with recognizing that you are always there, that what you discover is always seen, interpreted, heard, experienced by you as you are situated historically in the ongoing, never-stand-still of the social. It is the recognition that the social as your research phenomenon is to be found in that ongoing process of which you're part. Reifying the concepts that you may use to hang on to what you can observe and giving them substance in your written account is at odds with recognizing that what we're calling the social is only to be discovered among actual people and their ongoing activity. Concepts such as "social relations" or "social organization" have no corresponding reality as such. What is to be discovered is essentially in motion; concepts such as these freeze for inspection and analysis, dimensions of the complexly coordinated and historically embedded doings of people but must not be treated as if they refer to objects out there.

Institutional ethnography isn't about studying institutions as such. Rather it proposes a sociology that does not begin in theory but in people's experience. In avoiding theories that command interpretive allegiance it avoids commitment to the institutions of sociology that deploy the political effect of theory to master other voices. Writing a sociology for people doesn't just mean writing a sociology about matters of public concern. The phrase *for people* adapts an earlier statement I made when it was still central to recognize the masculine-centered character of the sociology of those earlier times in the women's movement and to propose to write by contrast a sociology *for women.* Taking women's standpoint in the everyday worlds of women's traditional work in home and with children meant beginning where we are as bodies in the actualities of our lives and exploring the society as it embeds, masters, organizes, shapes, and determines those actualities as we live them.

The idea is to reorganize sociology as a knowledge of society so that inquiry begins where people are and proceeds from there to discoveries that are for them, for us, of the workings of a social that extends beyond any one of us, bringing our local activities into coordination with those of others. The project is to extend people's ordinary good knowledge of how things are put together in our everyday lives to dimensions of the social that transcend the local and are all the more powerful and significant in it for that reason. We participate in them without knowing what we are doing.

From the beginning I have been writing about doing institutional ethnography as a method of research that followed from taking up women's/people's standpoint in the local actualities of the everyday. It is not meant as a way of discovering the everyday world as such, but of looking out beyond the everyday to discover how it came to happen as it does. A diagram I drew as part of my first explication of "institutional ethnography" (Smith 1987) displays these relations.

Our small hero, active in the work of mothering as a single parent, is implicated thereby in a complex of relations beyond her view. We, researchers, take up our inquiry from that site. Our research looks up through that complex from her standpoint, discovering just how it works so that she is engaged in it as she is. This is the project that Alison Griffith and I (Griffith and Smith 2005) undertook many years ago. Alison (Griffith 1984) explored first the "single parent" discourse (see chapter 7) that shaped both how we knew how to think of ourselves as single parents and how teachers and school administrators

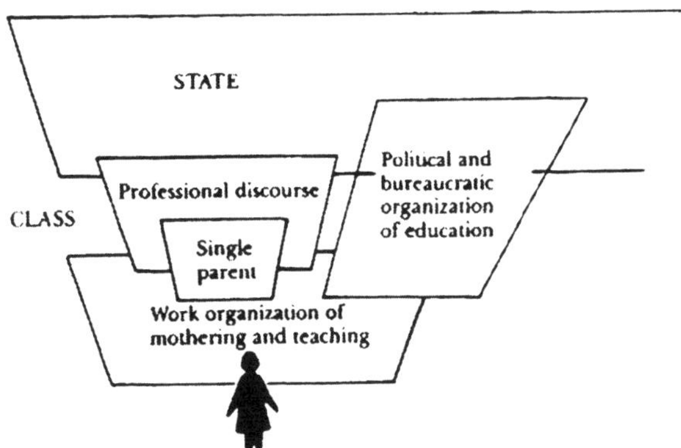

FIGURE 1.1.
A Woman's Standpoint: Single Parenthood and Educational Institutions

related to us and to our children. The "single parent" discourse is a subdiscourse of the professional discourse of educators establishing for them a common language that *knows* the world of children, parents, and schools and suspends or subsumes experiential knowledge. The work organization of mothering is articulated thereby to the work of schooling, both that of mothers and that of teachers, which in turn is organized politically and administratively as an extension of government or the state. In discovering these relations, we also discover (rather than presuppose) class and discover the relationship between the work of mothering, which is where we started, and how public schools operate to reproduce inequalities of class.

The reach of inquiry goes from where actual people are in their own lives, activities, and experiences to open up relations and organization that are, in a sense, actually *present* in them but are not observable. Institutional ethnography aims to discover and make visible so that from where our small hero stands, she can see how things are coming about for her as they do.[1]

Tim Diamond designed, for use in a graduate course on institutional ethnography, a schema (figure 1.2) for an institutional ethnography research

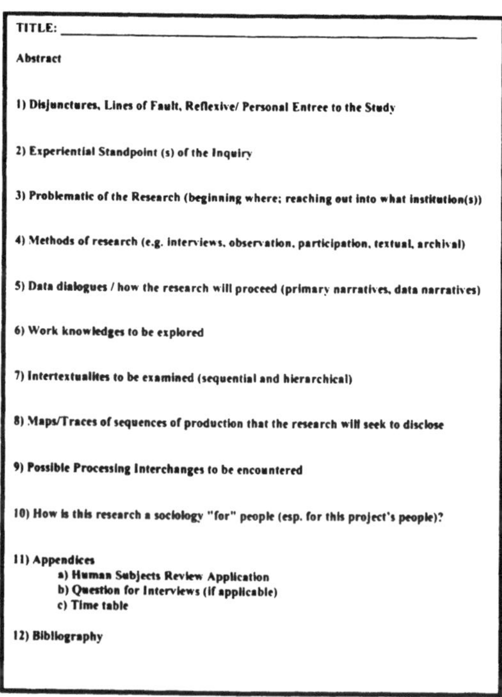

TITLE: ______

Abstract

1) Disjunctures, Lines of Fault, Reflexive/ Personal Entree to the Study

2) Experiential Standpoint (s) of the Inquiry

3) Problematic of the Research (beginning where; reaching out into what institution(s))

4) Methods of research (e.g. interviews, observation, participation, textual, archival)

5) Data dialogues / how the research will proceed (primary narratives, data narratives)

6) Work knowledges to be explored

7) Intertextualites to be examined (sequential and hierarchical)

8) Maps/Traces of sequences of production that the research will seek to disclose

9) Possible Processing Interchanges to be encountered

10) How is this research a sociology "for" people (esp. for this project's people)?

11) Appendices
- a) Human Subjects Review Application
- b) Question for Interviews (if applicable)
- c) Time table

12) Bibliography

FIGURE 1.2.
An Institutional Ethnography Research Proposal

proposal. It isn't intended as a proposal for funding. For that, readers should take a look at the proposal submitted to the National Welfare Grants program of Health Canada by George Smith, Eric Mykhalovskiy, and Douglas Weatherbee (chapter 9) in part III of this book. Diamond's proposal is a design for how institutional ethnographic research might proceed. I'm reproducing it here. You'll be able to see how it conforms to the diagram in figure 1.1.

That looking up from where you are, or from the where of some people whose experience of and in the everyday you've learned from and developed as the problematic of your study—it's that looking up and into as a process of investigation, of progressive discovering, and assembling what you've got as a base from which to move to investigating further and more widely that's the key to institutional ethnography.

The diagram of "A Woman's Standpoint: Single Parenthood and Educational Institutions" (figure 1.1) shows a small heroic figure standing there, at the bottom, peering into the ruling relations that tower above her. This diagram provides a frame for the papers collected as chapters in this volume. Each takes up a different aspect of or approach to the journey of exploration that starts where our small hero stands.

The first section is a collection of three papers focused on some of the different methods of research that institutional ethnographies have used and do use. Marjorie DeVault and Liza McCoy (chapter 2) have created a wholly new genre of methodological writing. Rather than drawing on a literature, consulting sources, or reviewing the current status of institutional ethnographic interviewing techniques in various studies, they have taken the innovative step of talking to institutional ethnographers about their interviewing practices. Using interviews, focus groups, and e-mail exchanges with institutional ethnographers, they not only draw on the experience of researchers in the field, but also exemplify interviewing strategies that explore people's work knowledge, in this case, the work knowledge of institutional ethnographic researchers. The variety of researchers' experiences with institutional ethnographic interviewing contributes to an overall consistency of interview objectives that combines with flexibility and responsiveness to the local settings and specific research objectives.

Tim Diamond (chapter 3) has written about participation as an ethnographic method in institutional ethnography. His chapter draws on his experience of doing an ethnography based on working as a nursing assistant in two senior citizens' residences in Chicago. He has written one of the great sociological ethnographies based on his work (Diamond 1992), and in this paper, he describes how he went about his study, focused his observations, located the institutional in the immediacy of observation, and what he learned. In addition he raises two major issues for institutional ethnographers: First, he addresses the topic of covert research, that is, of research that is done without the consent or knowledge of the organization or institution that is being observed. This was the situation of his original research. In writing his ethnography, he makes visible aspects of how residences for seniors work that are less than desirable, indeed that made him angry. It is unlikely he would have been allowed access to make those observations if he had sought consent. The ethical issues as well as the politics of ethical reviews are not so simple and he confronts them straightforwardly. A second major issue for institutional ethnography raised in his chapter is that of the centrality of taking a standpoint in the body, where someone actually *is* in the local settings of our/their lives. Because institutional processes are essentially mediated by and based in texts, it's easy for research to become preoccupied with the textual and, hence, to lose touch with the embodied actualities of people's work. Diamond does not leave this issue merely as critique but explores what might be done *in practice* to preserve what he calls the "corporeal incarnate."

The topics of interviews and of participant observation are treated by their authors as autonomous methods. My introduction to how texts may be incorporated into ethnographic practice (chapter 4) is put forward less as a method in itself than as a supplement to researches in which other methods may predominate. I am concerned in that paper with how to integrate texts into ethnographies that focus on people's actual activities and how they're coordinated. In institutional settings, texts are integral to the coordinating and institutional appropriation of what people are doing. But it's hard to think of texts as *occurring* in the local times and spaces of people's doings. This chapter suggests how that might be done and hence how texts could be incorporated into ethnographies as part of the action.

The second section takes up issues of what data looks like and when it's been gathered and what you can do with it. There are four papers: first, Marie Campbell (chapter 5) describes with examples from her own work just what *experience* can look like when it's captured by the inquiring researcher. Though she raises the postmodernist questioning of experience as a resource for researchers, she does not enter that debate. For the institutional ethnographer, the issue is not whether a subject's speaking about her or his experience of how things are and happen is shaped by how she or he is positioned and by the discursive contexts in which it is spoken. Rather Campbell, using her research into the introduction of new managerial strategies into a long-term care hospital, shows how institutional ethnography can draw on people's experiential—and diverging—knowledge of their work (in the generous sense of the term). Her ethnography discloses and analyzes just how the everyday work of the nurses in the hospital is reorganized as the new management approach is imposed.

Notice in her account how she captures those dimensions of people's experience that locate the institutional in the everyday of their work. Those she talked to were participating in processes of institutional transformation ("restructuring"); they had a piece of it in their hands, so to speak. The key, as she shows, is to recognize how the experience of informants can be drawn on by the ethnographer to show "how the experience came to happen as it did" (see chapter 5, p. 91). She learns of people's work experience by talking to them. In this respect, her approach differs from Tim Diamond's (described in chapter 3), who, as participant observer, was himself actually on the job, making his observations as he went along and working on them in his time off. His ethnography relies on his own experience and upon the work knowledge he developed in the course of learning and doing the job. Campbell constructs her ethnography by talking with those who are on the job and building an account based on their experience and work knowledges.

DeVault and McCoy (chapter 2) stress the centrality of starting with people's experience. Campbell shows how the experiential resources of those on the job can become the researcher's data. You can begin with your own, as Tim Diamond (chapter 3) does in his participant observational interview. You can expand from your own experience, as did Alison Griffith and I (see chapter 7), and then stretch out to engage with others similarly engaged in the institutional process that organized your own experience. Alison and I talked to other mothers about the work they did in relation to their children's schooling. That and our own experiences, as we rediscovered in this new light of inquiry, opened up the problematic of our study. McCoy in her paper (chapter 6) in this section proposes an alternative procedure. Studies often begin with interviews with a number of people focused on a theme or issues they have in common. McCoy, with her associates, interviewed or held focus groups with seventy-nine people, all with AIDS or being HIV positive. Her interest was in their experiences and thinking about the physicians they encountered. She shows us how easy it would be to focus on these as individuals, to create typologies of the different ways in which,they approached or responded to the physicians they encounter. An institutional ethnographic approach, however, does not study individuals; yet in this instance this is all the researchers have. Using examples from the interviews, she shows us first how to read what they talk about as work—the work of thinking about how to relate to a physician, the work of going to visit the doctor, of attending to what she or he says, and so on. The concept of work represents the informants as active and, from this point of view, we can begin to see them as encountering and working with and within health care institutions that are implicit in their accounts. Here then, for the institutional ethnographer, would be a place to open up inquiry into the institutional organization he or she encounters. Here is a problematic being given shape by the experiences of the people interviewed.

So McCoy shows how, starting in people's everyday lives, the institutional appears as a dark region remaining to be explored. Check back with the figure 1.1 diagram. Again we're starting where the small hero stands, only this time we have a number of different accounts. They are all, however, engaged with the same general institutional process. It is present; it is there; it can be found as a place to start investigation even when all you have is people's accounts of their everyday experiences. She shows us a place to start, a takeoff point for further study. In elucidating the institutional presence in people's experiential accounts, McCoy lays the basis for the complementary investigation into the institutional complex in which her informants were active.

McCoy's chapter demonstrates, though incidentally to its main topic, that discovering the problematic that will organize a piece of research will not usually depend on one person's experience. She shows an escape hatch out of institutional discourse: medical discourse can't take a standpoint such as that of our small hero of figure 1.1. Institutional discourse sets up a way of seeing in terms of its specialized functions. People aren't as they are in actuality but are expressions of pregiven categories: doctor, patient, nurse, pharmacist, and so on. Institutional ethnography, by contrast, shows us a place to start in the everyday as people experience it and a way to go in exploring the relevant dimensions of the institutions, which include the institutional discourse. From that standpoint, institutional discourse appears in its articulations to the institutional complex to be explored.

Here's where Alison Griffith's chapter (chapter 7) kicks in. She describes her discovery and systematic exploration of an institutional discourse she calls the *single parent discourse.* It was and is a discourse that organizes institutional practices. It creates an orthodoxy of interpretation among professionals who participate in it that can be applied to particular mothers without spouses in the home (and it is specifically applicable to mothers) constituting them and their children as "single parent families" and denying authority to those who might speak from their experience. This was the discourse that Alison and I had known how to apply to ourselves as well as how others were applying it to us. The small hero of figure 1.1, however, stands there *looking at it.* She's no longer hooked into it without knowing what it is. Griffith's chapter shows us how to *see* the single parent discourse; she provides in exemplary fashion, an account of how she discovered how the single parent discourse operates to organize institutional practices in various locations including public school systems. Uniquely, she addresses the texts of the single parent discourse as data; media stories, research studies, and educational policies are shown to coordinate and be coordinated by notions of single parent families as different.

Susan Turner (chapter 8) starts us on a different kind of journey. She has developed a method of mapping institutional process that is specific to institutional ethnography and that is a wonderfully powerful means of assembling the complex data of text-work-text or work-text-work sequences that make up institutional action. Our small hero gazes up into nothing as simple as a maze; the latter has at least a beginning and an end. She cannot find her way in there; she has to learn from the work knowledges of those who actually bring into being the processes she is caught up in and yet is trying to see and—imagining her now as researcher—explore and explicate. Turner's chapter shows us how to locate the pieces of institutional processes and assemble the interconnections of people's work and the texts that coordinate their work with that of others. The multiple interchanges (see Pence 2001) where texts come in to be processed and texts are sent forward for others to process are seen now as the interconnections of a complex sequence. The focus shifts from *position* to the *relations* that accomplish the institutional processes consequential for a small hero's everyday life concerns. The power of the institutional process is to catch her up in such a way that she too participates in its production. The power of Turner's method is to enable research to arrive at a map that is a *schematic representation* analyzing an institutional process, showing how it operates and its institutional properties. It is a method that makes it possible to see just how what happens is produced in the interrelations of people's work and the texts that coordinate it.

The final section looks towards how research might proceed. It provides three very different accounts. The first of these (chapter 9) is in the format of a research proposal that was made to a Canadian federal government department by George W. Smith, Eric Mykhalovskiy, and Doug Weatherbee. The proposal was successful in winning funding, though its outcomes did not fully realize the original objectives largely because of the death from AIDS of its senior author, George W. Smith. The proposal represents a tense and succinct practical realization of the principles of institutional ethnography. The topic of how government institutions of health care (I remind readers that this is Canada), welfare, and housing are coordinated in relation to people with AIDS or who are HIV positive could be imagined as one that examines, for example, the adequacy of information flows among them. That would be to take an institutional standpoint. This proposal is a radical inversion of that procedure. It proposes to explore the work involved in living with AIDS or being HIV positive from the standpoint of people who were, at the time of the proposal, doing it.

The concept of work has been emphasized in several chapters. It is an important one for institutional ethnography, expanding the ordinary usage of the term. Generally used in the context of paid employment, the women's movement discovered that somehow most of what is done in the home, traditionally a specialization of women, was not recognized as work. The institutional ethnographic usage builds on that conception to include anything or everything people do that is intended, involves time and effort, and is done in a particular time and place and under definite local conditions. Conceiving of living with AIDS as work was and still is a radical move. Tracking back to early chapters in this volume, you will find the same conception, notably in Campbell's and McCoy's chapters (chapters 5 and 6). Its application in the Smith, Mykhalovskiy, and Weatherbee funding proposal to examine how the institutional complex articulates to the work of living with AIDS is exemplary.

The second chapter (chapter 10) in this final section is an analysis developed by Lauren Eastwood to examine the processes within the United Nations that both enable Indigenous People to speak their experience and ensure that it can be heard and taken up only on terms already under its discursive control. Her chapter is written at an early point in the development of her ongoing research. Previously, she had done an institutional ethnography of the workings of the United Nations Forestry Forum (Eastwood 2005), taking up a problematic from the standpoint of nongovernmental organizations concerned with environmental issues. The ethnography she is opening up in this paper draws on her knowledge and analysis of the practical politics of documentation and the wording of documents in projecting past agreements, negotiations, and compromises into the future. Text and discourse are analytically opened up to show them as they create diffuse but significant organizational possibilities that others can take up and deploy in subsequent action. The potentiality for ethnographic explorations at levels such as these is radically enhanced by her studies.

The final paper (chapter 11) originates in Mending the Sacred Hoop, a group of Indigenous professionals who came together to address issues of the domestic abuse procedures of the U.S. judicial system. Institutional ethnography is drawn into and adapted to an Indigenous epistemology that shapes the research practice in ways that respond to the traditional cultures of the Indigenous community in that region (intersecting the border between Canada and the United States). Going beyond issues specific to Indigenous women's experience, Alex Wilson and Ellen Pence explicate critically the very character of judicial institutions and, by implication, beyond them. From an Indigenous People's standpoint, they raise issues for the very foundations of governing institutions in North America. Their chapter concludes with the natural next step that follows from an institutional ethnography, namely proposals for change, for doings things differently, for adopting approaches and measures that avoid the failures that research and analysis have brought to light.

So this is where this book ends. I'd like to conclude it with a "To Be Continued," as readers find in it ways of discovering how we are ruled and participate in our ruling and are then able to make plain to people (including themselves) just how it works.

Note

1. I strongly recommend that readers who want to get an institutional ethnography going consult Marie Campbell's and Fran Gregor's admirable lucid and practical introduction to institutional ethnography (Campbell and Gregor 2002). Their book is distributed in the United States by Rowman & Littlefield.

Part I

INSTITUTIONAL ETHNOGRAPHIC DATA: INTERVIEW, OBSERVATION, AND TEXT

INSTITUTIONAL ETHNOGRAPHY EXPLORES actual people's activities as they coordinate in those forms we call institutions. Ethnographers use whatever method is practicable (taking into account among other things, the research economy) and appropriate in opening up those aspects of institutional process with which they engage. Marjorie DeVault and Liza McCoy have assembled varieties of institutional ethnographic experience of interviewing, drawing on their own interviews with the ethnographers rather than on the literature; Timothy Diamond introduces participant observation; and Dorothy Smith proposes ways of making texts ethnographically accessible.

institutional ethnography → not about inner experience, but rather "relations of ruling" and how these relations shape local experiences

ontology = social as the concerting of peoples activities
↓
def = nature of existence

institutional ethnography → text based discourse
institution = clusters of text-mediated relations organized around specific ruling functions

inst eth → sequences of interconnected activities

inst eth interviewing → organized around "work"; point of interest is the informants activities and interconnected activities of others
have to move beyond institutional language
processing interchanges → where work processes intersect
focus not on theory building but on what actually happens

2

Institutional Ethnography: Using Interviews to Investigate Ruling Relations

Marjorie L. DeVault and Liza McCoy

SOCIAL RESEARCHERS USE INTERVIEWS in various ways, but they usually think of interviews as sources for learning about individual experience. In this chapter, we discuss interviewing as part of an approach designed for the investigation of organizational and institutional processes. In this alternative to conventional forms of interview research, investigators use informants' accounts not as windows on the informants' inner experience but in order to reveal the "relations of ruling" that shape local experiences (Smith 1996a).

We use the term *institutional ethnography*, following Canadian sociologist Dorothy E. Smith, to refer to the investigation of empirical linkages among local settings of everyday life, organizations, and translocal processes of administration and governance. These linkages constitute a complex field of coordination and control that Smith (1999) identifies as "the ruling relations"; these increasingly textual forms of coordination are "the forms in which power is generated and held in contemporary societies" (p. 79). Smith (1987) introduced the term *institutional ethnography* in writing about a "sociology for women," illustrating with her studies of mothers' work at home in relation to their children's schooling, but she understands the term as having wide application. Those who have followed Smith in developing institutional ethnography have investigated many different social processes, including the regulation of sexuality (Khayatt 1995; Kinsman 1996; G. W. Smith 1998); the organization of health care (Campbell 1988, 1995, 1999; Diamond 1992; Mykhalovskiy 2000; Mykhalovskiy and Smith 1994; G. W. Smith 1995), education (Andre Bechely 2005; Griffith 1984, 1992; Stock 2000), and social work practice (de Montigny 1995b; Parada 1998); police and judicial processing of violence against women (Pence 1996); employment and job training (K. M. Grahame 1998); economic restructuring (McCoy 1999); international development regimes (Mueller 1995); planning and environmental policy (Eastwood 2005; Turner 1995); the organization of home and community life (DeVault 1991; Luken and Vaughan 1991, 1996; Naples 1997); and various kinds of activism (Ng 1996; Walker 1990).

Over the past two decades, a loosely organized network of institutional ethnographic researchers has emerged in North America, the members of which meet regularly to share developing projects and refinements of these methods.[1] This chapter surveys the work of that network. In preparing the discussion that follows, we have examined published examples of institutional ethnographic research, interviewed practitioners (individually and in small groups), and collected accounts of research practices and reflections via e-mail. We understand institutional ethnography as an emergent mode of inquiry, always subject to revision and the improvisation required by new applications. Thus we wish to emphasize that we do not intend any prescriptive orthodoxy. Rather, we hope to introduce this approach, provide practical information about it that is often unarticulated in published work, and reflect on unresolved issues of research practice. Because many of the specifics of institutional ethnographic interviews are the same as the "good practices" used by researchers conducting other kinds of interviews (methods of gaining access, building rapport, probing for specific accounts, listening carefully, and so on), we highlight distinctive practices associated with institutional ethnographic studies.

In the following section, we provide an introduction to this research approach and consider various uses of interviewing in institutional ethnography projects. Next, we discuss the conduct of interviews. The subsequent section foregrounds the key role of texts and institutional discourses in institutional ethnography, showing how interviews can be oriented toward these aspects of social organization. We then turn to analysis and writing in relation to institutional ethnographic interviews.

Institutional Ethnography as a Mode of Inquiry

Dorothy Smith proposes institutional ethnography as part of an "alternative sociology," an approach she describes as combining Marx's materialist method and Garfinkel's ethnomethodology with insights from the feminist practice of consciousness-raising. "In different ways, all of these ground inquiry in the ongoing activities of actual individuals" (Smith 1999: 232, n. 5). Analytically fundamental to this approach is an ontology that views the social as the concerting of people's activities. This is an ontology shared by phenomenologists, symbolic interactionists, and ethnomethodologists. Smith expands this through the concept of social relations, which, as in Marx, refers to the coordinating of people's activities on a large scale, as this occurs in and across multiple sites, involving the activities of people who are not known to each other and who do not meet face-to-face.

In contemporary global capitalist society, the "everyday world" (the material context of each embodied subject) is organized in powerful ways by translocal social relations that pass through local settings and shape them according to a dynamic of transformation that begins and gathers speed somewhere else (e.g., if the local hospital closes, the explanation will not be wholly local). Smith (1990b) refers to these translocal social relations that carry and accomplish organization and control as "relations of ruling":

> They are those forms that we know as bureaucracy, administration, management, professional organization, and the media. They include also the complex of discourses, scientific, technical, and cultural, that intersect, interpenetrate, and coordinate the multiple sites of ruling. (p. 6)

A central feature of ruling practice in contemporary society is its reliance on text-based discourses and forms of knowledge, and these are central in institutional ethnography (a topic we return to later).[2]

Building on this conception of ruling, Smith's notion of institution points to clusters of text-mediated relations organized around specific ruling functions, such as education or health care. Institution, in this usage, does not refer to a particular type of organization; rather, it is meant to inform a project of empirical inquiry, directing the researcher's attention to coordinated and intersecting work processes taking place in multiple sites. For example, when health care is considered as an institution, what comes into view is a vast nexus of coordinated work processes and courses of action—in sites as diverse as hospitals, homes, doctors' offices, community clinics, elementary schools, workplaces, pharmacies, pharmaceutical companies, advertising agencies, insurance companies, government ministries and departments, mass media, and medical and nursing schools. Obviously, institutions cannot be studied and mapped out in their totality, and such is not the objective of institutional ethnography. Rather, the aim of the institutional ethnographer is to explore particular corners or strands within a specific institutional complex, in ways that make visible their points of connection with other sites and courses of action. Thus Timothy Diamond is studying the organization of health benefits in the United States, which he examines in its character as a text-mediated relation connecting the activities of individuals, their employers, insurance companies, hospitals, pharmacies, and so on (focus group, August 1999).

Institutional ethnography takes for its entry point the experiences of specific individuals whose everyday activities are in some way hooked into, shaped by, and constituent of the institutional relations under exploration. The term *ethnography* highlights the importance of research methods that can discover and explore these everyday activities and their positioning within extended sequences of action. When interviews are used in this approach, they are used not to reveal subjective states, but to locate and trace the points of connection among individuals working in different parts of institutional complexes of activity. The interviewer's goal is to elicit talk that will not only illuminate a particular circumstance but also point toward next steps in an ongoing, cumulative inquiry into translocal processes. As Peter Grahame (1999) explains, "The field continuously opens up as the researcher explores the institutional nexus that shapes the local" (p. 7; see also P. R. Grahame 1998).

The researcher's purpose in an institutional ethnography is not to generalize about the group of people interviewed, but to find and describe social processes that have generalizing effects. Thus interviewees located somewhat differently are understood to be subject, in various ways, to discursive and organizational processes that shape their activities. These institutional processes may produce similarities of experience, or they may organize various settings to sustain broader inequalities (as explored in DeVault 1999: chap. 5); in either case, these generalizing consequences show the lineaments of ruling relations. For example, George W. Smith (1998) treated the gay young men he interviewed not as a population of subjects, but as informants knowledgeable about school life for gay youth. He explains:

> The interviews opened various windows on different aspects of the organization of this regime. Each informant provides a partial view; the work of institutional ethnography is to put together an integrated view based on these otherwise truncated accounts of schools. (p. 310)

The general relevance of the inquiry comes, then, not from a claim that local settings are similar, but from the capacity of the research to disclose features of ruling that operate across many local settings.

Institutional ethnographies can "fit together"—much like the squares of a quilt (Smith 1987)—because they share the same organizing ontology and the same focus on generalizing processes of ruling. Thus Janet Rankin's (1998, 2003) study of nurses' work and administrative categories in a British Columbia hospital extends the analysis in Eric Mykhalovskiy's (2000) study of health services research and hospital restructuring in Ontario, and both extend the analysis in Liza McCoy's (1999) study of accounting texts and restructuring in another area of the public sector in Canada. This does not mean that the three studies consciously locate their analyses in relation to one another, but that through the analytic frame they share they can be seen to be describing different moments and aspects of the same generalizing set of relations.

Dorothy Smith's work on the social organization of knowledge predates the emergence of feminist sociology, but her formulations gained increasing power as she situated them within a community of activist feminist scholars seeking a transformative method of inquiry (DeVault 1999). Institutional ethnographers generally have critical or liberatory goals; they undertake research in order to reveal the ideological and social processes that produce experiences of subordination. For example, in Smith's classic feminist text *The Everyday World as Problematic* (1987), the idea is to "begin from women's experiences" and to take as the problematic for the research the question of how such experiences are produced. This notion shares with much feminist writing an interest in women's previously excluded views, but it uses women's accounts only as a point of entry to a broader investigation. The idea is to shift from a focus on women themselves (as in a sociology "of women") to a kind of investigation that could be useful in efforts to change the social relations that subordinate women and others.

Institutional ethnographers aim at specific analyses of social coordination; the liberatory potential of the approach comes from its specification of possible "levers" or targets for activist intervention. Some institutional ethnographic research has emerged directly from the researcher's position as activist (Pence 1996; G. W. Smith 1990); these projects may be driven and targeted directly toward questions arising from activist work. Some academic researchers work collaboratively with activists: Roxana Ng with garment workers' unions, Marie Campbell with people who have disabilities, and Mykhalovskiy and McCoy with AIDS activists, for example. And some academics (and other professionals) research processes that shape their own work settings, often exploring the peculiar ways in which they themselves are implicated in ruling relations despite their intentions (de Montigny 1995b; Parada 1998). Whatever the position of the researcher, the transformative potential of institutional ethnographic research comes from the character of the analysis it produces; it is like a "map" that can serve as a guide through a complex ruling apparatus.

Possible Shapes of Institutional Ethnographic Projects

Institutional ethnography is driven by the search to discover "how it happens," with the underlying assumptions that (a) social "happening" consists in the concerted activities of people and (b) in contemporary society, local practices and experiences are tied into extended social relations or chains of action, many of which are mediated by documentary forms of knowledge.

Institutional ethnographic researchers set out to provide analytic descriptions of such processes in actual settings. There is no "one way" to conduct an institutional ethnographic investigation; rather, there is an analytic project that can be realized in diverse ways. Institutional ethnographies are rarely planned out fully in advance. Instead, the process of inquiry is rather like grabbing a ball of string, finding a thread, and then pulling it out; that is why it is difficult to specify in advance exactly what the research will consist of. Institutional ethnographers know what they want to explain, but only step-by-step can they discover whom they need to interview or what texts and discourses they need to examine. In the discussion that follows, we describe some common "shapes" or trajectories of institutional ethnographic research.

Beginning with Experience

A common—even a "classic"—approach to institutional ethnography (recommended by Dorothy Smith 1987) begins with the identification of an experience or area of everyday practice that is taken as the experience whose determinants are to be explored. The researcher seeks to "take the standpoint" of the people whose experience provides the starting point of investigation. For example, George Smith (1988) begins from the experience of gay men who were arrested by police in a series of sweeping raids on gay bathhouses; Didi Khayatt (1995) begins from the experience of young lesbian women in high school; Campbell and her associates begin from the experience of people attempting to live independently with physical disabilities (see Campbell 1998b, 1999); Diamond (1992) begins from the experience of people, mostly women, who work as nursing assistants in nursing homes for the elderly; and Susan Turner (1995) begins from the experience of community residents seeking to stop a developer from destroying a wooded ravine. In all of these studies, the researchers go on to investigate the institutional processes that are shaping that experience (e.g., the work of policing, the work of teaching and school administration, the organization of home care services, the administration of Medicare and nursing homes, the organization of municipal land use planning). The research follows a sequence: (a) identify an experience, (b) identify some of the institutional processes that are shaping that experience, and (c) investigate those processes in order to describe analytically how they operate as the grounds of the experience.

The researcher can employ a range of data collection techniques to explore the experience that provides the starting place and identifies the problematic. Most common among these techniques are interviews and focus groups, participant observation, and the researcher's reflection on her or his own experience, all of which serve to generate descriptions of what people do in their everyday lives. The analytic enterprise is paramount, however, and ways of realizing it are diverse. Many institutional ethnographers use individual and group interviews. For example, Khayatt (1995) conducted interviews with young lesbians. Campbell and her associates conducted interviews with people living with disabilities (see Campbell 1998b). Paul Luken and Suzanne Vaughan (1998; Vaughan and Luken 1997), along with older women informants, generated oral histories regarding the women's housing activities. Dorothy Smith, Liza McCoy, and Paula Bourne (1995) conducted focus group interviews with girls in secondary school. Bresalier and associates (2002) conducted focus groups with men and women living with HIV/AIDS about their experience of looking after their health. Through informants' stories and descriptions, the researcher begins to identify some of the translocal relations, discourses, and institutional work processes that are shaping the informants' everyday work.

Some institutional ethnographers spend considerable time at this point of entry (for it can take time to understand the complexity of an experience, and data from this exploration can provide material with much analytic potential). In other cases, a researcher may begin from an experience that he or she knows something about, or where the problematic is already clear (e.g., G. W Smith 1990; Walker 1990). Eventually, however, the researcher will usually need to shift the investigation to begin examining those institutional processes that he or she has discovered to be shaping the experience but that are not wholly known to the original informants. Thus a second stage of research commonly follows that usually involves a shift in research site, although not in standpoint. Often, this shift carries the investigation into organizational and professional work sites. At this stage, other forms of research and analysis may come to be used. The researcher may employ observation and the analysis of naturally occurring language data to examine institutional work processes, for example. Or the researcher may use text and discourse analysis to examine the textual forms and practices of knowledge that organize those work processes. But interviews continue to play an important role here as well, whether as the primary form of investigation or as a way of filling in the gaps of what the researcher can learn through observation and document analysis.

A common aspect of institutional ethnographic research at this second stage involves the researcher's investigating institutional work processes by following a chain of action, typically organized around and through a set of documents, because it is texts that coordinate people's activity across time and place within institutional relations. For example, Turner (1995) traced the trajectory of a developer's planning proposal as it passed through a review process involving the city planning office, the local conservation authority, the railroad company, and a meeting of the city council.

Research Focused on "Ruling" Relations

In some institutional ethnographic research, the point of entry is in organizational work processes and the activities of the people who perform them. Rather than arriving at these processes through an exploration of the experience of people who are the objects of that work or who are in some way affected by it, the researcher in this type of institutional ethnography jumps right into the examination of organizational work sites. The researcher knows about a set of administrative or professional practices and sets about studying how they are carried out, how they are discursively shaped, and how they organize other settings. For example, Mykhalovskiy (2000) investigated health services research and its use in health care restructuring. Dorothy Smith and George Smith (1990) researched the organization of skills training in the plastics industry. Elizabeth Townsend (1998) studied the work of professionals in the mental health system and the contradictions between their professional goal of empowering people and system processes organized to control deviance. Alison Griffith (1998) investigated the legislative and policy bases for educational restructuring in Ontario. This type of institutional ethnography emphasizes the detailed examination of administrative and professional work processes.

Conceptualization and Place of Interviewing

Interviewing is present in some form in just about all institutional ethnographic studies. But "interviewing" in institutional ethnography is perhaps better described as "talking with people," and institutional ethnographic uses of interviewing should be understood in this wide sense as stretching across a range of approaches to talk with informants. At one end of the continuum are planned interviews, where the researcher makes an appointment with someone for the purpose of doing a research interview. Then there is the kind of "talking with people" that occurs during field observation, when the researcher is watching someone do his work and asks him to explain what he is doing, why he did what he just did, what he has to think about to do the work, where this particular document goes, and so on. "Informal," on-the-spot interviews can be combined with later "formal" or planned interviews, in which the researcher brings to the longer interview a set of questions or topics based on the earlier observation and talk. Yet in institutional ethnography investigation through "talking with people" is not necessarily confined to settings and occasions that occur during formal field research. Because institutional ethnographers are investigating widespread institutional and discursive processes in which the researcher is located as well as the informants, opportunities to talk with people about institutional processes can arise for the researcher serendipitously, as it were, in her or his daily life of going shopping, talking with friends, seeking medical care, and so on, depending on the topic of the research.

Further, "talking with people" is not necessarily done one to one. At the planned end of the continuum, a number of recent institutional ethnographies have used focus groups to generate group conversations about shared experiences (Bresalier et al. 2002; Campbell 1999; Smith et al. 1995; Stock 2000). And Timothy Diamond reports that his research into health insurance draws on collective interviews he holds with his students during class, in which participants collaborate in developing an account of how health care is covered in the news and on television (focus group, August 1999). Such an approach works in institutional ethnography because institutional processes are standardized across local settings, so any group of informants encounters those processes in some way. *Talking with people* is also a wide term in the sense that it includes more than the usual research format (whether formal or informal) of asking questions and listening to answers. Eric Mykhalovskiy comments: "Describing interviews as a set of questions doesn't get at the actual work involved. For me, analytic thinking begins in the interview. It's like an analytic rehearsal. I'm checking my understanding as it develops; I offer it up to the informant for confirmation or correction" (interview, September 1999).

Conducting Institutional Ethnographic Interviews

Institutional ethnographic interviewing is open-ended inquiry, and institutional ethnographic interviewers are always oriented to sequences of interconnected activities. They talk with people located throughout these institutional complexes in order to learn "how things work." In many investigations, informants are chosen as the research progresses, as the researcher learns more about the social relations involved and begins to see avenues that need exploration. Given that the purpose of interviewing is to build up an understanding of the coordination of activity in multiple sites, the interviews need not be standardized. Rather, each interview provides an opportunity for the researcher to learn about a particular piece of the extended relational chain, to check the developing picture of the coordinative process, and to become aware of additional questions that need attention.

Dorothy Smith reports that when she conducted interviews jointly with George Smith, in their study of the organization of job training (Smith and Smith 1990), they thought of their talk with informants as a way to build "piece by piece" a view of an extended organizational process. Rather than using a standard set of questions, they based each interview in part on what they had learned from previous ones. She explains: "You have a sense of what you're after, although you sometimes don't know what you're after until you hear people telling you things. . . . Discovering what you don't know—and don't know you don't know—is an important aspect of the process" (interview, September 1999). As in any qualitative interviewing, there is a balance to be achieved between directing the interview toward the researcher's goals and encouraging informants to talk in ways that reflect the contours of their activity. The distinctiveness of institutional ethnographic interviews is produced by the researcher's developing knowledge of institutional processes, which allows a kind of listening and probing oriented toward institutional connections. Again, Smith explains, "The important thing is to think organizationally, recognizing you won't know at the beginning which threads to follow, knowing you won't follow all possible threads, but noting them along the way."

Institutional ethnographic researchers often think of interviewing as "coinvestigation." Such an approach is evident in Gary Kinsman and Patrizia Gentile's (1998) discussion of the oral history narratives they collected from gay men and lesbians affected by Canadian national security campaigns of the late 1950s and early 1960s. They see the first-person narratives as both a "form of resistance to the official security documents" (p. 8) and a basis from which to build a critical analysis of those documents. Because people were affected differently, the narratives took different shapes, and the researchers found that their providing some historical context often helped informants remember and reconstruct their experiences. They describe their interviewing as "a fully reflexive process in which both the participant and the interviewer construct knowledge together" (p. 58).

Most institutional ethnographers tape conversations with informants, both as an aid in making notes and to preserve details whose relevance may not be immediately obvious. Transcripts of interviews are important texts in themselves, facilitating analysis and providing a way for research participants to "speak" in published accounts of the research. Diamond, however, is concerned about privileging the textual representation over the embodied actuality of the research conversation. We are always in our bodies, he reminds us; in fact, Smith's concept of the "everyday" begins from that fundamental fact. People's descriptions of their work activities and lived experiences are often produced gesturally as well as verbally, and our understanding of that work and that experience arises for us, in part, through our bodily response to their gestures. "[Institutional Ethnography], in insisting on bodies being there, sensitizes us to bodies as part of the data. . . . It's not about just words but how the words live in embodied experience" (T. Diamond, personal communication, December 1999).

Interview Strategies

Institutional ethnographic interviewing is typically organized around the idea of work, defined broadly, or "generously" (Smith 1987). Whether it is the paid work of an organizational position, the activist work of challenging a regime, or some "everyday life work" such as caring for children or managing an illness, the point of interest is the informant's activity, as it reveals and points toward the interconnected activities of others. The idea of work provides a conceptual frame and guides interview talk; the point is not to insist on the categorical status of any activity, but to hold in place a conception of the social as residing in the coordination of people's actual activities.

The generous understanding of work deployed by institutional ethnographers is related to early feminist insights about women's unpaid and often invisible work—the recognition that although various kinds of work sustain social life, some are uncompensated, unacknowledged, or mystified as aspects of personality (e.g., women's "caring" work, as explored in DeVault 1991). An institutional ethnographic study aims at a picture that displays all the activity sustaining a particular institutional nexus or arena, and this analytic goal gives rise to several distinctive strategies for the conduct of interviews. In the following subsections, we identify several kinds of work and discuss strategies associated with each.

Work Practices of Everyday Life

Some researchers conduct institutional ethnographic interviews with a view to understanding the everyday/everynight experiences of people living particular lives—single mothers, people with AIDS or disabilities, older women, or immigrant women, for example. In these interviews researchers seek detailed accounts of activities: What do mothers do when their children have trouble at school? How do individuals work at managing their health? What work do older women do to maintain their housing? How do immigrant women seek employment, education, or training? Ellen Pence began her research by "talking to women who used the police and courts. I would ask what went right or wrong". These conversations gave her a view of the efforts battered women made to seek help (focus group, August 1999). Similarly, Nancy Naples (1998) studied the implementation of the 1988 Family Support Act in an Iowa jobs program that allowed recipients to work toward a college degree. She collected interview, observational, and documentary data on the policy, but the grounding for her study came from interviews with women in the program. Her interviews produced accounts of the women's everyday routines, which she used to uncover the tensions between their lives as mothers and college students and the demands of the program—thus bringing an "everyday life" dimension to policy analysis.

Given the conceptual frame discussed above, the interviewer approaches these conversations as explorations of work practices in everyday life; the point is to learn about what the informant actually does. Informants may or may not think of what they do as a form of "work"; the interviewer may use the rubric of work in questioning, but there is no need to insist on explicit talk of work or agreement about the status of the activity. When Smith and Griffith interviewed mothers, for example, "it worked well to take them through the school day, to ask them what they did at each point, such as what is involved in getting the kids ready for school, getting them there on time." Smith finds that guiding the interview in this way often has the result of "training the informant": "I tell people what I'm interested in, things I'd like to hear about, rather than asking questions. . . . Some people happily go on at a level of expanding practice, and some don't. So that's maybe a good reason to do multiple interviews" (interview, September 1999). Similarly, Diamond elicits "stories" as the basis for his research into the organization of health care: "Sometimes I just say, I want to talk about health insurance in the U.S. People jump in with long stories. . . . Invariably people will talk about employment, because that's the intervening institution—people need to be employed or connected to someone employed to have health insurance" (focus group, August 1999). In a study of a public school choice program, Lois Andre Bechely interviewed parents using the program. She notes:

> Getting people to continue to talk about the details of their "work" can be a challenge. . . . And in the case of parents (and this is almost always the mothers), not all of them saw their involvement as work—it was just what they did—while others did actually use words like, "it's my job," etc. (e-mail communication, September 1999)

Mykhalovskiy and McCoy (2002) and their associates found that although the notion of work was useful to them, conceptually, in establishing the framework of their group interviews, it was counterproductive when used with informants, for whom it evoked a prevalent normative standard of the "good patient" who conscientiously works at "managing" his or her health, against which many informants perceived themselves as delinquent. The researchers had the delicate job of figuring out how to ask people what they did around their health without suggesting that they should have been doing more or otherwise.

Interviews about everyday life work may also be used to point toward the work practices of others. For example, George Smith (1998) emphasizes that the gay students he interviewed were not meant to be "objects of study";

although their narratives could be interpreted as accounts of "work" they do as students (e.g., to "fit in" or pass), he uses their stories as windows on the work processes that affect them—both the "everyday work" of students upholding a heterosexist regime through surveillance and gossip and the paid work of teachers and administrators, which was not organized to interrupt that regime and sometimes reinforced it. Some institutional ethnographers attempt to conduct such interviews with a view to more than data collection, seeking to share insights with informants in the course of interviewing. Diamond says of his interviews on health insurance, "Together we construct a critique of benefits" (focus group, August 1999). And Gerald de Montigny, commenting on his studies with youth in state care, reports:

> My big challenge is that when I do an interview, I do so not only as an ethnographer, but from the standpoint of wanting to be a skilled social work interviewer. . . . I do not feel that I am able to explicate in my interviews the complex social forces at play in these youth's lives, though as a social worker, I do try to help them to understand the play of forces across the landscape of the everyday experiences. (e-mail communication, September 1999)

Whether such dual goals are achievable—and if so, how—appears to be among the unresolved questions of institutional ethnographic interviewers.

Frontline Organizational Work

Frontline professionals, such as teachers, nurses, trainers, social workers, community agency personnel, and other bureaucrats, often become informants in an institutional ethnography. Individuals in such positions are especially important because they make the linkages between clients and ruling discourses, "working up" the messiness of an everyday circumstance so that it fits the categories and protocols of a professional regime. In some studies, such individuals are interviewed as intermediary actors in an institutional complex: Kamini Maraj Grahame (1998, 1999), for example, interviewed intake workers who screened Asian immigrant women into job training, showing that funding formulas organized their work such that they tracked the women into employment streams compatible with local employers' needs. Similarly, Smith and Griffith's interviews with teachers showed how they are located between parents and concerned with particular children and school district practices, designed for standardized processing of groups (Smith 1987). And Yoko Ueda (1995) interviewed human resource professionals to learn about corporate personnel policies that shaped the family work of Japanese expatriate wives in Toronto. In other studies, researchers may be more directly focused on the work situations of these frontline workers and concerned with the organization and control of such work. Campbell's (1988b, 1992b, with J. M. Rankin 2006, and chapter 5 of this book) studies of nursing work are designed to illuminate the mechanisms of managerial control that have increasingly limited nurses' autonomy in care work. Similarly, Ann Manicom's (1995) examination of "health work" undertaken by teachers in low-income schools explores how these teachers are drawn into work that goes beyond official accounts of their jobs.

Here again, institutional ethnographers seek detailed accounts of work processes, but interviewing frontline workers presents its own distinctive challenges. These workers have been trained to use the very concepts and categories that institutional ethnographers wish to unpack, and they are accustomed to speaking from within a ruling discourse. Thus the interviewer must find ways of moving the talk beyond institutional language to "what actually happens" in the setting. Campbell teaches such interviewing strategies in part by offering the following advice:

> Listen to the person tell her story. Pay attention to the sequencing. Then ask yourself, can you tell exactly how she gets from one point to another? If not, ask questions, clarify so that you can. (interview, January 2000)

Such strategies require practice, because "we're all very good at filling in the blanks." But the organizational orientation of institutional ethnographers leads them, with practice, to see both gaps in these accounts and the kinds of filling in necessary for a fuller organizational analysis. The challenge of moving beyond institutional language is so central to institutional ethnographic interviewing that we return to it in the following section.

In some studies that are focused more explicitly on change, interviews might include discussion of possible modifications of frontline work. For example, Pence's (1997) study of safety for battered women involved interviews with the various workers who serve the women as advocates and hospital and criminal justice workers. As she gained an understanding of the interlocking activities of these workers, she could see that women's safety was only one of the concerns that shaped their work and, in fact, was often subordinated to organizational imperatives. She and her team began to ask workers not only how the system operated, but also how it might be organized differently. She explains:

> We ask, "Is there something you don't have in your job, that if you did have, would help prevent that woman getting beat up?" "If you were going to build victim safety into this process, how would you do it?" It's an eye-opener. People in an institution rarely get asked, "Do you want to change something as basic as a form you fill out every day?" "How would you change it?" And when you ask

> them, "Why is this on the form?" they can be quite insightful [about how the form works in the system], even though they might never have thought about it that way before. (focus group, August 1999)

As with everyday experience interviews, then, some researchers orient toward the dual goals of analysis and change; but these intriguing possibilities require partnerships with activists and practitioners that are not easily established and may not always be feasible.

"Ruling" Work

Institutional ethnographic researchers are always interested in moving beyond the interchanges of frontline settings in order to track the macroinstitutional policies and practices that organize those local settings. Thus interviews are often conducted with managers and administrators who work at the level of translocal policymaking and implementation, and these interviews also require a distinctive orientation and strategy. Kamini Maraj Grahame (1998, 1999), who studied federally funded job training for immigrant women in the United States, emphasizes the complexity of this kind of institutional process and the amount of "legwork and conversation" required, even to have a sense of where in the structure one might need to conduct interviews. She learned about various parts of the institutional complex of job training while working in and with community organizations and eventually conducted interviews not only with clients of and workers in those organizations, but also with managers working in the local, state, and federal agencies that funded and oversaw the programs. With each interviewee, she focused on that worker's role in the overall job training system. She would ask, "What do you do?" Recognizing that she was interviewing each at a particular point in time, and therefore at a particular point in what she came to call "the training cycle," she would ask what the interviewee was doing that day or week, and then, "Why are you doing this now?" Whenever someone mentioned a document, she would ask to see a copy of it and then ask what the worker did with that document. In these ways, she built an accumulating understanding of how work processes were textually linked across sites and levels of administration. (We address this kind of textual coordination again below.)

Grahame found that she often had to proceed without a clear sense of where interviewing would take her: "Someone in the federal government says something I have no way of making sense of—seeing the relevance of—until I go back to an interview I did at a community organization. Then I can put it all together." Because the information gained in interviews requires this kind of synthesis, she feels it is very important to tape and transcribe whenever possible.

"Taping allows me to go back and forth and have things make sense in a way they did not initially," she explains. "It's a very complex enterprise, and there's no time to go back and redo interviews" (focus group, August 1999).

Often, interviews with managers and administrators are conducted in the later phases of institutional ethnographic studies, so that researchers can use information gained from clients and frontline workers to direct the interviewing. For example, Lois Andre Bechely reports:

> As I got farther up the chain of command, I had already done preliminary analysis of parent interviews and policy documents and my questions were focused on trying to uncover the social and textual organization of school choice practices that parents encounter and participate in. (e-mail communication, September 1999)

Andre Bechely used her knowledge as a former teacher to organize questions for administrators, but the talk still proceeded in the searching and open manner characteristic of institutional ethnographic interviewing.

The openness of such interviewing allows informants to speak in the forms appropriate to their work. For example, McCoy's (1998, 1999) study of restructuring in Canadian community colleges and the forms of accounting coordinating that process is based on interviews conducted almost entirely with managers. Her informants often talked about new cost accounting documents by enacting speech situations, that is, reporting what was said in the past or what might be argued in future negotiations. McCoy (1998) points out:

> It is not to be supposed that these enactments exactly match what was said or what will be said; their usefulness as data in this kind of study lies in what they suggest about what can possibly or appropriately be [said], and especially, how what can be said depends on and is oriented to the textual forms through which events and activities are known in authoritative ways. (p. 416–417)

Such reports give a strong sense of the discursive character of the work of ruling in this kind of setting.

Processing Interchanges

Institutional ethnographers are especially alert to the points where work processes intersect, points that Pence (1996) has labeled "processing interchanges":

> Processing interchanges are organizational occasions of action in which one practitioner receives from another a document pertaining to a case (e.g., a 911 incident report, a warrant request, or a motion for a continuance), and then makes something of the document, does something to it, and forwards it on to the next organizational occasion for action. It is the construction of these pro-

> cessing interchanges coupled with a highly specialized division of labor that accomplishes much of the ideological work of the institution. Workers' tasks are shaped by certain prevailing features of the system, features so common to workers that they begin to see them as natural, as the way things are done and in some odd way as the only way they could be done, rather than as planned procedures and rules developed by individuals ensuring certain ideological ways of interpreting and acting on a case. (p. 60)

In her study of the processing of domestic violence cases, Pence attends to the spaces and tools that organize the tasks of workers—how dispatchers use computers, police use Dictaphones, and so on—and to the forms required at each point of connection. As she points out, it is not "the woman who was beaten who moves from one point to the next in the stages of case processing"; rather, the "file stands in for the woman who was assaulted" (p. 67). In studying how this extremely important file is produced, Pence watched workers in these processing interchanges and also asked them about their work, querying police officers, for instance, on "how they decide when to write a report, how they decide what to record in their narratives, and how much leeway they have in making these decisions" (p. 71). At each processing interchange, she explains, "an institutional investigation helps to determine how such an objective (i.e., accounting for victim safety) could be incorporated into the design at each of these occasions" (p. 89). Working with practitioners in the system, Pence has developed an "audit" procedure—basically, an institutional ethnographic investigation to be used collaboratively to provide "a place for advocates and practitioners to work together" (p. 187).

Campbell (1998b, 1999) has used a similar approach in her participatory research project on home support for people with disabilities. Her team used interview material to identify processing interchanges they wished to examine in detail, and Campbell and her assistants arranged for team members to conduct observations of these moments in the management of home support. Watching a scheduler work at a computer screen, for example, they asked questions to help her make explicit the kinds of choices she was making. "People think the computer does it," Campbell notes, "but that glosses the judgment involved in her work" (interview, January 2000). The researchers found that "continuity" in scheduling home support workers was important for people with disabilities and a goal shared by workers in the system. As they observed the scheduler, however, they found that "her talk open[ed] up the organizational priorities that interfere with the Client-focus of her work" (p. 6).

Both Pence and Campbell have found that working with a team to investigate interchanges provides opportunities for participants to come to a fuller shared understanding of organizational action. Campbell reports that team members would sometimes clash over the differing perspectives: "The professionals would say, 'You're not seeing this right; this is what's happening.'

And people with disabilities would say, 'But it doesn't feel that way; here's how it feels'" (interview, January 2000).

As facilitator, Campbell would let such discussion proceed, and then ask, "Now whose standpoint are we taking?" Team members could then respond, "Oh yes, the standpoint of people with disabilities" (interview, January 2000). In this kind of exchange, Campbell is reminding her research team of the way that a notion of "standpoint" anchors the research in the relevancies of a particular group. The point is not that "people with disabilities" share a determinate standpoint, or that the perspectives of the professionals should be ignored or discounted. Rather, the idea is to consider how the perspectives from different locations illuminate the relevant social relations while keeping in mind the questions focused by the concerns of people living with disabilities.

Selecting Informants

The preceding discussion provides some context for understanding institutional ethnographic approaches to the selection of interviewees. Because institutional ethnographers are not oriented toward descriptive reporting on a population, they do not think of informants as a "sample." Still, when exploring the ground of everyday experience, some institutional ethnographers seek informants who can report on varied circumstances and situations. For example, Smith and Griffith (1990) interviewed both middle-class and working-class mothers; Manicom (1995) spoke with teachers in schools serving middle-class and poor students; Smith and colleagues (1995) sought high school girl informants in different kinds of school situations. Some researchers make special efforts to include perspectives they believe are missing: Didi Khayatt, for example, found it relatively easy to interview middle-class lesbians in Egypt but had to make special efforts to find working-class informants (focus group, October 1999).

Such efforts are common to many kinds of interview studies. However, institutional ethnographers aim not for categorical descriptions, but for analyses that trace how the people living in these different circumstances are drawn into a common set of organizational processes. Some report that attention to differences among informants can easily pull them toward the kinds of categorical analyses embedded in ruling activities, as when Smith and Griffith (1990) found themselves thinking much like school administrators about the class composition of student groups. One solution is for researchers to conceive of this kind of selection in terms of diversity of experience rather than categorically. For example, when interviewing people living with HIV/AIDS about their health work, Bresalier and associates (2002) thought about diversity among their informants' circumstances, reasoning that they needed to include women caring for children, people living in prison, people on welfare, and so forth.

As discussed above, institutional ethnographies are rarely based solely on such a group of interviews; rather, they almost always use such interviews as pointers toward informants working in other settings. Those interviewees might be chosen in more varied ways. Some researchers follow "chains of action" (e.g., K. M. Grahame 1999; McCoy 1998). Some choose informants in and around sites of confrontation: George Smith, for example (1990), located the field of the AIDS bureaucracy through work with other activists attempting to gain access to treatments. And in some studies, it seems useful for researchers to select "good thinkers" as interviewees. When Pence interviewed police, for example, she sought those who wrote especially complete or useful reports:

> If you read fifty police reports, you can say, "I want to talk to the cop who wrote these four." But I also try to interview one dud, so I can see how much is the institutional process and how much is the person. (focus group, August 1999)

Often, as George Smith (1990) explains, researchers simply rely on informants they encounter as their investigations proceed, using each conversation to expand understanding of the terrain.

Clearly, the selection of informants is more open-ended in institutional ethnographic investigations than it is in more conventional positivist studies, but the process is not haphazard. Rather, fieldwork and interviewing are driven by a faithfulness to the actual work processes that connect individuals and activities in the various parts of an institutional complex. Rigor comes not from technique—such as sampling or thematic analysis—but from the corrigibility of the developing map of social relations. When George Smith (1990) was learning about placebo-controlled trials of experimental AIDS treatments, for example, he did not need to identify recurring "themes" in the accounts of multiple physician informants. Rather, he sought their help in filling in his knowledge of how such trials work, continuing to "check" the account he was building as he proceeded with the investigation, and returning to physician (and other) informants as needed when questions or inconsistencies arose.

Interviewing about Textual Practices

A prominent aspect of institutional ethnography is the recognition that text-based forms of knowledge and discursive practices are central to large-scale organization and relations of ruling in contemporary society. To use an organic metaphor, textual processes in institutional relations are like a central nervous system running through and coordinating different sites. To find out how things work and how they happen the way they do, a researcher needs to find the texts and text-based knowledge forms in operation. Thus institutional ethnographic investigation often involves close attention to textual practices, and interviewing is an important strategy in this regard.

When institutional ethnographers talk about texts, they usually mean some kind of document or representation that has a relatively fixed and replicable character, for it is that aspect of texts—that they can be stored, transferred, copied, produced in bulk, and distributed widely, allowing them to be activated by users at different times and in different places—that allows them to play a standardizing and mediating role. In this view, a text can be any kind of document, on paper, on computer screens, or in computer files; it can also be a drawing, a photograph, a printed instrument reading, a video, or a sound recording.

Much institutional ethnographic research has focused on standardized texts used in professional and bureaucratic settings, such as care pathway forms in hospitals (Mykhalovskiy 2001), intake forms and applications at an employment agency (Ng 1996), patients' charts (Diamond 1992), nursing worksheets (Rankin 1998), forms for calculating teachers' workloads (McCoy 1999), course information sheets used in competency-based education reform (Jackson 1995), and safety assessment forms used by child protection workers (Parada 1998). Other bureaucratic texts studied have included job descriptions (Reimer 1995) and developers' maps used in land use planning (Turner 1995). Griffith (1998) and Ng (1995) have examined legislative texts. Sometimes institutional ethnographic researchers look at the creation or generation of texts, such as the work of producing a newsletter for doctors (Mykhalovskiy 2000), creating materials for job skills training (Smith and Smith 1990), or taking wedding photographs (McCoy 1987, 1995).

Institutional ethnographers are also interested in the text-mediated discourses that frame issues, establish terms and concepts, and in various ways serve as resources that people draw into their everyday work processes, for example, health services research (Mykhalovskiy 2000), the literature on child development (Griffith 1984, 1995), the literature on "deviant" sexuality as an aspect of the policing of gay men (Kinsman 1989), the terms of an international development regime (Mueller 1995), and popular cultural discourses of femininity (Smith 1990b: chap. 6). Whatever the text or textual process, in institutional ethnography it is examined for the ways it mediates relations of ruling and organizes what can be said and done.

Listening for Texts

At the early stages of research, when researchers are just beginning to learn about the institutional processes that shape the relations they are studying, they are alert to catch informants' references to texts or text-mediated processes. Sometimes these are fairly easy to catch, as when an informant mentions a specific document and how it functions. In the following extract, for example, a college administrator mentions something he refers to as a "D form":

> Well, that's the problem. We mounted programs and the last thing that's looked at is the return. Because the ministry—when we mount a program—has a little clause at the bottom of the D form that simply says, "You've got to make this work; we're not going to give you any more money than the funding units for it." So, if you want to put it on, fine. It's a disclaimer by the ministry of any acceptance of any debts that this program-mounting creates.

At this point, or perhaps later in the interview, the researcher might ask to see a copy of the D form and, if possible, get one to take away with her. She will also want to learn more about how the D form is used: When is it filled out? By whom? What resources and future activities depend on the D form? In this way, the researcher begins to see how local settings are tied into extended institutional relations and at the same time lays the groundwork for future interviews ("Whom could I talk to about that?").

Sometimes the researcher suspects that a textual process lies behind the description an informant is giving. It is not uncommon for informants who work in bureaucratic settings to use glosses and metaphors, as in the following example, where a college administrator is describing the work of a committee that recommends "per diem prices":

> And they report to the College Committee presidents who agree or disagree with their recommendation. And then that's sent on to the Ministry of Skills Development, who again have to nod their approval. And finally to the federal government, who have to pay the per diem. And they nod their approval or whatever.

Experience suggests that this "nodding" occurs textually, and an institutional ethnographer interested in this process might go on to ask explicitly what form the reporting and the approval take. She might also want to discover which office or person does the approving on behalf of the ministry.

Not all the texts mentioned will become focal in the analysis, but in the early stages of studies some researchers like to map out the main textual processes at work in an institutional setting. In some cases, "mapping" might precede the initial interviews. Pence explains:

> We get together a prep work of documents and legislation. We used to start by going out and blindly interviewing. Now we prepare. But we do find out things [about texts] when we interview that we didn't know were there. (focus group, August 1999)

Asking about Texts

However texts come to be identified as central to the relations under study—whether through exploratory interviews, through prep work, or through the researcher's prior knowledge—the research at some stage may involve interviews with people who can talk in detail about a text or those aspects of a textual process they know. One effective way for an interviewer to structure such an interview is to sit down with the informant and the text in question and talk very concretely about what is in the text and how the informant works with it. Diamond reports: "I ask people to bring a pay stub to the interview, so we can look at that text. We explore together: Where is health in this pay stub?" (focus group, August 1999).

If the document in question is a standardized form, some researchers like to do the interview around a form that has been completed, rather than a blank one, as that will result in more concrete description. For example, when Dorothy Smith was interviewing a probation officer about a presentencing investigation form, she worked from an actual, completed form to ask about the sources of information (predominantly textual) and the practices of judgment that went into filling it out (interview, September 1999). When McCoy (1987) was interviewing a wedding photographer, she and the photographer worked from a set of photographs he had recently taken; as they looked through the stack of proofs, he talked about how he had worked with actual people and actual equipment on that specific day to make those pictures.

In other cases, the text in question is not one the informant creates or completes, but one he or she activates in some way, such as a report or a memo. Here the interviewer might focus on practices of reading to learn how the text is taken up in an actual setting, within an accountable work process. A transcript excerpt provided by Eric Mykhalovskiy illustrates this:

> **Eric Mykhalovskiy:** So when you get those reports, what are you looking for? How do they inform your thinking?
>
> **Hospital administrator:** Hmm. Well, certainly we look at the average length of stay, the timeline. So if all of a sudden, I mean, we're averaging around five days, so if all of a sudden we're up to six, then that would concern me.

What the researcher wants to learn about the text and the practices of making or using it will vary, depending on the nature of the text and the focus of the investigation, but in general, institutional ethnographers are after the following:

1. How the text comes to this informant and where it goes after the informant is done with it.

2. What the informant needs to know in order to use the text (create it, respond to it, fill it out, and so on).
3. What the informant does with, for, and on account of the text.
4. How the text intersects with and depends on other texts and textual processes as sources of information, generators of conceptual frames, authorizing texts, and so on.
5. The conceptual framework that organizes the text and its competent reading.

The Problem and Resource of Institutional Language

Institutional work processes are organized by conceptual schemes and distinctive categories. These are the terms in which the accountability of the work is produced, and procedures of accountability provide one of the main ways that various local settings are pulled into translocal relations. Institutional ethnography therefore pays strong attention to institutional categories and the interpretive schemata that connect them.

In interviews, it is common—and understandable—that people in an institutional setting describe their work using the language of the institution. This is especially the case with people who have been taught a professional discourse as part of their training or people whose work requires them to provide regular accounts of institutional processes. "Some people do jobs where public relations is part of their job, so they are doing that work while talking to me" (K. M. Grahame, focus group, August 1999). The challenge for the institutional ethnographer is to recognize when the informant is using institutional language. Not to do so is to risk conducting interviews that contain little usable data beyond the expression of institutional ideology in action, because institutional language conceals the very practices institutional ethnography aims to discover and describe. Dorothy Smith elaborates:

> These terms are extraordinarily empty. They rely on your being able to fill out what they could be talking about. During the interview, you do that filling in while you listen, but when you look at the transcript afterward, the description isn't there. (interview, September 1999)

As an example, Ann Manicom reports:

> One challenge I've faced in interviewing professionals is . . . to get them beyond saying something like "Well, I have a lot of ADHD kids" to getting them to actually describe day-to-day work processes. The discourses are of course also interesting and an important piece of the analysis, but shifting them out of the discourse is important for actual descriptions of the work process. (e-mail communication, September 1999)

An informant's comment that she has "a lot of ADHD kids" would not be treated by an institutional ethnographer as a straightforward description of her work, although it does show the teacher using institutional concepts to make sense of and to talk about her day-to-day actuality. Within the institution of schooling, it is certainly a competent description; other teachers would nod in sympathy and feel that they knew exactly what the teacher was talking about. A school administrator would understand something about that classroom relevant to her work of allocating resources. This is because the term references a discourse and practice of knowledge operative within the institution. An interviewer who knows something about teaching and professional discourses might also find, as Smith suggests above, that she too knows what the teacher is talking about. An alert institutional ethnographer, however, would try to get the teacher to describe, for example, what these "ADHD kids" are like: what they do or need, and in what ways their needs complicate or add to her teaching work. The researcher would try to learn how the teacher uses the ADHD concept to organize her work with the children and her conferences with their parents. Furthermore, the researcher might try to learn how ADHD as a category operates in the administration of schooling: for example, in some school districts, classroom assistants and other resources are allocated through a procedure that takes into account the number of students in a class who are entered in school records as having "special needs," such as ADHD. An institutional ethnographer encountering institutional language has thus a twofold objective: to obtain a description of the actuality that is assumed by, but not revealed in, the institutional terms, and, at the same time, to learn how such terms and the discourses they carry operate in the institutional setting.

Analysis and Presentation

As institutional ethnography is fundamentally an analytic project, we cannot terminate this discussion of interviewing at the moment when the tape recorder is turned off and the researcher packs up her or his notes to go home. In this section we briefly address the work that comes after the interview has been taped and transcribed. The studies we have referred to and cited throughout the chapter provide further advice and models for analysis. Institutional ethnographers tend not to use formal analytic strategies such as interpretive coding. Some use qualitative data analysis software to group chunks of transcript, sometimes pages in length, by theme or topic; others contend that the logic of these programs runs against that of the institutional ethnographic approach. The software seems to work best for institutional ethnographic analysis when the grouping is done rather simply, something like the indexing for a book (D. Smith, personal communication), sticking closely to topics of talk and references to institutional sites and processes. For example, a researcher might collect in one file everything informants said about using AIDS service organizations, in another the informants' stories about the work and challenges of finding suitable doctors, and so on. A researcher examining chains of action or process interchanges could use the software to group informants' comments around particular sites, texts, or moments in the process. This kind of computer-aided sorting works at a fairly primary level and offers researchers a manageable way to work with large numbers of interviews; it still leaves the analytic work to be done, as always, through writing, thinking, and discussion with collaborators and colleagues.

Just as projects have different shapes, institutional ethnographers aim toward different kinds of analyses. Some use their data to map out complex institutional chains of action; others describe the mechanics of text-based forms of knowledge, elaborate the conceptual schemata of ruling discourses, or explicate how people's lived experience takes shape within institutional relations. John McKendy (1999), who interviewed men incarcerated for violent crimes, focuses his analysis on the informants' stories and the interview itself as a conversation, but in a way that makes visible the juxtaposition of primary narratives and ideological, institutionally oriented accounts.

> In doing the analysis now . . . I am on the lookout for segments of the interviews where "fault lines" can be detected, as the two modes of telling—the narrative and the ideological—rub up against each other. I want to examine how such junctures are occasioned within the flow of the interview, what kinds of narrative problems they pose for the speakers, and what methods speakers improvise to handle (overcome, resist, circumvent) these problems. (p. 9)

Townsend (1996, 1998) took her data—participant observation notes, interview transcripts, and documents—and addressed them through three analytic processes. First she "undertook the rather arduous task of describing the everyday world of occupational therapy" (Townsend 1998: 19). Then she "trac[ed] the social processes that connect the work being studied with the work of others. . . . Through a back-and-forth method of exploration, [she] traced connections between what occupational therapists do and the documentation and other processes that govern that work" (p. 21). Finally, she examined the "ideological character" of the institutional process: the ways that "occupational therapists and the people with whom occupational therapists work are conceptualized and categorized in mental health services, then coordinated and controlled through textual facts about these categories rather than through face-to-face supervision" (p. 24).

In general, institutional ethnographic analysts look at interview data as raising questions; according to Khayatt, the key is to ask, "How is it that these people are saying what they're saying?" She adds, "This methodology allows you to go back to a political-economic context for the answer" (focus group, October 1999). Ng and Griffith agree that analysis is always a matter of moving back and forth between collected speech and the context that produced it. For Ng (1996, 1999), whose research explores the work experiences of immigrant women, the analytic focus is how these women are drawn into institutional processes. She believes that conventional analyses of immigrants' lives often "produce ethnicity" through particular kinds of analytic work on interview data, linking informants' comments back to their "home cultures." Her goal, instead, is to find clues to "how things happen" for the people identified as immigrants in Canadian institutions. Griffith says of analysis: "It's never instances; it's always processes and coordination. It's all these little hooks. To make sense of it, you have to understand not just the speech of the moment, but what it's hooked into" (focus group, October 1999).

Many institutional ethnographers find that they collect considerably more information than they use in a single analysis because the analysis eventually follows some more specific thread of social organization. Dorothy Smith explains: "You don't have to use the whole interview. You can be quite selective, because you're not interested in all aspects of the institutional process" (interview, September 1999).

Writing Strategies

Two general strategies for presenting interview-based analyses can be discerned in published institutional ethnographies. In one, the writer uses interview data to produce a description, in the writer's voice, of the institutional processes under examination. Usually this account is a composite built up from multiple sources: people's explanations, documents, and so on. Knowledge gleaned through interviews with informants in different institutional locations is rolled together into a description of how a complex institution "works." The individual informants, however, do not "speak" in the text.

Researchers employing an alternative strategy use quoted excerpts from interviews to carry forward the description and analysis in the final text. George Smith (1998) uses the notion of the "exhibit" to specify a distinctive use of interview excerpts:

> As exhibits, the excerpts create windows within the text, bringing into view the social organization of my informants' lives for myself and for my readers to examine. Though what is brought into view emerges out of the dialogic relations of the interview, excerpts must not be read as extensions of my description. As

> exhibits, they make available the social organization of the everyday school lives of the individuals I interviewed. Dialogically they enter the actual social organization of schools into the text of the analysis. (p. 312)

Some writers combine these strategies, using composite accounts where analytically appropriate as well as bringing forward exhibits, descriptions, and life stories from the transcripts.

> In general, I use informants' descriptions when the matter is their actual work and the experience of doing it; I use my own description (based on multiple sources) when I am describing generalized relations or chains of action that transcend the local experience of any one informant. (McCoy 1999: 47)

Institutional ethnographers try to maintain a focus on institutional relations not just during interviews, but in analysis and writing as well. This can be a challenge because apparently minor features of presentation format, such as the identification of speakers, can support or interrupt that focus. For example, writing procedures that tag all quotes, regardless of topic, with the gender, race, and class status of the speaker risk inviting an individualizing line of analysis, in which class and ethnicity are treated as inherent in individuals rather than produced through coordinative social processes. Consequently, some institutional ethnographic writers suppress personal information about informants in order to keep the focus on the institutional processes they are describing; they identify quoted speakers only by their location in the institutional work process of which they speak (e.g., nurse, client, teacher, administrator). On the other hand, institutional ethnographers using life stories to examine an experience and elaborate a problematic usually find it analytically important to include biographical details and to distinguish speakers from each other through the use of pseudonyms. It is sometimes useful for writers to instruct their readers in how to read interview excerpts. Campbell (1999) introduces her team's report with some comments about how excerpts should be understood:

> Viewed from the standpoint of what might be called "the official work processes" of community health, people with disabilities are clients. . . . In Project InterSeed's research we found that the person on the receiving end is not passive but must claim his or her place as an active participant in health care. . . . We ask you to think differently about clients and to read the word *client* in this report as a job title (i.e., Client). It signifies that Clients work, including conducting relationships with people in the health care system, orienting Home Support Workers, managing different workers in their home in order to work towards having their individual health needs met. The understanding of people with disabilities as actively engaged in Home Support work helps set the frame for our discussions. (p. 1–2)

As in most aspects of instituional ethnography, there is no fixed writing format to which all practitioners adhere; instead, writers have the goal of keeping the institution in view and different ways of realizing that goal.

Conclusion

In one view, our brief discussion here risks misrepresenting institutional ethnography because of the artificiality of separating out the "interview" parts of the approach. For practitioners, institutional ethnography always combines theory and method, and these are understood not as dichotomized "ingredients" for an analysis, but as constituting a coherent approach to "writing the social" (Smith 1999). We have also been concerned with the danger of reifying the approach as technique. Indeed, the institutional ethnographic focus on "ruling" prompts de Montigny to ask, skeptically, "What social forces of funding, or recognition, or careers compel us to label and name that which we do as 'institutional ethnography'?"(e-mail communication, September 1999). These risks seem worth taking, however, because we believe that institutional ethnography approaches offer distinctive advantages for researchers seeking to unmask the relations of ruling that shape everyday life.

Dorothy Smith's writing has been taken up in sociology as critique and revision of core theoretical concerns of the discipline, but the institutional ethnographic approach to empirical investigation has fit less comfortably within academic sociology because its focus is not on theory building but on "what actually happens."[3] Much of the work we have discussed here, and much development of institutional ethnographic approaches, has occurred among professionals concerned with their relations to clients and the forces shaping their work or among activists working to understand the institutions they confront and seek to change. In addition, many institutional ethnographers have found that the approach is a powerful teaching tool because it can provide anyone with a strategy for investigating the lineaments of ruling (Naples 2002).

Institutional ethnography is one of the new modes of inquiry that have grown from the cracks in monolithic notions of "objective" social science, as women of all backgrounds, people of color, and others previously excluded from knowledge production have found space and "voice" to explore their experiences and pose questions relevant to their lives. In this context, the distinctiveness of institutional ethnography lies in its commitment to going beyond the goal of simply "giving voice."

Ann Manicom reports that her feminist students—sensitized to the occlusion and misrepresentation of women's experience in so much traditional social science—sometimes worry about "imposing" extended analyses:

> So the work to be done is to help them think more deeply, first about the notion of "women's voices," and secondly about the notion of going "beyond" voice. The first process makes problematic any simplistic notion of "experience" arising in any one of us as individuals; the second brings into view how the traces of social relations are already in women's accounts of their experience. Thus, what is called for in [institutional ethnography] is not so much "going beyond" as it is tracing more intently what is already there to be heard. (e-mail communication, September 1999)

Such analyses are directed toward ruling processes that are pervasive, consequential, and not easily understood from the perspective of any local experience. But the institutional ethnographic approach suggests that an understanding grounded in such a vantage point is possible, and necessary, if we are to build upon excluded perspectives the kind of "map" of institutional processes that might be used in making changes to benefit those subject to ruling regimes.

List of Interviews

Campbell, Marie. Telephone interview with M. L. DeVault, January 2000.
Diamond, Timothy. Focus group conducted by L. McCoy, Duluth, MN, August 1999.
Grahame, Kamini Maraj. Focus group conducted by L. McCoy, Duluth, MN, August 1999.
Griffith, Alison I. Focus group conducted by L. McCoy, Toronto, October 1999.
Khayatt, Didi. Focus group conducted by L. McCoy, Toronto, October 1999.
Mykhalovskiy, Eric. Interview conducted by L. McCoy, Toronto, September 1999.
Ng, Roxana. Focus group conducted by L. McCoy, Toronto, October 1999.
Parada, Henry. Focus group conducted by L. McCoy, Duluth, MN, August 1999.
Pence, Ellen. Focus group conducted by L. McCoy, Duluth, MN, August 1999.
Smith, Dorothy E. Focus group conducted by L. McCoy, Duluth, MN, August 1999.
Smith, Dorothy E. Interview conducted by M. L. DeVault and L. McCoy, Toronto, September 1999.

Notes

1. The group includes several generations of Smith's students from the University of British Columbia and the Ontario Institute for Studies in Education (University of Toronto) and has attracted increasing numbers of other scholars. During the past decade, informal meetings have evolved into more regular conferences at York University and OISE, including a 1996 workshop sponsored by the American Sociological Association's Sex and Gender Section. Members of the group have collected exemplars

of the approach in publications such as Campbell and Manicom's (1995) edited collection; a special symposium in human studies titled "Institutions, Ethnography, and Social Organization" (1998); and a special issue of *Studies in Cultures, Organizations and Societies* on institutional ethnography (Dobson and Smith ed. 2001). In addition, two recently published texts provide useful overviews (Campbell and Gregor 2002; Smith 2005).

2. Although this approach shares with Foucault an interest in texts, power, and governance, there are some central differences that are particularly significant for empirical research. In Foucault's work and in work taking up his approach, for example, the notion of discourse designates a kind of large-scale conversation in and through texts; Smith works with a wider notion of discourse that is consistent with her social ontology and her commitment to grounding inquiry in the activities of actual individuals. For Smith, discourse refers to a field of relations that includes not only texts and their intertextual conversation, but the activities of people in actual sites who produce them and use them and take up the conceptual frames they circulate. This notion of discourse never loses the presence of the subject who activates the text in any local moment of its use.

3. Smith's critique involves seeing the enterprise of theory building as implicated in ruling relations. The revision it calls for is one of orientation: Rather than building theory, the researcher seeks to explicate how the categories of social theory work, in concert with related institutional processes, to regulate activities in local sites.

3

"Where Did You Get the Fur Coat, Fern?" Participant Observation in Institutional Ethnography

Timothy Diamond

Introduction

THIS CHAPTER DISCUSSES participant observation as part of the range of methods open to institutional ethnographers. The first part of the chapter is an edited version of a conversation between Dorothy Smith and me. The second part consists of my reflections on the conversation and generally about the benefits of participant observation for the development of institutional ethnography.

The conversation was suggested by Smith as a way to draw out some of the methodological strategies that had gone into a participant observation research project I had done some years earlier. It was called *Making Gray Gold: Narratives of Nursing Home Care* (Diamond 1992). I did research working as a nursing assistant in a series of nursing homes. Smith framed the conversation by asking four questions: how I came to do the work, how it became an institutional ethnography, how I did the ethnography, and how I wrote the book. We taped the conversation. I transcribed it and excerpted it into the dialogue that follows.

In the second part of the chapter, drawing from some of the themes of the conversation and from Smith's recent writings, I suggest potential contributions of participant observation for institutional ethnographers. These types of studies can help refine skills pertaining to telling stories, the presence of the author, and the author's embodiment. They can also enhance institutional ethnography's goals of incorporating place, time, motion, and the presence of larger social organization within local situations.

Part I. The Conversation

Where Did the Nursing Home Study Start?

Dorothy: How come you got interested in talking with the nursing assistants in the first place?

Tim: Hmm. I'm trying not to answer in too abstract a way. Some of the reasons included wanting to engage in some work that had connections to the feminist sociology I was studying and, being a man, needing somehow to get my hands dirty in some fieldwork, to proceed from a specific standpoint. Some of the reasons were actually to find secure work in a new city. And I had read your classic pamphlet, *A Place to Begin, A Way to Go* (Smith 1977), and it offered back then, as it does today, the outline of a genuinely materialist inquiry.[1]

D.: But did you meet the nursing assistants by accident?

T.: Yes, we did meet by accident, but prior to meeting them I was "ready" to meet them. My first post-PhD job was in a medical school. I was reading a lot about nursing and exploring its social organization. I observed a fascinating graph. It was of all nursing personnel in the United States. It was clear from this graph that nursing assistants outnumbered registered nurses and licensed practical nurses by vast numbers. Yet in the six years I had studied medical sociology up to that point, I had scarcely seen nursing assistants mentioned in the professional literature. So you could say that the study began with a visual image, a statistical graph. Conceptually, that would be true.

But in the flesh and blood sense, it had fascination as both a sociological project and a very high probability of a job that would provide a base of survival. On this last I was only partly correct, for well into a full-time job I realized the net pay fell far short of that base.

Initially, I had begun an interview study with nursing assistants who took their breaks at a coffee shop near where I lived. Suddenly they stopped appearing. A rule had come down in the nearby nursing home where they worked that no one could leave the building even during breaks. I can see their empty booth now. It was a local and particular moment hooked into ruling relations, and I set off from this disjuncture to explore them. If the nursing assistants couldn't come out of a nursing home for a break or an interview, I was determined to go into some to find out why.

There was a pull to participant observation, but I stumbled around for quite a while. Surely they are difficult to design.

D.: Wait. Let's stop at the stumbling. Wouldn't you think that's the way an ethnography should develop? You aren't able to previsage what it is you are going to do, or what you are going to discover. Isn't stumbling around integral to the process?

T.: But it's difficult to write a proposal saying you don't know what you're going to do.

D.: Yes, that is a difficulty with institutional ethnography because you actually don't even know what questions you're going to ask. It's a problem for research funding, but let's be clear, it's not a problem with the research process.

T.: And sometimes I would notice some material object and wonder how to incorporate it into analysis, how it might contain the social relations I was trying to uncover. For example, in Fern Parillo's closet I noticed an expensive fur coat. But the home was full of very poor people, supported by Medicaid, the poverty/health care program in the U.S. Eventually I was able to discover that she had become poor under the social policies. In listening to the residents, the outlines of the policies are there. "Where did you get the fur coat, Fern?" "Oh, I had it for years when I lived in (a suburb). I used to wear it to church with my husband." She went from her suburban home to a hospital, then to one home where she lost all her money, and to this one as a pauper. I can see now this extra-local ruling relation right there intrinsic to that coat in that closet and to our conversation about it.[2]

Hmmm, "participant observation" and "observation" seems almost an inappropriate duality. In a sense all observation is participant observation.

D.: Yes, I agree, but I can see why the distinction is made. It inherits a particular kind of epistemological issue which I suppose is rooted in positivism that if you're "just" doing observation then you can be objective, whereas in participant observation you can't be objective because you're positioned in the process and that's a basis that I think we wouldn't accept in institutional ethnography, so the distinction is troubled, I would agree with you.

T.: So we might think about observing as a continuum, positing on the one hand this objective observer . . . well, but now we even see her there in an embodied way. I don't think you can write the author out anymore, even the so-called objective ones.

D.: No.

T.: Now very quickly along that continuum comes a huge political problem. In an earlier era one could contemplate doing covert research. The nursing home work, by the way, did not start out with that intent but *became* covert. And I'm sort of proud of that part of it. But covert research seems to have lost its legitimacy. Some of that body of research was so very good. And much of it was deeply ethically reflective; it just didn't have to pass through that scrutiny of the ethics review boards, which now would never let it though. I don't know, do you think it is a tradition that still has hope in these times?

D.: Well, it's more problematic, if you were doing it for your thesis, or funding, for example.

T.: I'd like to see it not abandoned. Do you feel the same?

D.: Very much so.

T.: So this work became covert. I went along a step at a time.

I remember asking you, at the start of the research, "If this stuff is to proceed from women's standpoint, can a man do it?" "Sure," was your immediate response. You now define "women's standpoint" as a subject position referring to the local, particular, and embodied. Roughly translated, then and now, that meant it is a research strategy open to men provided they do the work women do, or take up that embodied position in some form, some grounding, in order not just to be operating in their heads.

So I knew in broad outline what I wanted to learn about: everyday work practices of nursing assistants. But I did not know any of the circumstances under which I would learn them. For example, I did go to school. At first I didn't even know I had to do so in order to become certified. So that was about eight to nine months added on to the research "design."

And the schooling became a chapter. I was laughing on the way to this interview about a little secret I have carried since those days, and whether it would come out today. What made that bizarre circumstance in that schoolwork as well as it did? How could a white guy, midthirties, go to this class and get along in a joking way with at least some of the African American women in their early twenties? Many reasons, maybe. I mean I liked them, and that always shines through. But there was something deeper, a bonding, a ritual, a connection that worked. It was outside of class. It was down in the alleys on breaks, out in the dark and cold winter nights where we four or five would huddle around, to keep warm, to tell jokes about the teachers. And to share a joint.

D.: Oh dear! (Laughing.)

T.: That part didn't make it into the book, but it was the social bonding that glued us.

So this student-nurse with whom we had shared this kind of transgression could then confide, heart to heart, about what to do about this bedridden patient she met on the clinical practicum. The guy had this erection and was asking her for help in tending to it. She honestly didn't know what to do as a nurse. For sure they had never dealt with such matters in class (where we were once asked on a test, "What is the function of the penis?" the correct answer to which was "to urinate"). She couldn't mention the issue in the classroom, but she could with someone with whom she'd just shared a smoke out back.

But then, after I got the certificate, I still couldn't find a job.

D.: Oh, really?

T.: They saw the certificate but also this white man. They were sure I was a newspaper reporter or some such.

D.: Oh.

T.: So I spent another three or four months trying to get a job, knocking on doors. I thought I was a complete failure as a sociologist. There I was with a certificate and no one would give me a job. Not much of a project. A book about going to nursing assistant school—and then not working—might have been a bit thin.

So over time I said less and less about my background and eventually got hired. Speaking as we do of local moments articulated to translocal relations of ruling, there was that crucial Friday afternoon that I was hired, just at shift change. They saw a man and needed men. The head nurse was eager to get a male nurse who would work evening shift. Off the cuff she mentioned that normally the administrator and his assistant interview prospective workers. At the time, though, she would do it and be done with it, and I was hired on the spot. The administrators, meanwhile, were in the Philippines, arranging for contract workers. Here was this nursing home, with a pretty name, apparently poor to judge from the economies of its residents, connected multinationally into the indentured servitude of Filipino nurses. This home, its administrators and workers, were part of a global industry.

D.: How long did you work?

T.: For four months at that home.

D.: When did you know you were done?

T.: Well, I had three jobs in all. I had learned from Fern's story that there are rich and poor homes, and often in lived experience they were linked. I knew I needed to get some sense of the class dynamics of this institution. I needed to work in a rich home as well as a poor one. So I went to a rich one, too. In all, I worked in three homes, one for eight months, one four, another about four. As I look back it was enough to get to know people as they were day in and day out. It seemed important, as well, to work all three shifts—and that surely is a standpoint issue that came screaming at me. Most social science is about daytime life. Here a lot happened at night.

How Did It Become an Institutional Ethnography?

T.: We very quickly want to talk about work practices. I knew enough to look for them.

I knew something about how to look for a tiny gesture containing wider relations beyond it. Anyone who reads about the dog doing his business on the wrong lawn learns to look for these things, like the child pointing to the bird and fish, or the train rolling across Canada and looking so different from the standpoints of the First Nations people who watched and the whites who rode it. So I had these concrete images.[3] Besides, I knew immediately as I read that anyone who dared to write "shat" in an academic paper, that was the social science for me!

And I had Marie by then. Marie does not describe much of the flesh and blood of the actual work of nursing, all its pain and emotional tensions, and all the actual work that get leeched out of the accounts. But Marie is great for the work that nurses must coordinate textually, so I had her going in.[4]

I also had your "generous conception" of work.[5] Nursing assistant work, I found out, is far more complex than it is written about in the charts. The experience is full of physical and emotional turmoil, and it is suppressed. "If It's Not Charted, It Didn't Happen" read the sign above the nursing station. But what happened to what happened that wasn't charted? So the investigation was about seeing, explicating, doing, and writing about work where we didn't think it existed.

And I knew I could write about residents as active in constructing their own lives, not all of them perhaps, and productive in the daily order of the place, if only in compliance with, or resistance to, the rules. And I could raise the potential of revolution in nursing homes, having realized that some of the things I was observing could be radically changed. I often say in lectures that I was born for a nursing home and that I look forward to being in one. But mine will have whirlpools, pot, whisky, and daily massage. Ridiculous, yes, but said to contrast the stories that these residents told, which so often were about just contending with the consummate boredom of the life. "Not much to do around here," David Forsythe often bemoaned. "Guess I'll go take a nap."

And I could spot contrasting standpoints. Lots of outsiders, visitors, doctors, state people would come in and see the bulletin board, strategically placed to be seen right as one exits the elevator, displaying all the "Activities": Tuesday, bingo; Wednesday, birthday party; Thursday, sewing ("Why would I want to sew?" asked Mary Mcguire. "I sewed all my life. Always hated it."). But for the visitors, smiling and satisfied by the text they had activated it was altogether different. "Isn't it wonderful; they have everything for them here," Anne

Karney concluded after a brief encounter with the fifth floor, as she left behind the nothingness of the other twenty-three hours.

D.: Sounds like boarding school.

T.: People are there all day long. And night. But outsiders can come in and the experience is mediated by text—the actual having been leeched out, the textual popped up on the board, "Party today."

D.: Yes.

T.: I want a full staff of activities' directors, with an infinite array of activities, again like massage, whirlpools, martinis, and marijuana—well, that's my personal list. Yes, we can only laugh at such foolishness now. But the revolutionary potential is there, or it surely seemed to me to be, proceeding from everyday work practices.

Also I talked with the workers and residents and then wrote their words as conversation, as they originally occurred, hoping the people would come across with some subjectivity. It doesn't matter who was doing what or what they were doing, but that some were doing something. The beautiful thing about the generous conception of work is that it can include the doings of all kinds of things, including the work of doing nothing, which may be the hardest work of all. This generous conception has such a liberating potential. In this case it frees the researcher from the conceptual chains of the "done-tos" and "acted-upons," as residents are so often considered, into seeing them as doers, actors, agents.

It was almost downhill once that conceptual apparatus was in place; then I could just concentrate on the details of what the nursing assistants and residents were doing, like these former homemakers now eating with plastic forks and spoons, which many despised, while tens of thousands of dollars were transferred from banks or governments to these corporations.

Another focus was on how the local work is accomplished in its enormous complexity, like the essential but essentially distasteful work of cleaning someone's bodily messes, over and over, and still carrying on—still a marvel to me—yes, but that can't be the whole contribution for institutional ethnography. No, for us, we have to follow this all up with the how—how it is there but made invisible, made objective, made true. "If It's Not Charted, It Didn't Happen" seems to be a phrase widely familiar among nurses and nursing assistants. I got to that point. But if I had it to do again, I would pay more attention to the sequencing and activating of the texts, which is new.

D.: Yes. Yes, we've learned quite a bit.

How Did You Do the Ethnography?

D.: How did you record your notes?

T.: All the field notes were on an eight-and-a-half-inch paper, folded in eighths, folded into my back pocket, which to this day I still carry.

D.: And what did you record?

T.: All kinds of things, not just words, but they had to be encoded with key words. In order to scribble some words on one of those scraps of paper, I went to the bathroom often. Given the setting, most people seemed not to mind. Then in the off-hours I would tear up these eighths and sort them, picking out themes of what was said, and pasting them in some preliminary scheme up on the wall, literally, with scotch tape. I moved them around, like a big puzzle. Eventually, they got sorted around and shuffled into chapters, still on the wall. The wall became a book in progress.

D.: How did that help?

T.: Well, it made of the writing a whole body physical act. I always find that in describing institutional ethnographies, there's gesturing and moving around going on, like Adele Mueller's women in Peru weaving their blankets, or Marj DeVault's women feeding their families, or Paul Luken and Suzanne Vaughan's women moving whole households. I move because these studies are always linked back to embodied experiences and activities.[6]

We may want to make a distinction here between observation and observational research. Institutional ethnography is a materialist method; it searches out the social relations contained within materials and studies the relations as themselves material.

D.: Yes, it's a bit different when you set out to do a research study of something. You go into the field and you're in there not just as a nursing aide but as an observer, which gives meaning to the term *participant observation*. You're working and you're observing and the observing has this kind of double consciousness, where you've got a little pocket full of notes that you're going to carry away or that you're running off to the washroom with.

T.: Yes, observation becomes a sensual activity, of setting and people's bodies. As the administrator stood six inches away from my face, bawling me out loudly for drinking coffee on the ward, I could feel my heart and perspiration, in fear and anger. And the first observations were of physical revulsions from everyday processes of messy bodies, and I tried to write about messiness, and the hard work of cleaning it all up. So these were some of the sensual dimensions of this observational work.

D.: Yes. I'm wondering how you did this move from working as a nursing assistant to putting it in writing.

When I did observational work, I wrote a lot. I kept this journal and more formal notes, evenings, weekends. I'd write up everything: feelings, reflections, whatever—also observations that I saw or heard.[7]

T.: You wrote them?

D.: I typed them.

T.: And then reread and rewrote them?

D.: No, I don't think I rewrote them. I didn't sort of frame them up; they just sort of accumulated—in this big, fat thing which was sort of like a journal and that was really the basis of my thesis, the material in that more than anything more official.

T.: I can distinctly remember wanting to make the writing a physical act. I mean physically enjoyable rather than the contortions and torture we usually enact in this act. And I was committed to the mandate of "preserving the presence of the subject" that is still such a vital part of it all.[8]

D.: While you were doing the work, you were working on the book. I didn't do that. I think the way people were taught to do fieldwork, inasmuch as you were taught to do fieldwork, was that you collected data and then you figured out what the hell to do with it. And that was a big problem.

I bring this out because I think it's an interesting thing to bring out in terms of people reading how to do observations, not necessarily institutional ethnography observations, but the different ways of approaching the kind of observational process in terms of how you are writing about it. I wasn't trying to set up a model on the basis of the way I did it but rather to ask you to explicate a little more about how you went about it. Because I think you did it differently. And I think that's something that's interesting to people.

T.: Yes, I was into participant observation but never took a field methods course.

D.: They hardly existed.

T.: You mean you didn't even have one with Goffman?

D.: No. They didn't tell you what to do in the field. Nobody told you what to do.

T.: My trick in "preserving the presence of the subject" was to quote people in their talk and build around their speech. While rapidly rousing and dressing residents at 7 a.m. on a cold morning, I would regularly encounter Irene O'Brien's plaintiff cry, "Why can't I get a little rest around here?" She thought she'd entered a rest home; over time I concluded that she was wrong. She had entered a factory-like, three-shift, understaffed, efficiency-driven manufacturing plant, and she was the product. . . . Oh, sorry, where was I?

D.: Go on.

T.: Also I was angry at the obscenities in the organizations I was observing, a great driving force. I was not a passive observer. Subdued, close to the chest, secretive (which is what covert means), yes. But there were so many everyday emotions, like grief, actively suppressed in the institutional order of things. I, of course, had the special privilege of being able to write all that out, and it was comforting, expiating.

I put the quotes in various chapters, holding on to a chapter outline as a skeleton. Then I went about the business of dropping these quotes into the chapters, putting meat on the bones so to speak.

How Did You Write the Book?

D.: I'm still searching for an explicit account of how you went from the work of observation to the work of writing, the production of the writing, which was different from how I did it.

T.: I'm thinking about one way. We're talking about writing, not acting, not dramatization. But in this work they come close. Drama unfolded in front of me a bit at a time. It was fun to realize that in acting out these tales I could elicit emotional responses from audiences, as the events had done in my experiencing them. I could make people laugh sometimes. I wrote up some of these activities as performance.

And sometimes I was the butt of the humor. For example, there was the highly skilled nursing assistant balling me out for getting soap in this guy's eyes. So I acted it out as it occurred and wrote down how I was acting it out. ". . . and she grabs the washcloth out of my hands and gives me this double-take, eyes darting back at me. 'You ain't had no babies, have you?'"

I've gotten huge mileage out of the leap that residents and nursing assistants were "active." Maybe they don't speak to the connections between everyday life and the translocal relations of ruling with which it is coordinated, that's our job. That's what I feel I should have been better able to speak to.

D.: Well, I'm not so sure you have to when you're writing it up as institutional ethnography; you found that you could find the extra-local ruling relations *in* the small, daily routines. Were you conscious of writing that into the text?

T.: Well, I tried to be, as in the Philippines connection, with this home as part of a global industry and a carefully managed international labor force.

D.: You know, there are a number of ways of doing this. You can start out with . . . well, Alison and I[9] started with our own experiences, yes, then we talked to the women about the work they did in relation to their children's schooling, and then we talked to the administrators and they each put complementary readings on the situation. That would be different from writing an observational account in which you are showing the presence of the translocal in the every day.

In the observational situation you're directly participating, so you have a different kind of ground. I was rereading some of your chapters and I remember you describing the business of the chart, and how some of the work didn't make it to the charts—so that is a different kind of way of showing the institutional in the local, where there is a work process and part of that is doing the charts. And the charts are what hook that work process into the extra-local organization. You didn't actively pursue that. I'm not saying you should have; I just want to bring out what is distinctive about the ways in which you found the institutional in the local.

T.: And what I heard, experienced, and tried to capture was so much of the local erased.

D.: And that is worth giving prominence to; it's distinctive to your work.

T.: And I think we want more of that kind of thing, don't you, more of the actual, the everyday life.

D.: Yes, I would agree.

T.: I was poor, and that was a driving force, and the nursing assistants were poor, and the residents were poor. How can this be? I kept asking.

And institutional ethnography gave me the tools to show some of the complexities of this work and watch it get erased, as itself a work process, vested in texts. So that by the time you read a chart of what the nursing assistant work involved, it became on the page robot work that anyone could do.

Also, at that level of degraded life, I hated going to work on those hot, non-air-conditioned Saturday afternoons, off to the evening shift. Like meeting the woman who was begging for a quarter on the street, but turns out she was also a resident of the nursing home. At first I couldn't even understand the words of her request, for she had only a few teeth, so her speech was slurred—teeth care being very low on the available services—a moment completely connected to the Medicaid regime.

And I remember people being divided up by their body parts, some parts cared for, some not. I remember lining up residents in chairs and taking off their shoes and socks so the foot doctor could come in and, in assembly line style, scan down one foot after another, scarcely looking up at the people to whom they were connected. He was out the door after scribbling the requisite transformation of human life into measures that fit the medical codes. These are things you saw every day and in turn every day was ruled by these codes. "How has Mary Ryan been eating lately?" asked a nurse pouring over a chart.

"Well," I pondered, "She's not very hungry at mealtime. In the middle of the night, though, when there's no food available, that's a different story."

"No, no. I'm not interested in any of that," she snapped, eyes riveted on the boxes to be checked. Is she "independent," "requires assistance," "dependent on staff," or a "tube feeder?"

We can see, especially through the institutional ethnography lens, that the question was not about Mary at all, but about how much labor was required—for the whole floor, where people's idiosyncratic eating habits were made over into textually based patterns and generalized to the whole.

D.: Is that in the book? It's interesting.

T.: Yes, though maybe not those exact words. And it brings up again the different kind of data that is represented here in this project, whereas most institutional ethnography relies heavily on interviews thus far in its development.

D.: Yes. It's going to have to. It's simply an economic thing. It's so much cheaper. Time is money, that's the reason. It would be great to have more observational work, yes, and to combine them. Institutional ethnography isn't going to be stuck with just one.

I'd also be interested in seeing someone develop some quantitative work, so you can if you want to say something quantitatively about nursing homes. We never looked at it as though each study were to have one kind of method. It would be lovely to have more observational stuff.

T.: I want to make note of your emphasis on the materiality of the text. Of course, pointing to the materiality of the text implies being able to point to the materiality of anything. Here we draw a line from the Marx and Engels writing that you richly invoke in the companion volume. It's always interesting to see how actual materials come into play. Observations find their way from the reader back to a material base, local and particular situations, marking a ground from which observations are made—some of your major points are based in observations.

D.: Yes.

T.: Still one more topic I wanted to touch on before we wind down was this lingering question, what is the place of the author in the writing?

D.: I think the author should be there in just an ordinary way, not present in a way that obscures what the author is trying to tell or show; there can be too much.

T.: How institutional ethnographers handle themselves in the text is an open question. I like what you do. You enter into a sentence often in a passing phrase. You aren't the object, but you appear with some material references, just sort of dropped into a sentence.

D.: But why did you raise the topic of presence?

T.: Well, it's a problem. Twenty years ago authors weren't supposed to mention themselves. Now in this postobjective era, "Where is the researcher here?" and "How does the researcher come into the discussion?" are significant questions. For example, feelings of embarrassment and self-consciousness were pervasive in my experience; it was liberating to be able to write about them. What about violence and patient abuse? Looking back I say, "Yes, I did both!" No, not really, but I was very, very close. I could tie knots behind residents' backs with some skill learned in the army; we would boast about our knots. That fierce need for control was organizationally produced.

D.: Yes, those are important things to record.

T.: I didn't steal, and never saw anyone who did, and it may be blown way out of proportion. But at that pittance of a wage, you're pissed—that sets the stage.

D.: Did you write that in the book?

T.: No, I don't think so. This understanding came later amid questions, since everyone wants to know about the violence that they've heard and read about.

D.: Yes, it's been interesting writing the mothering book. We have this notion of a trajectory—so that we can position ourselves now at the moment of writing in relation to what we've learned since, and reflect on it. There are some things you're perfectly stupid about, but now it's obvious.

T.: I always think about the two of you walking the ravines, feeling deficient as mothers.

D.: Oh yes, that's where the study comes from, in that experience.[10]

Part II. Potential Contributions of Participant Observation

Just while preparing some summary comments to this conversation, I was asked to visit a sociology class at the nursing school of a university in the eastern United States. The students had been reading *Making Gray Gold* and were eager to relate their own experiences. Four particularly engaged students stayed after the class for more discussion. Perhaps not coincidentally, all were or had been nursing assistants.

One leaned toward my ear and asked with a sly smile, "I have one question for you. Tell me the hardest thing there was for you to learn about this job."

I had no hesitation in knowing my answer, but I felt shy to blurt it out to this person I had just met. Until I remembered she was a nursing assistant.

In like manner, turning toward her ear, I whispered back, "To clean someone."

"Yes," she laughed robustly and pointed at my chest, "that's it. I completely agree!"

From there we rolled into other agreements, like how the whole operation of nursing homes needed revolution and that we wanted to start it with about three times the staff that they have now.

It was a validating moment, occurring many years after the original research, but reaffirming not just the substantive content upon which we agreed but that there was a standpoint from which we could "look up into" the social organization of nursing homes.

Embedded in that conversation were certain dimensions that highlight the specific invitations into data-gathering that are offered by participant observation as a way of doing institutional ethnography. Of course there are many ways of doing participant observation and it has a long tradition in the social sciences. But there are aspects of the nature of its inquiry that are particularly helpful for institutional ethnography.

In the previous chapter, DeVault and McCoy discussed how interviewers can enter into the local settings of people's doings. In Smith's research that follows in the next chapter, readers get to see texts entering and moving through local settings. Here in between them the inquiry has concerned how participant observers enter into local settings to see beyond them, or rather to see the beyond within them.

I would suggest, reflecting on the materials in both this volume and the one by Smith (2005) that accompanies it, that participant observation studies are to be encouraged in institutional ethnography because they have the potential to refine our appreciations of at least the following dimensions of the craft: stories, authors, bodies, place, time, motion, how ruling relations work, and particular ways for seeing the social organization in the local.

Participant observation is grounded in actual events from which descriptions and stories are derived. As we struggle with our research designs, it is always good to bear in mind the actual stories that constitute the base of a problematic. Behind every good problematic there sits an author and the stories she or he has to tell.

If there are stories, there has to be an author/researcher active in their production; there's no room in this method for an invisible author. In a sense almost all institutional ethnography begins in participant observation. Authors' own experiences consistently form the bases for research problematics. For example, studies like those of nurses by Marie Campbell (1984, 1988, 1992b), Dorothy Smith and Alison Griffith's (2005) of mothers, Nancy Jackson's (1995) of community college teachers, Ellen Pence's (2001) and Gillian Walker's (1995) of battered wives, and Susan Turner's (1995 and chapter 8 of this book) of neighbors—all begin in various ways with the researcher's own experience whether as a nurse, a mother, or a community college teacher, or in the women's movement working to change the situation for battered women or organizing with other residents to protest a local development. Taken together we now have a whole corpus of work that orients researchers toward beginning in everyday experiences to trace connections to extra-local ruling relations.

In the current institutional ethnography literature we have some very clear starting points. Readers learn where the authors are "coming from" as entrée to their investigations, and this method insists that researchers always be able to refer back to the original experiential base. But in following textual sequences, researchers have decided not to spend too much time fleshing out the everyday world, or discussing their own positions in it, or their part in the production of their accounts. Presently, therefore, the place of the author in institutional ethnography remains an open issue, one that wants to be worked out with a variety of methodological approaches.[11]

In participant observation the author has to come out in certain ways, or perhaps we might say is free to come out, and is openly part of the production of the data itself. In so doing there are special invitations in this method to incorporate physicality, bodies in motion, the authors', and others. Putting one's body on the line as part of a research project seems to give rise to discovery *in* one's body of relevant data. Its specific aches and pains, its emotions, the messiness of the flesh and blood events—these provide a corporeal, incarnate base with which to ground the author's and others bodies in action and coordination.[12] In the work reported here, I wrote about the smells that seemed to linger in my consciousness long after a shift and a shower were over, or of the hunger in the middle of the night experienced by both resident and worker, or the boredom of the routines, or the challenges of the close-up bodily contact—all provided grist for analysis and for organizational and policy critique.

This method also offers possible insights to the challenge of how to begin in everyday life. Almost always in participant observation there is a *place* that provides the starting point. To begin in a standpoint as a methodological device remains one of the breakthroughs of this method, but how to do it is still there to be explored; far from a given, how to start there remains somewhat uncharted territory. Participant observation begins in a specific setting, a starting point on a map, a "you are here" point. It provides a way to start in local particularities to establish a problematic with a focus on how actualities of people's lives come to be hooked up with institutional relations.

As with place, *time* is immanent in participant observation research. The opposite of snapshot methods, this research form goes on in a specific place and time, and over time. As such, participant observation explores the social *in motion*, as an ongoing concerting of activities. This dimension of social life is foundational to the social ontology of institutional ethnography; how to capture it in research is a challenge. The stories that appear in interview research can be full of action, for sure. Yet they are by definition reconstructions, first by the teller and then by the researcher. But in participant observation the primary narratives are different. They happen in an actual time and place and in motion.

Participant observations, as they are developed in the future in institutional ethnography, may also have unique contributions for understanding how ruling relations work. Very often they provide a position for exploring ruling relations from the outside. In the research discussed here, the work was done "outside" in the sense of "under" ruling relations, from a particular subordinate position in an organization. Subordination itself can yield some insights and passions. When I got caught with that cup of coffee on the ward, which was against the rule that staff were not allowed to eat or drink on shift, I could have been "written up," or suspended or gotten into all kinds of trouble.

"Are you finished with your coffee yet, fella?" the administrator scowled sarcastically, and loud enough for other workers to hear the reprimand.

I cowered appropriately but seethed inside. Eventually I could fit this stingy little rule into a whole array of incidents that, tiny in themselves, went together to make up an organization under intense social control. The initial problematic of the study, how nursing assistants could be forbidden from leaving the workplace on break or lunch, seemed extreme initially, but less and less so as I experienced, literally face-to-face, many more rules that reflected and reinforced the coffee ban. Where are the ruling relations? Often right there in the rules and their local practices.

One feature of the participant observation in this paper is that it became a *covert* research. I decided to study the ruling by immersing myself in its subjugation rather than getting administrators' permissions, which would have been conspiring with them, to be on the side of the ruling. The present conditions of research in North America may well preclude such a posture, with the human subjects review committees acting as gatekeepers of permissions from authorities. Researchers now have to explore creative ways to pose an investigation that does not involve overt deceit.

Whether covert or overt, the method lends itself to figuring out how to locate the institutional *in* the local, at the point of contact with the actual. As we search for how to collapse the dichotomy of micro and macro, to find the latter in the former, in people's doings, it can help to be anchored in specific doings. The researcher can proceed from that ground to identify texts that tie people's work into the institutional and to study how institutional processes are coordinated *as* people's work mediated by texts. Being there, one can see texts being read and come into play in a sequence and regulatory hierarchy.

Participant observation can open up the analytic aperture away from individuals and toward the *coordination* of their doings observed while doing them. One can observe (some of) the texts as they occur in the course of a work sequence in which the researcher is involved. As the charge nurse leaned over her desk, at pains to get the right precoded option to her closed-ended question of "How has Mary been eating lately?" there was no reason for her to look up at me. Her question was asked by the text and required the text's answers, not mine; she was its proxy and respondent. Mary's erratic eating wishes and needs found no place in this interrogatory devise, where "requires assistance" became her assigned slot.

And from an insider's position, one can watch as texts get activated. I can see the smiling visitors arrive to spread good cheer, indeed providing vital services of a material, social, and emotional nature, yet perpetuating the ideologies that silence residents. We could see them walking off the elevator to come face-to-face with the bulletin board, which told them of all the activities of the day. "Oh, they have activities for these people all the time" was a common reading. It was one in sharp contrast to those of us who lived and worked amidst the consummate boredom of it all. Visitors, as readers, brought to full circle the ideological production of the discourse of activities. The visitors, we can now say, activated those texts, became their proxy, and participated in the ruling relations that permeated the rooms they entered and left.

Finally, there's Fern. She and her coat might have entered into analysis through some other method, or not so, but they did emerge as a result of participant observation. Reaching into her closet was also one way to reach into the local practices that hook to categories and frames of an institutional discourse tied to funding. There the coat hung barren and alone, shorn of all the other fine clothing that she later told me she once owned. Now a pauper, the question I was asking, "Where'd you get the fur coat, Fern?" was really about what it was doing there amid the emptiness that surrounded it. But looking out from within the closet, as Fern, this story's hero, might do, we could see the coat's journey as a journey of policy in motion. From the rich home in the suburb, through hospitalization, then a Medicare home, then the depletion of all personal resources, only then to Medicaid support and its penniless life, Fern's story is one of a general social relation, lived then and now throughout the United States. While preserving her presence as a subject, an institutional ethnography shows the answer to the question to be an identifiable and traceable set of textually mediated social relations.

We now know that the charge is to begin in a problematic and go from there. Drawing texts into ethnographic investigations is essential for looking up into the translocal organization of the everyday. Institutional ethnography has advanced considerably in the "going from there" part, especially in its textual analyses—in being able to work up accounts of extended relations.

Still, although we want to travel beyond the experiential bases and their stories, we always want to be able to hold on to them, to be able to return back to them, to the "you are here" point on the map from which we began. We want to keep experimenting with trying to portray everyday life and experience—how to do this is not a given but an invitation. Smith has often noted that we don't want to lose sight of the embodied that is foundational. Participant observation invites and insists on a portrayal of action. In this sense it helps us in our search for the act-text-act sequences by helping us to flesh out what we mean by the "act" part, and in so doing, to keep in touch with the embodied activities of people's work.

Notes

1. Smith reinvigorates the method of historical materialism, outlined in Marx and Engels, that all history begins with actual individuals and the conditions of their exchange. She has broadened the social ontology to refer to coordination between individuals, including textual coordinations. See the companion volume to this book, Dorothy Smith's *Institutional Ethnography: A Sociology for People* (2005), chapter 2, and Marx and Engels's *The German Ideology* (1976).
2. Here is where this kind of materialist analysis begins, with actual materials, and the social relations contained within them.
3. Smith's writing is frequently grounded in concrete images from her own experiences: the dog on the lawn ties local settings to property relations (Smith 1987: 155); the train going by introduces the standpoint of the researcher seeing through one side of the window (Smith 1974b: 10); the child pointing to the fish shows the making of meaning *as* a social act (Smith 1999: 115).
4. Campbell (1984, 1988).
5. One of its earlier articulations is in *The Everyday World* (Smith 1987: 165).
6. Mueller (1995); DeVault (1991); Luken and Vaughan (2003).

7. Smith's dissertation was about a mental hospital, with supervisor Erving Goffman, at Berkeley in 1964.

8. Preserving the presence of the subject, as found in *Everyday World* (1987), p. 151.

9. Griffith and Smith (2005).

10. From "Institutional Ethnography" in Tim May, *Qualitative Research in Action* (2002), p. 24: "On long walks through the ravines of Toronto we shared the stories of our mothering work, of our children's struggles, of our fears about interfering, of pushing teachers too hard, of not pushing them hard enough. Our explorations opened up the social relations and organization of schooling as those in relation to which women's work as mothers is done."

11. For a recent discussion that takes up the place of the author, in this case the author being George Smith, and his "Political Activist as Ethnographer (G. W. Smith 1990), see Mykhalovskiy and Church, forthcoming.

12. As in Kathryn Church's *Forbidden Narratives: Political Autobiography as Social Science* (2005).

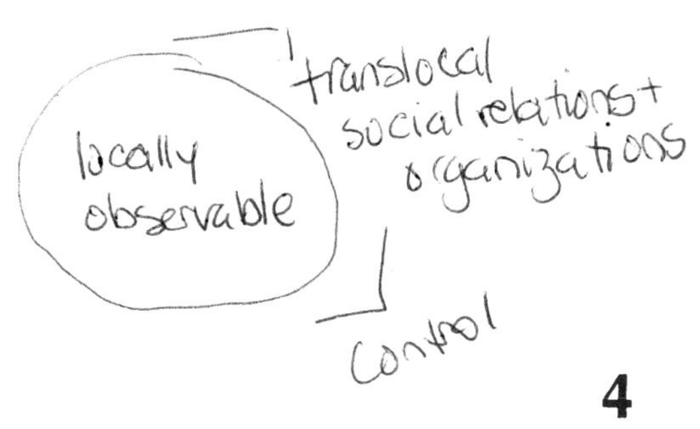

4

Incorporating Texts into Ethnographic Practice[1]

Dorothy E. Smith

INCORPORATING TEXTS INTO ethnographic practice is essential to institutional ethnography. It is what enables it to reach beyond the locally observable and discoverable into the translocal social relations and organization that permeate and control the local. Enunciating this principle is one thing; creating a practice or practices that realize it is another. In this paper I'm going to introduce some ways in which texts (or documents) can be recognized as part of the action, as what people do, or as occurring in particular local settings of people's activities. The importance of texts, as of any phenomena of language, to the social is as coordinator of the diversities of people's subjectivities, their consciousnesses. People, as individuals, arrive at any moment with their own distinctive histories, their distinctive perspectives, capacities, interests, concerns, and whatever else they may bring as a potentiality to act in a given setting. Among those sharing the same local setting, actual diversities may be both generated by and coordinated through physical movement, work processes, gesture, language (talk and text), and so on. Diversities of perspective and activity may be mediated by technologies of all kinds; technologies of all kinds, as they expand, enhance, and transform human work activities, also coordinate them. While institutional ethnography can certainly address any technology from this aspect, the technologies of texts and textuality as these enter into the coordinating of people's work are foundational to its project. Texts do something rather special as coordinators of people's activities, and this paper aims to suggest how we might investigate the ways in which they operate in particular local settings.

Of course, texts must be defined before we can move further. Institutional ethnography uses the notion of text to refer to words, images, or sounds that are set into a material form of some kind from which they can be read, seen, heard, watched, and so on. Of course, I'm addressing those most commonplace objects of our contemporary world, so much present that we take them and their ubiquity entirely for granted. They are the books, the bus tokens, the airline reservations, the radio, the CDs, the e-mail messages, the advertisements, the movies, and so on and so on and so on. Their material forms are such that a given form of words, images, or sounds is replicable; that is, anyone else anywhere else can read, see, hear, and so on the same words, images, or sounds as any other person engaged with the same text. The magical character of replicable texts from the point of view of institutional ethnographic interest is that they are read, seen, heard, watched, and so on in particular local and observable settings while at the same time hooking up an individual's consciousness into relations that are translocal. For the ethnographer individuals' engagement with a text is locally observable and, at the same time, it is connecting the local into the translocality of the ruling relations. Discovering, then, how texts articulate our local doings to the translocally organized forms that coordinate our consciousnesses with those of others elsewhere and at other times is the objective. Ethnography stretches beyond the locally observable to describe and explicate in the text a local coordinating of people's consciousnesses that hooks in to the ruling relations within which institutions form functional complexes. Drawing texts into the scope of ethnographic investigation is an essential step in exploring the translocal organization of the everyday.

But how to do that? Our ordinary practices of reading, watching, hearing, and looking at texts absorb our consciousness in the text itself and in our conversation with it. It takes us out of our local experience and the direction of our action in which our experience arises. This makes it difficult to envisage texts as part of ongoing everyday activity and as themselves active through or in us in how that activity is coordinated with that of others.

This paper does not claim to provide comprehensive solutions to this problem. It collects instances of institutional ethnographic research procedures that have solved it in particular ways and puts forward principles that might govern how texts can be taken up in ethnographies of the local presence of the ruling relations. I have grouped the examples under two main headings, each of which locates an important dimension of how texts coordinate sequences of action. The first considers research practices that exhibit texts as coordinators of sequences of action; the second, research practices that operate in a regulatory hierarchy of texts I call the *intertextual hierarchy*. The two types of research practice are complementary, overlap to some extent, but each attends to rather different aspects of how institutions are brought into being in the translocal coordinating of people's local work. In some instances, both types of research practice could be used. And, of course, the researcher may develop others that have not been envisaged here. Whatever the research practice, however, it is essential that the text be recognized as a local occurrence articulated to and articulating people's doings.

Texts as Coordinators in Sequences of Action/Work

In the accompanying book, *Institutional Ethnography: A Sociology for People,* I used a diagram that I'm going to reproduce here. My diagram was intended to help fix the notion of texts as happening in time and place and as integral to organized sequences of action.

It's a simple notion but harder to realize in ethnographic practice. Notice that it is a sequence in time, a course of action. In our ordinary practices of reading we forget that it is done in time as well as in a particular local setting. We forget our own bodily presence and location in the act of reading. The sequence formalized in the above diagram places the text as an *occurrence* embedded in what is going on and going forward. The notion of the text as occurring is intended specifically to make it observable as in an ongoing activity. It suggests as a simple rule that texts should not be analyzed in abstraction from how they enter into and coordinate sequences of action. Some texts, such as case files, are a product of and make accountable the coordinating of multiple institutional functions, for example, the work of

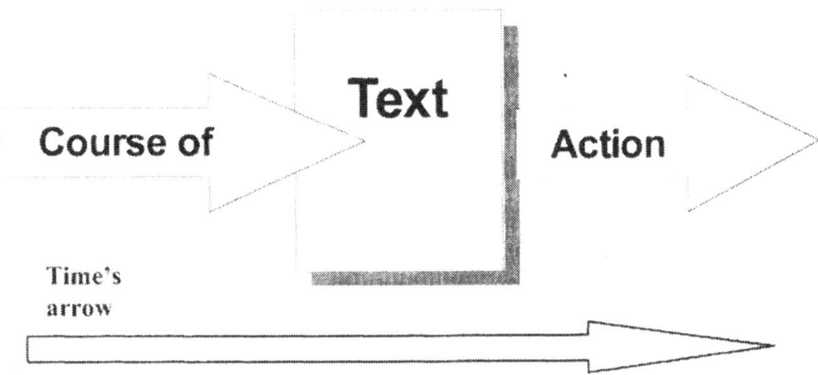

FIGURE 4.1.
Conceptualizing Texts in Action: The Act-Text-Act Sequence

nurses, physicians, social services, occasionally police, and so on in relation to a hospital patient. They are not made to be read as a continuous text like a novel. Rather they are read selectively for different purposes, articulated to various sequences of action, and it is these selective readings for which the text is constructed and which, in a sense, analyze it to find the sense it can make in particular settings of action.

In what follows, I have developed two examples of research approaches that realize this sequence and preserve the temporal movement from one stage or step in a sequence (the left side of figure 4.1) through the text and into stage two of the action which *incorporates the text.* The first[2] of these illustrates a very straightforward procedure. It involves interviewing both those involved in the work processes that bring the text into play in the sequence, *and* those who take up the text to enter it into the next phase of action. The example used is that of the completing of a form used to evaluate students in relation to applications for admission to graduate school. The research, by Edouard Vo-Quang (1998), involved an interview with a faculty member familiar with the work of completing such an appraisal (left side of figure 4.1) and a second interview with the graduate admissions officer (GAO) who would read such appraisals (right side of figure 4.1) in the context of coming to decisions about whether to admit the student.

The second uses essentially the same model—the act-text-act sequence of figure 4.1. It works, however, with a situation in which interviewing was not possible. There was only the text of a court-ordered psychological evaluation of a woman contending for custody of her child. Analysis draws on the same temporal sequencing, examining first the traces *in the text* of how it was produced and, second, explicating what it projects as organization for what comes next.

Example 1: The Appraisal Form

My account here is based on Edouard Vo-Quang's research, done when he participated in a graduate course on textual analysis I gave some years ago.[3] I had suggested that one very straightforward procedure would be to do interviews, either leading into the text (the left side of the figure 4.1 diagram), about how the text entered into what came next (the right side, figure 4.1) in an ongoing sequence of action, or both. Edouard chose the last of these. He interviewed a faculty member in his department (not sociology) about what was involved in completing the form established for appraising graduate students applying for admission to graduate school. He then went on to interview the graduate admissions officer (GAO) about how the completed form was read.

The form opens with the usual interrogatory structure of the genre—the student's name, address, phone number, and so on. It structures the referee's responses with a grid that asks her or him to evaluate the student on a set of attributes. Here's what that section of the report looks like:

	Top 5%	Top 10%	Top 25%	Top 40%	Average	Below Average	No information
Academic Preparedness							
Ability to communicate: orally							
in writing							
Creativity and the capacity for independent thinking							
Industry and reliability							
Initiative and seriousness of purpose							
Intellectual capacity							
Research skill or potential							
Teaching ability							
Professional expertise							
Overall rating							

FIGURE 4.2.
The Evaluative Grid

The referee's work is to decide where to locate a particular candidate, known to him or her in the context of teaching. The job is to rate the individual in relation to other students that the referee has known. Edouard talked to the faculty member about how she or he would go about completing the form, focusing on a portion (represented in figure 4.2) that calls on the referee to examine her or his experiences with this individual in the light of the categories provided. The referee has to figure out how to call up from memory or records what can be fitted into this framework, recognizing its intention, that is, that when it's read it will contribute to a decision of considerable significance in the life of the individual thus evaluated.

I've drawn a diagram (figure 4.3) based on Vo-Quang's findings that show the sequence. The attributes listed in the evaluation grid that the referee completes can be seen as a kind of filter selecting the categories in which the referee's experience is to be expressed (the left-hand side, corresponding to the left-hand side of the earlier figure 4.1) diagramming the conceptualization of a text as coordinator of a sequence of action. It is the filtered evaluation that arrives for the graduate admissions officer's (GAO) reading. The GAO explained to Vo-Quang how the completed form would be read in the context of the work of appraising a student in order to arrive at a decision as to whether to admit. We do not have an account of the GAO's work to the point of its completion, but the GAO's reading, as Vo-Quang describes it, is clearly oriented to the work of coming to such a decision.

What has been put through the filter from the referee's side (the left side of the "filter sequence" diagram, figure 4.3) has been reconstructed as the standard categories and system of ranking of the form. How the rankings selected are read on the other end of the process isn't available to the referee. Similarly at the next stage of the sequence, the GAO has no access to the kind of knowledge of the student on which the referee has drawn in completing the form. This textually generated disjuncture is made particularly visible here by the striking differences in the referee's reflections and intentions and how they are interpreted by the GAO. Though there are significant transformations in the referee's intended message when it arrives at the GAO's reading, the latter has no difficulty in treating his or her interpretation as if it were what the referee intended.

The diagram, figure 4.3, next page, explicates the operation of the text as a filter in the course of a sequence of action. The referee's work is represented in the left column of the diagram, the categories of the text lifted from figure 4.2 in the central column, and the GAO's reading in the right-hand column. Notice at the top of the figure the *time's arrow* that reminds us that what we are being shown analyzes a temporal process, a sequence in time from the collections and recollections of the referee confronted with the categories and ranking procedures of the form and then the form itself that is presented for reading by the GAO.

The referee and the GAO have different procedures for operating the filter: the referee operates the filter to assemble relevant aspects of his or her experience of the student to be evaluated; the graduate admissions officer operates the filtered product in relation to the process of deciding whether this student should be admitted. The filter cleans up the potential clutter of the detail that the referee brings to the work of evaluation. More important, it standardizes it. The GAO can read it in relation to other forms completed by other referees, some (a restricted number) for the same student, others of other students with whom a given application can be compared. Instead of referees' letters written in different styles and varying terminologies, the text allows comparisons to be made in standardized terms, regardless of how adequately they represent referees' views.

Notice that the term *application* in this context locates a collection of texts, a *file*, of records constituting the representation of a person that will be read and perhaps discussed (if there's a committee at work with the graduate admissions officer) as the reality of that person's potentialities for graduate work. That is how the representation is read and interpreted by the GAO. The disjunctures that the filtering procedure is capable of generating are discovered by Vo-Quang's research procedure. Figure 4.3 shows that, at a number of points, the referee's intentions and experience are translated into the categories of the evaluative grid that are read very differently by the GAO. In more

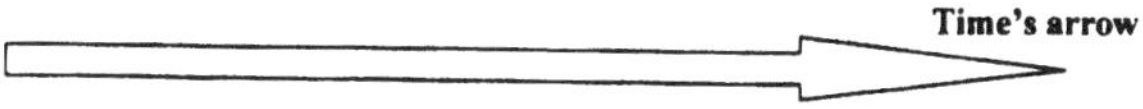

Time's arrow

Faculty Refereeing	Grid items	Graduate Admissions Officer
Academic preparedness refers to how prepared the student was for the class: ". . . in terms of academic preparedness, if it's a seminar course, um, I would think about the extent to which they were prepared every week for the seminar and, um, I would assess how they asked questions in class, that sort of thing."	**Academic preparedness**	*Academic preparedness* is less important to the assessment of the applicant since it is redundant with respect to a careful reading of the transcripts (courses taken, level, etc.)
Creativity and capacity for independent thinking "is usually reflected in the marks."	**Creativity and a capacity to independent thinking**	*Creativity and a capacity for independent thinking* "is very important."
". . .'*industry*' is evaluated according to whether or not the student was a 'hard worker,' and the student's '*reliability*' and to how regularly she attended class."	**Industry and reliability**	*Industry and reliability* and *initiative and seriousness* "filter flakiness."
Initiative and seriousness of purpose is an indicator of a student's "initiative," whether or not or how often the student would lead discussion, start debates, or "take initiative to do something. unusual in class." *Seriousness of purpose* "reflects upon the commitment [of the student] to the discipline or the subject matter or scholarship more generally." Taken together, these indicate the extent to which the student will be a "dedicated graduate student."	**Initiative and seriousness of purpose**	
Intellectual capacity as well as *research skill and potential* are reflected in the work/marks of the student: "If they're really gifted analytically or theoretically, it usually turns up in their papers or work."	**Intellectual capacity**	"*Intellectual capacity* translates into 'Is the applicant bright?'"
"*Research skill and potential*, again, here I look at their research papers and the extent to which I think they've got talent in this area."	**Research skill and potential**	
Being honest about how students are ranked is very important to this referee: "I always give . . . a purely accurate . . . because these go on to other people, and they look at it, colleagues in other universities, and they know that, you know, um, they're relying on me to give an accurate assessment of [the student's] capabilities."	**Overall Ranking**	Referring to the percentage ratings at the top of the columns in the frame, the GAO comments, "Everybody lies." Thus, "Top 25% is ranked low; top two columns, Top 5% and Top 10% are acceptable."

FIGURE 4.3.
The Filter Sequence

than one instance the referee treats a category with careful reference to a student's conduct as participant in courses. The category *Initiative and seriousness of purpose* is an example. The referee looks for specific kinds of behavior in the classroom (he or she must have been keeping records) that would indicate a special relation to the discipline, to learning, and to scholarship. Further, the referee treats this category as drawing on quite a different range of observations than the previous, *Industry and reliability.* The GAO, however, treats these in combination as filtering "flakiness." The most striking disjuncture occurs in the final item, *Overall Ranking*. The referee understands the rating she or he gives a student as a responsibility to colleagues; the truth must be told. The GAO by contrast interprets referees' ratings as *lies*.[4]

The consistencies and disjunctures mark how the form mediates an instructor's everyday experiences with and observations of a student who is making an application to graduate school and the assessment procedures used by a given university department to decide whom to admit. The completed text *transports* the referee's observations and experience from one setting to another at a distance; at the same time the particularities of that experience disappear. The local and everyday work of undergraduate teaching in universities is reduced, specified, and subject to standardization in producing what becomes *information* at the later stages in the sequence. The term *information* is itself deceptive. It hides the production and reading of texts that have a specifically standardized form enabling them to be treated as equivalent to one another and to be read using procedures that *read through* (Smith 1990a) the words and/or numbers to an imputed actuality beyond them.

Example 2: A Court Psychological Evaluation

Vo-Quang was able to interview both a person responsible for producing completed appraisal forms and a person responsible for reading them in the course of a specific work sequence. Of course, it is not always possible to talk both to those active in producing the text and those who read to enter it in some way into what gets done next. However, the movement from act to text and from text to act (figure 4.1) is built in the text. Thus even when you have only the text and no one to talk to, you may be able to find out quite a bit about how the text enters into the organization of a sequence by exploring traces of how the substance of the text as assembled, that is, where it came from, how it was put together, and how it projects organization into what follows. This analysis works with the text of a court psychological evaluation, performed by a psychologist we shall call William Graham, of a woman, Emma Merwin—also a pseudonym—claiming custody of her son. The evaluation was ordered by the court as part of child custody proceedings in which Emma Merwin eventually lost custody of her child.[5] There is no information about how the evaluation was produced other than that internal to the text; nor is there information about how the text was used in the court setting.

Similarly, apart from the information that Emma Merwin lost custody of her child, there is no information about how the texts were used in the court setting. Analysis sticks closely to what can be found in the text itself, focusing on finding something about the production process in the text itself and on "evaluation" is projected into readings that will be focused on whether Ms. Merwin or her husband should have custody of their children.

Emma Merwin's Psychological Evaluation

COURT PSYCHOLOGICAL EVALUATION

EXAM:
[4 dates of meeting]
DOB: * * * *
AGE: 34

REASON FOR REFERRAL: Assessment requested in custody issue.

TEST ADMINISTERED: Bender Gestalt, Projective Drawing Series, Sentence Completion, Rorschach, Thematic Apperception Test, Comprehensive Clinical Interview

CLINICAL DESCRIPTION: This 34-year-old married woman, currently separated from her child, impressed as a woman with marked emotional difficulties clinically. She spoke in a very soft, controlled manner as if she were trying to hold onto emotional controls. She was not successful. Tears came very quickly. She presented as one whose thinking was loose, confused, and tangential. There was a loss of distance. When she looked at some of the cards, they took on an air of reality. At the very least, her defences displayed serious deterioration and she reacted by being overcome by emotion and not being able to continue. At times, too, she was seductive—But, most of all, the picture of pathology was so overwhelming that I felt myself with enormous compassion for this disturbed woman.

EMOTIONAL FUNCTIONING: The test data confirm the distinctly pathological nature, which was hinted in her clinical behavior. Tests reflect that she is a disorganized, chaotic woman prone to occasional perceptual distortions but more towards illogical conclusions in her thinking. She can best be described as a borderline individual who fades in and out of reality. I was unclear whether she actually believed some of the things she said, or whether she was using them as a way of attempting to keep her child from his father. However, I was convinced that she is likely delusional about some issues.

Specifically, she feels victimized, she feels deceived, and she feels deception is multiplying in her environment. She feels that Judge X is also a victim of this deception and that others are being taken in by it. Specifically, she feels that she and her son were the victims of abuse from her husband (the child's father) and that she has no control over it. She feels emotionally and physically abused and harassed by her husband. She is fearful that her husband is going to harm her child by his control. She does not feel that he will harm the child when he is in the presence of others, but behind closed doors danger lurks for the child.

She is a woman who is paranoid in her perceptions, whose defences are defective, whose obsessive-compulsive defences falter and she is left feeling overwhelmed, overcome, chaotic, and anxious. She truly loves her child but her difficulties are such that she cannot act in the child's best interest. When she questions her child about possible abuse, it is likely that she is causing the child harm because she begins to feel that things are happening which in reality are not. One would conjecture that she is capable of causing her child marked emotional harm by her behavior.

She is a narcissistic, self-absorbed, and egocentric with much referential thinking. She thinks that things that happen in her environment refer to her and this is quite illogical. She feels burdened by authorities, unwhole and unfinished as an individual, and she is markedly enraged at and frightened of men. She perceives threat when it does not exist, again in an illogical way. Her ex-husband is viewed as abusive, as a fraud, and as being involved with [a cult organization].

She became extremely overwhelmed and had to stop the session when she began to talk about the [cult organization]. She felt that something ominous was going to happen if she continued talking about it. Her reaction was quite bizarre and unrealistic.

I see this woman as one who is capable of reacting in very unusual, uncontrolled, impulsive and labile—perhaps even dangerous ways. I cannot pinpoint any violent behavior on her part but her defences are so fragile that she is a capable of any behavior. I believe, too, that her need to keep her child from the father could result in her absconding with him. Hence, the safest course would be for supervised visitation. I also believe that she is capable of saying things to her son which are illogical and could cause him harm as well.

It is my impression that she truly loves her son. I saw her with him and it is clear that her feelings for her son, her love and her need to be with him are real. She related to him in a manner which suggested deep feelings for him. The two clung to and hugged each other, reflecting the time that elapsed since they had last seen each other and the love each had for the other. Mother was mostly appropriate, but at times had to be stopped by [sic] saying things in front of the child which were inappropriate for him to hear.

SUMMARY AND RECOMMENDATIONS: In conclusion, then this is a woman who is quite disturbed. She is a borderline individual who is currently delusional and who fades in and out of reality. She is capable of outrageous behavior of an impulsive, chaotic nature. She has boundary problems. She is illogical in her thinking and thinking [sic] is characterized by looseness, tangentiality, and losses [sic] of distance. She is narcissistic, self-referential and self-absorbed. Because of her emotional condition, she presents as a danger to her child and hence I feel strongly that the father should maintain custody and that visitation for Mrs. Merwin should be on a supervised basis.

[signed] Wm.A Graham, Licensed Psychologist

Once we've taken up the sequence act-text-act represented as a course of action in figure 4.1, we can find a good deal of this process in the text itself. Some of what we find draws on some background in what is involved in the writing of a psychological report; four dates were listed at the head of the text presumably representing four meetings between the psychologist and Emma Merwin. I was also told when I was asked to analyze the report that it was part of a child custody proceeding, that it was court ordered (i.e., Emma Merwin was required by the court to subject herself to evaluation), and that the result of the proceedings was that Emma Merwin lost custody of her child. My analysis here focuses on uncovering the process of production present but not enunciated in the text and on how the text projects organization into the future. With respect to the latter, I want to make clear I am not assuming that the text determines what comes next. I've rather carefully chosen the term *projects* to preserve the analytic constraint of remaining with and within the text itself. Just how a text is taken up and incorporated into a sequence or sequences of action is always an empirical question.

The Buried Dialogue

The evaluation takes its source from a series of dialogues between Graham and Merwin. Yet the account is written as if Merwin's behavior is independent of the interchange between them and of the overall context in which their dialogue proceeds. Merwin may lose custody of her child; she is required by a court order to meet with the psychologist for evaluation. Dialogue is implicit or buried. The character of the dialogue is suggested in the heading that introduces the abbreviated EXAM, presumably short for *examination*. Control of questions, tests, and product are with the examining expert; the examined is subordinated.

Mikhail Bakhtin (Bakhtin 1981) has introduced the notion of hybrid utterances, that is, utterances, whether spoken or written, that contain two voices. There are many ways in which these can be written: sometimes in the form of reported speech, such as "she told me that her husband had abused her" (not from Merwin's evaluation). In reported speech it's easy to extract what she said from the speaker's role" in other and more interesting instances, dialogue is buried in a sentence structure, in phrases and even in descriptive terms so that we may not be aware of the hybrid organization

In this report, one voice masters the other, a magisterial voice, which shifts to a level of language that subordinates the other. A term such as *illogical* carries an implicit and suppressed dialogue. "I don't understand what she's talking about" as a response to what someone says is converted into the objectified representation of the subject as illogical [24, 49, 51, 65]; tests reflect that she is a disorganized, chaotic woman prone to occasional perceptual distortions but more towards illogical conclusions in her thinking [22–24]. Notice that statements of this kind are made without reference to a formally independent set of criteria. Concepts such as *denial* in clinical settings are also implicitly dialogic, describing or reporting situations in which the psychologists' or psychiatrists' interpretations are rejected or avoided by subjects. The psychologist suggests an interpretation of some aspect of her story; she rejects or denies it. It is the privilege of the magisterial voice to translate this dialogue into psychological discourse as denial. The psychologist is removed from the scene and so is the original dialogue that has been buried in this phrase. What it was that she has denied disappears. His authority as an expert is built into the representation of her side of whatever story as denying his.

The distinctive speech genre (Bakhtin 1986) of psychology as it is deployed by Graham translates experiences arising in a series of conversations or interactions into objectified statements about the other. Brief descriptions of what Merwin said or did are described as if they were generated out of her personal attributes without connection to the situation of examination, the presence and activity of the psychologist, and the threat hanging over her of losing a child. For example, her breaking down into tears during a test is described thus: "at the very least, her defenses displayed serious deterioration and she reacted by being overcome by emotion and not being able to continue" [16–17]. It is her reaction to deteriorated *defenses* that lead to her being overcome by emotion rather than what she is going through.

The dialogic ground of the above example is complicated by the implied presence of the texts of the various tests [7–8] that Merwin was given. They are technically developed standardized psychological tests. They insert a distinctive third party into the dialogue between Graham and Merwin. Merwin is required to engage with the texts of the test in Graham's presence—Merwin "looked at the cards" [15]. She reads and responds without knowing or being able to correct or modify how her responses will be understood and recorded. It is Graham's work outside the setting of their dialogue to read Merwin's responses and from them derive a characterization *of her* in terms of objectified attributes: "The test data confirm the distinctly pathological nature, which was hinted in her clinical behavior. Tests reflect that she is a disorganized, chaotic woman prone to occasional perceptual distortions but more towards illogical conclusions in her thinking" [21–24].

The psychologist also generates hybrid statements in which statements attributed to Merwin are embedded in statements about her subjective states, as in sentences opening with "she feels . . . "

> Specifically, she feels victimized, she feels deceived, and she feels deception is multiplying in her environment. She feels that Judge X is also a victim of this de-

> ception and that others are being taken in by it. Specifically, she feels that she and her son were the victims of abuse from her husband (the child's father) and that she has no control over it. She feels emotionally and physically abused and harassed by her husband. She is fearful that her husband is going to harm her child by his control. She does not feel that he will harm the child when he is in the presence of others, but behind closed doors danger lurks for the child. [30–37]

We can envisage more clearly what such stylistic constructions achieve if we extract from this account a series of statements as if in Merwin's voice:

> I feel that I am being victimized. The judge and others involved are getting a false picture of my situation and of what is going on. My son and I were abused by my husband, and I could not control the abuse. He abused me emotionally and he abused me physically. I am afraid my husband will harm my child by how he controls him. My husband won't let others see him harming the child but behind closed doors, my son is in danger.

This fiction helps us to trace Graham's work on the materials created in his dialogue with Merwin. Her story is not admitted *as such*. The implied statements that the psychologist embeds as feelings are not treated as representations of how her husband has behaved towards her and her son in the past and of her fears for the future based on these experiences. The issue of whether such statements are accurate accounts of what was going on *never even arises*.

The Role of Discourse

In the section on *intertextual hierarchy* that follows this, I introduce the notion of a regulatory text. I shall not expand on that topic here. I want, however, to direct attention to the operation of the discourse of clinical psychology in Graham's report. I do not suppose that every clinical psychologist would produce a report of Emma Merwin as she goes through the court process that eventually denies her custody of her child. What the discourse does, however, is establish procedures for telling stories about people that isolate them from their own lives and the settings of their lives and constructs what is going on with them *as it is expressed in the psychologist's office* (or other situation of observation) as if it were an attribute of individual personality. Though not every psychologist writing an evaluation would proceed as Graham did, the discourse he shares with others does enable him to detach Emma Merwin from the fearful threat of losing her child, from her history of living with an abusive partner who, she believes, may also be a danger to her son, from the deep anxieties of the court proceedings, among them the experience of being subjected to *tests* that may be critical to the outcome without having any idea of what is involved in "passing" them successfully. If these conditions and circumstances had been drawn into the evaluation, would not her tears and fears make ordinary sense as responses to the situation in which she encounters William Graham, psychologist?

Projecting Pathology

The temporal movement schematized in figure 4.1 is preserved in this textual analysis by attending to aspects of the report that can be explored as projections into what comes next. The evaluation has been ordered as part of the court proceedings and will presumably be read and participate in the outcomes of that sequence of action. Pathological behavior is also constituted in this report by establishing a pathologizing interpretive frame to contextually isolated accounts of the subject's behavior in the interview or to something she has said. A pathologizing sequence can be found that has three steps: (1) an introductory pathologizing interpretation; (2) a description of the subject's behavior; (3) a follow–up pathologizing interpretation that tells the reader to see the foregoing as symptomatic. Here is an example:

> *Interpretive frame:* This 34-year-old married woman, currently separated from her child, impressed as a woman with marked emotional difficulties clinically. [10–12]
>
> *Description:* She spoke in a very soft, controlled manner as if she were trying to hold onto emotional controls. She was not successful. Tears came very quickly. She presented as one whose thinking was loose, confused, and tangential. There was a loss of distance. When she looked at some of the cards, they took on an air of reality. [12–16]
>
> *Follow-up interpretation:* At the very least, her defenses displayed serious deterioration. [16]

Devices of this kind produce the described behavior as *symptomatic* of the general state of emotional disturbance ascribed to the subject. Merwin's inability to control her tears is symptomatic of her emotional difficulties. The same pathologizing sequence can be seen in Graham's version of Merwin's story of domestic abuse. The psychologist's account of her story is introduced by his statement that he is "convinced that she is likely delusional about some issues" [27–28] and followed up by "she is a woman who is paranoid in her perceptions, whose defences are defective, whose obsessive-compulsive defences falter and she is left feeling overwhelmed, overcome, chaotic, and anxious"[39] [40–41].

Pathologizing activates a discounting procedure that suspends the ordinary efficacy of what people have to say. Once psychopathologized, what Merwin says and does are not received and responded to in the same way as those recognized as *normal.* What she says and does are taken up not for what is actually said but as an expression of her imputed psychopathology. The "we" relation in which is taken for granted that "we" share the same social and temporal coordinates and experience things from the base of a shared set of conditions is suspended (Smith 1990a). Under this description, what Merwin says and does will not be taken as a basis on which others can rely in how they respond.

Clearly a report of this kind, if received without critique by a court, would seriously undermine any claims to custody of a child or children a woman might make. The story told from her viewpoint is already discounted, as indeed it is in the psychologist's report. At the simplest and yet most powerful level, this is what the evaluation projects into what comes next in the course of action that determines whether Merwin will lose custody of her child.

Intertextual Hierarchy

In the introduction to this paper, I described the second topic of research into texts as coordinators of institutional activity as the intertextual hierarchy in which texts regulate other texts. An important dimension of the textual organization of institutional processes and the ruling relations in general is regulatory. Higher-order texts regulate and standardize texts that enter directly into the organization of work in multiple local settings. The presence of regulatory texts can be identified in the examples given in the first section. It is not so clear, perhaps, in Vo-Quang's study, but the psychological evaluation is permeated with the regulatory texts of the discourse of clinical psychology. The very organization of an account based on a dialogue between psychologist and mother which can be represented as an unmediated representation of *her* psychological states is discursively structured.

Figure 4.4 provides a diagrammatic sketch of the regulatory hierarchy. In what follows I fill out the diagrammatic sketch with an analysis of a specific text to show, in this instance, how it can be seen to locate people's doing as organizational/institutional procedure over and above particular settings, people, and activities.

The text of a grade appeal procedure, installed in the department of sociology of a Canadian university, is examined as a regulatory text. The text that I

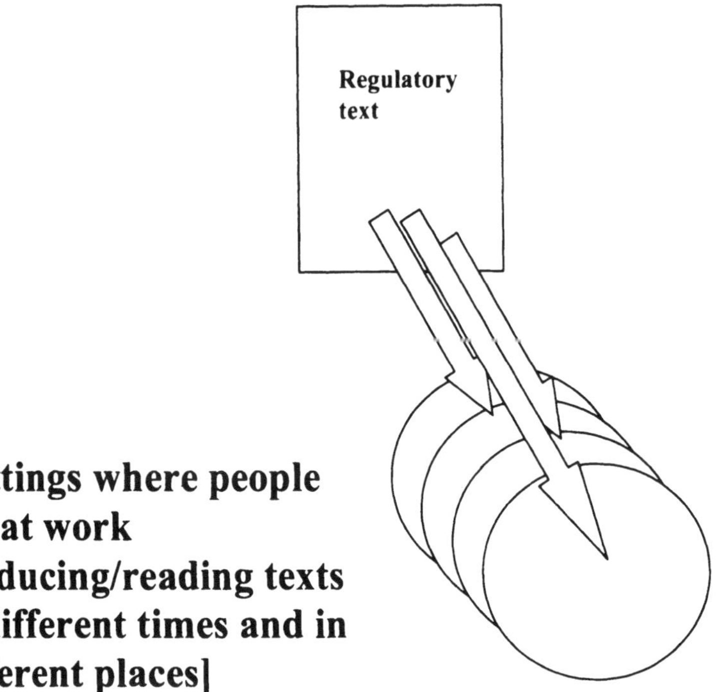

FIGURE 4.4.
Regulatory Texts Reach into Local Settings of People's Work

examine was introduced to me by Katarzyna Rukszto (1994). In addition to Rukszto's brief ethnographic account written from a student's experience of making a grade appeal, I draw on my own knowledge of such procedures.

GRADUATE PROGRAMME IN SOCIOLOGY

Grade Appeal Procedure

1. It is the responsibility of the instructor to clarify, early in the course, the assignments, their weighting and the deadlines which students are expected to observe. Where a student's appeal indicates that members of the class were unclear about these matters, fair decision-making becomes much more difficult.

2. Students have the right to appeal the grades they receive on written work, but not on seminar presentations or for seminar participation. This must be done within two weeks of the date when notification of the grade is sent to the student. Grades submitted by May 15 are mailed to the student in June. When a grade is submitted to clear an incomplete, a copy is placed in the student's mailbox in 2071 Branksome Hall.

3. When a student is dissatisfied with a grade, the first step should be to discuss it with the instructor. There may have been a misunderstanding which can be cleared up between them. The instructor may be able to suggest changes which the student is willing to make, if the paper has been handed in well before the deadline for clearing incompletes. Where there is little time, it may be possible for the instructor to give the student an oral exam on those aspects of the topic which were judged to be inadequately covered. Should the student and instructor find it difficult to reach an agreement (e.g., consensus on course expectations) the Graduate Director may be asked to act as mediator.

4. Where student and instructor are unable to reach agreement, the student may appeal to the Director for a re-evaluation of the paper(s). The Director will then try to find an appraiser who is acceptable to both instructor and student. Before any appraisal is made, the student and the instructor have the right to communicate in writing to this person any matters relevant to the appraisal, such as instructions about coverage, style, and length or agreements about the scope of the paper. The appraiser will send an evaluation of the paper with reasons to the Programme Director, who will communicate these to the Executive Committee of the Programme.

5. Where student and instructor cannot agree on a neutral appraiser each has the right to name one reader. The Executive Committee of the Programme will see the paper, be told of the two names, and appoint a third person who will join them to form and will chair the Appraisal Committee. The persons appointed will normally be members of the Faculty or Graduate Studies in good standing. The Appraisal Committee will meet and report its decision, with reasons, to the Executive Committee of the Programme.

6. If the Appraiser's evaluation differs from the instructor's enough to alter the grade for the course, the decision whether to make the change rests with the Executive Committee. A judgement must be made, whether the difference between the evaluations is small enough to be due to reasonable variation in judgement between one instructor and another, or is large enough to justify overruling the instructor's verdict. In the past, a half grade difference was considered small and a full grade large, but this is not a binding guideline.

7. The Executive Committee makes the final decision at the Programme level. There is provision for appeal of a Programme's decision to the Dean of Graduate Studies and/or the Senate. Such appeals are likely to be heard, however, only if there is evidence of irregularities in the procedures which the Programme Director or Executive Committee followed. Appeal procedures beyond the Programme are currently under revision.

Revised and approved by Executive Committee January 27, 1993.

Texts don't achieve the capacity to regulate just by their existence. The Grade Appeal Procedure would have no *force,* that is, no capacity to effect a change in grade, had it not an authorization by some body established under university rules having itself *under these regulatory texts* been accorded the capacity to create and authorize such a procedure. In this document, authorization is provided in its last line [52] "Revised and approved by Executive Committee January 27, 1993." In the absence of the authorizing text, modes of authorizing and *appropriating* the interplay as *of* the organization or institution do not operate. And, of course, the text has no force until it is activated, as the grade appeal was by Rukszto's letter to the Director of Graduate Studies in her department.

The text formulates a process. People's doings are no longer just that but become interpretable as expressions or instances of a higher source of organization, independent of particular people. The texts that they produce, including the change in grade if that is the outcome, are regulated and interpreted by the text of the Grade Appeal Procedure (GAP). Though the exact character of the reevaluation of the student's work is not specified, it must be fitted to its function in the procedure, that is, to produce a recommendation that either denies a change of grade or proposes a change that goes forward to the decision-making body.

The sequence of textually coordinated moves is foundational: the appraiser's work is to review the assignment (a text) and to produce a text (the evaluation); the evaluation if it recommends change goes to the Executive Committee for review; if the recommended change is approved, it goes to the Dean of Graduate Studies. The process is essentially one of handling, reading, and passing on texts from one stage to the next. It begins with the student's course assignment; it has been accorded a grade that is unsatisfactory to the student; the student launches an appeal—in the case in which my analysis originated the appeal was made in writing to the Director of Graduate Studies in the department. The various texts are passed on among formally designated categories of persons—the *student's* assignment goes to the *appraiser*, the *appraiser* prepares an evaluation; the *Executive Committee* reviews the evaluation and makes a decision—which must also be a text of some kind or a modification of the appraiser's evaluation as by stamping it "approved." The latter then goes to *Graduate Studies* where further work will be done to change the *student's* grade record. The texts produced coordinate and warrant the transfer from one stage to the next of the process. The GAP is itself subordinated within a complex intertextual hierarchy that includes rules about the conditions that must be met for particular individuals to be fitted to the categories and assume the capacities and agency assigned to them—an instructor or faculty member must, for example, hold (or have held during the appropriate period) a proper contractual position in the university for the course taught to count as part of a student's program for her or his evaluation of a student's work to be valid.

In making observable how such a regulatory text might operate to produce out of particular actions done by particular people in a particular time and place an organizational/institutional process, I've drawn on Harold Garfinkel's (1967) treatment of the everyday work of the Suicide Prevention Center staff, of jurors, and of people at work coding sociological data. The work of people employed in such settings is to determine the correct verdict in someone's death, to decide by what criteria patients were chosen for psychiatric treatment, and so on. Garfinkel moves radically away from the paradigm that treats the "patterning" or "typicality" or "repetitiveness" of social activities as an effect of conforming to norms or rules. Rather he explicates an ongoing open-ended development of concerted activities that is aimed at producing what participants can *recognize* as the rational processes of investigating whether a death should be categorized as a suicide or whether a given person should be admitted as a patient and so on. The rationality of the inquiries done by those at work in such settings is not a simple property of their activities. Rather the "*recognizably* rational properties of their common sense inquiries . . . are *somehow* attainments of members' concerted activities" (Garfinkel 1967: 10); that is, those who participate produce for themselves and others what they can recognize as rational and objective. It is the *recognition* of what is said and done that produces it as accountably accomplishing the rationality and objectivity of a given institutional order.

In most of Garfinkel's examples, rationality and objectivity are achieved in settings that are textually regulated. He does not, however, recognize the role of texts. Rather he extrapolates rationality (objectivity, facticity, etc.) as a general feature of how order is accomplished among and by members. Rationality isn't treated as a property of action but as an accomplishment of how people recognize and make sense of what they and others are doing. In an analogous fashion, institutional ethnography treats texts not as prescribing action but as establishing the concepts and categories in terms of which what is done can be recognized as an instance or expression of the textually authorized procedure. In a sense, it recovers the textual that remains implicit in Garfinkel's account. It is the recognizability of what is done or being done as an instance or expression of the regulatory text (rather than rationality) that accomplishes an institutional process or procedure.

Thus the text of the appeal procedure presented above wouldn't be read prescriptively. Rather the reader's work is to find what might be recognizable as a proper instance of its categories.[6] In deciding to write a letter to the Director of the Graduate Program, Rukszto oriented to what she and other participants could recognize, under the terms of the text, as *initiating a grade appeal*. Notice how it is already possible to write of the "grade appeal" as if it had objective existence—which, of course, it had but not without the text. We can imagine a sequence of action that, in the absence of a text, doesn't add up to an appeal of a grade: a student goes to the Director of Graduate Studies, telling her that the grade awarded isn't justified; the Director says, "Okay, I'll get so-and-so to check it," and so on. There's no procedure here. It is the authorized text of the GAP that establishes the set of terms, formalized sequences, and so on providing methods standardized for all participants for analyzing and recognizing what might be done and what has gotten done. In this way the work of different parties in an actual appeal process is coordinated *to produce what can be recognized as proper instances of steps in a grade appeal procedure.* What people actually do can be analyzed and evaluated by others as "discussing the grade with the instructor" [14–15], "appeal to the Director" [23–24], "finding an appraiser acceptable to both instructor and student" [25], and so on. And in projecting their own actions, participants attend to how others will be able to recognize them as instances or expressions of the text. The grade appeal text does not prescribe in the sense that actions can be derived from it. Different experiences can be analyzed and recognized under the phrase, "discuss[ing the grade] with the instructor" [14–15]. Do student and instructor actually have to meet? Would a telephone call suffice? Possibly. The actual discussion might differ greatly from case to case. Perhaps one instructor receives the student coldly, virtually refuses discussion, reiterates her right to give the grade as she sees it, insists on the validity of her comments, and refers the student to the original course outline in which the criteria applicable to the assignment have been specified. Another may be open and responsive, discusses the comments but isn't persuaded to change the grade, in part because she feels it would be unfair to other students. Similarly the Director's arrangements with the instructor, the student, and appraiser might be on the telephone, via chats in hallways or in the cafeteria, by e-mail, and so on. Activities involving any of these kinds of contacts can be recognized as "finding an appraiser acceptable to both student and instructor" [25]. Certainly the encounter may be very different in different instances or cases. Indeed the very notions of "cases" or "instances" rely on the existence of the formalized text as bearer of the paradigm that constitutes them as cases or instances. Those who read this and who have had some experience with such a procedure will be able to fit their experience into the intertextual of this GAP.

Just as the various actions taken by those who, in any actual case, people the categories of the GAP, the texts that coordinate are read and interpreted in its terms. The various subordinate texts that are produced and that coordinate the stages of the appeal must also be fitted to the GAP as the regulatory text. The appraiser's evaluation would have to be recognizable as an evaluation of that student's assignment in that course, would have to take into account the

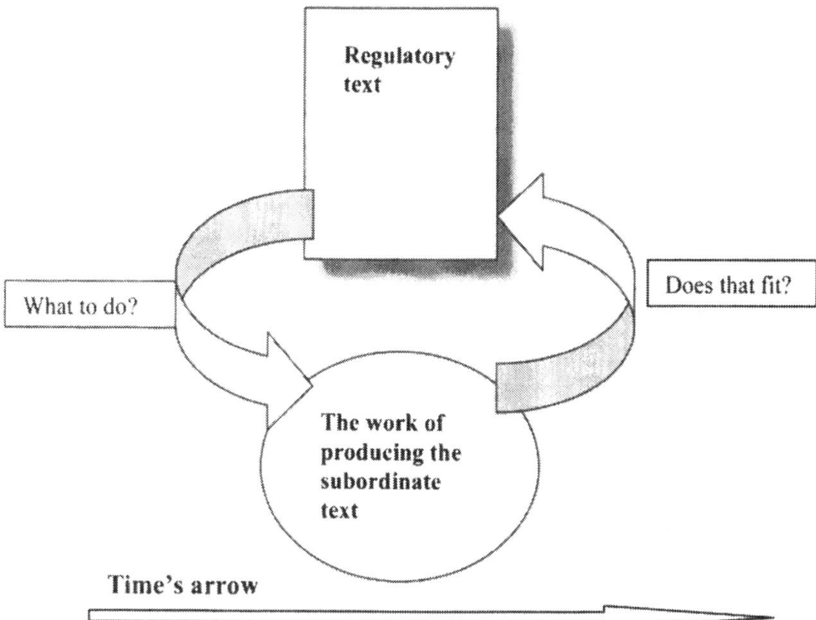

FIGURE 4.5.
Intertextual Circles

specification of the assignment given by the instructor, and would have to give reasons based on that assignment for what is recommended. It creates a textual bridge between the assignment, the recommended grade, and the Executive Committee's decision.

The above account of how the text of the Grade Appeal Procedure works when it is put into practice has reinserted a temporal dimension that was absent from the figure 4.4 schematization of the intertextual hierarchy. This is made explicit in figure 4.5. The term *intertextual circles* refers to a characteristic circularity discernible in the ongoing organization of this intertextual hierarchy. What is produced as text under the regulatory authority of the superordinate text, in this case, the GAP, must be capable of being interpreted/understood as a proper instance or expression of its regulatory categories and concepts. Figure 4.5 pictures this circular process; it is, as the "time's arrow" at the base indicates, a process in time, an organization of people's work. From activating/reading the regulatory text, the question arises of what to do that can be fitted to the framework of that text; the work that is done to produce the appropriate text, the appraiser's evaluation in the case of the GAP, must then be readable as a text that fulfills the function ascribed to it in the regulatory text. The circularity of intertextual hierarchies is integral to the organization of the contemporary ruling relations in general, including large-scale organization and those functional complexes we have called *institutions.*[7] Such intertextual circles have, for example, been developed as technologies of accountability as methods of bringing the ambiguities of the work of human services under financial control.[8]

Conclusion

The examples that I have worked through here should not be taken as exhaustive as models of how texts might be introduced into ethnographic research, particularly, of course, institutional ethnography. The texts and the mini-ethnographies that extended them were not part of more general ethnographic studies. They were exercises or performances introduced here as demonstrations of how texts can be incorporated into such ethnographies using the basic act-text-act sequence that locates a text as embedded in and coordinating a sequence of action. It is recognizing texts as in action that is key.

Two approaches to investigating texts-in-motion have been presented. One is a straightforward investigation of sequences in which the text is given a central role. Vo-Quang's small study of how an appraisal form to accompany applications for admission to graduate school is first read and completed by the referee and then read by the person in charge of admissions illustrates a textual sequence which is very general in some form or another in contemporary society. A form is filled in; the form becomes the institutional representation of a person; its properties are read back into the actuality of the person it represents. Vo-Quang's procedure was simple and effective; he interviewed the person who completes the form and then its reader in the context of the course of action in which the text plays its part. A second example in the first section was intended to suggest how to incorporate the act-text-act sequence when the ethnographer has only a text to work with. The text was that of a psychologist's evaluation of a woman caught up in court proceedings consequential for her custody of her son. In this instance, analysis focused on what could be learned from the text itself using the sequential model of a text embedded in and coordinating a sequence of action that I have set up as paradigmatic (figure 4.1).

The second type of textual coordinating in sequences of action was described as an intertextual hierarchy. Here I opened up a key dimension, namely how texts regulate other texts. Intertextual hierarchies are very generally at work in texts such as those represented in the first section. They would be at work, for example, in the psychologist's evaluation of Emma Merwin.

The discourse of clinical psychology would clearly have been operative as regulator in the psychologist's evaluation. The regulatory text brought under analysis was that of a Grade Appeal Procedure. Analysis emphasized how it operates to subsume the actualities of what people do as well as organizing subordinate texts (such as the appraiser's evaluation). What is done becomes recognizable as an instance of the procedure within the intertextual hierarchy. The sense a subordinate text makes is found in the interpretive frame the regulatory text establishes.[9] This is a process in time and of people's work.

These examples of how texts can be incorporated into ethnography have been presented as exercises that isolate a particular text. They are meant to be suggestive, to show what can be done when texts are seen as integral to courses of action. I do not intend to suggest that texts should always be isolated in the settings of the courses of action in which they participate. Rather the examples are meant to suggest some of the ways in which texts cañ be incorporated ethnographically. Nor do I intend to confine the researcher to the kinds of examples I have made use of here. The region is wide open to discovery, and I encourage those interested in taking up institutional ethnography to exploit its possibilities, hanging on always to the foundational model represented first in figure 4.1, of seeing texts as occurring in locally developing courses of action, as in motion, as integral to coordinating ongoing action, breaking thus with texts' deeply rooted and functional disposition to precipitate the reader out of time.

Notes

1. Marie Campbell and Tim Diamond read the original draft of this paper. Their comments were immensely helpful both in uncovering buried themes and clarifying the examples and how they were interpreted for the reader. Of course, muddles that survived are mine.
2. Susan Turner's paper in this volume shows how the articulations of work and text sequences can be mapped to explicate complexes of institutional process.
3. Given in the sociology department of the University of Victoria, British Columbia.
4. Of course, if everybody lies, their relative rankings can still be compared.
5. The analysis of Emma Merwin's psychological evaluation was originally developed as a report for Praxis International (Smith 2000). I am very much indebted to them for permission to quote the text of Merwin's evaluation and the passages of my original report for them that have been incorporated into this paper. The text of the evaluation exemplifies the genre of such texts, though, of course, not every such instance projects pathology. Names of Emma Merwin and William Graham are fictional. Details that could be misidentified with an actual person have been changed or removed.

6. See chapter 5 in my *Institutional Ethnography: A Sociology for People* (Smith 2005) for an extended treatment of this procedure analyzed as a distinctive text-reader conversation.

7. See McCoy (1998), Parada (2002), Rankin (2004) for instances in a variety of institutional settings.

8. For further discussion and examples see Smith (2005).

9. Institutional ethnographers have incorporated texts in various ways, and I shall not attempt a comprehensive list. Here follow some examples that might be useful to those interested in pursuing research of this kind:

> Campbell, Marie L. 2001. "Textual Accounts, Ruling Action: the Intersection of Knowledge and Power in the Routine Conduct of Community Nursing Work." In *Studies in Cultures, Organizations, and Societies* 7(2): 231–50; McCoy, Liza. 1995. "Activating the Photographic Text." In *Knowledge, Experience, and Ruling Relations: Essays in the Social Organization of Knowledge*, ed. M. Campbell and A. Manicom, 181–92. Toronto: University of Toronto Press; Rankin, J. M. 2003. "'Patient Satisfaction': Knowledge for Ruling Hospital Reform—An Institutional Ethnography." *Nursing Inquiry* 10(1): 57–65.

Of course, there are others, but these are particularly lucid and various and, above all, do something rather different from the examples included in this paper. In this book, you will find a more expansive treatment of texts used in mapping governmental process in Susan Turner's paper.

Part II

ANALYSIS

THERE ARE MANY DIFFERENT WAYS in which institutional ethnographic data analysis is taken up: Campbell shows how to ground ethnography in the experience in and of people's specific work setting; McCoy's paper emphasizes the differences between how interviews based on individual experience are taken up in an institutional ethnographic frame and more familiar and standard sociological analyses; Griffith's chapter explores a discourse ethnographically—in this case the discourse of single parenthood—showing how it comes into play in various educational settings; and Turner explicates a method of mapping major sequences of work-text-work and shows how to produce an ethnographically based cartography of local governmental process.

5

Institutional Ethnography and Experience as Data[1]

Marie L. Campbell

Institutional Ethnography and "Experience"

THIS PAPER DISCUSSES HOW, in institutional ethnography, a researcher goes about exploring and understanding her own or someone else's everyday/everynight life in a methodical way. In the theoretical approach known as social organization of knowledge (where institutional ethnography is located as a research strategy), experience is the ground zero of the analysis (Smith 1987, 1990a, 1990b, 2005). The analysis begins in experience and returns to it, having explicated how the experience came to happen as it did. The objective of making the analysis is to open up possibilities for people who live these experiences to have more room to move and act, on the basis of more knowledge about them. Dorothy E. Smith, long ago, called her work a sociology "for women"; more recently, she and other researchers who use this approach (e.g., Campbell and Manicom 1995: 7–12) have claimed that this form of analysis offers something for all those whose lives are subject to ruling relations.

Recently, questions have been raised by postmodernists and poststructuralists about feminists' use of "experience" as a basis of knowing, in the context of a broader reexamination of earlier feminist scholarship. Some have usefully argued against the notion of a "unitary subject" of women's experience and against white, heterosexual, middle-class feminists' appropriation of women's experience as normative or exclusionary (e.g., Alarcon 1994). A related critique of feminist analysis shows up the inadequacy of explanations that ground feminist knowledge claims in something essential or ideal arising from "women's experience" and for which authorizing women's voices might seem to be a solution (Bar On 1993). Another set of important postmodernist and poststructuralist concerns (e.g., Scott 1991) I take to be about the questionable status of experiential accounts produced by people whose knowing is discursively organized. Experience is one of the concepts, along with agency, subjectivity, discourse, and identity, whose contestation has generated within feminism a fruitful rethinking of some of the traditional disciplinary methods[2] in which feminist scholars have been trained and through which their conversations still take place.

While these debates have motivated this paper, my goal here is not to add to the theoretical discussions around the possibility of knowing from experience. Rather, I am making a demonstration of what Dorothy Smith means when she enjoins us to "begin from the actualities of people's lives" if we want to understand what is happening to them. Smith is one of the feminist scholars for whom women's experience remains of key methodological importance, even as it has become contentious in postmodern/poststructural circles.[3] The aim of this paper is to show how to put personal experience into the center of a trustworthy analysis. I want to illustrate how the use and status of experience as data in an institutional ethnography sets it apart from "the authority of experience" that Scott (1991) challenges, and from Clough's (1993) view that experience is a construction of sociological conventions.

Institutional ethnography, like other forms of ethnography, relies on interviewing, observation, and documents as data.[4] Institutional ethnography departs from other ethnographic approaches by treating those data not as the topic or object of interest, but as "entry" into the social relations of the setting. The idea is to tap into people's expertise in the conduct of their everyday lives—their "work," as Smith wants us to think of it (a concept discussed later in this chapter). The conceptual framing of everyday experiences heard or read about, or observed, constitutes one of the distinctive features of an institutional ethnography. Another is its political nature. Exploring how people's lives are bound up in ruling relations that tie individuals into institutional action arising outside their knowing, "institutional ethnography allows one to disclose (to the people studied) how matters come about as they do in their experience and to provide methods of making their working experience accountable to themselves . . . rather than to the ruling apparatus of which institutions are part" (Smith 1987: 178).

The Study

The setting of the study[5] I discuss here to illustrate my argument about experience as data is a long-term care hospital[6] in Victoria, Canada. The experiences analyzed are those of some nurses observed and recorded by a researcher in the context of a study of the implementation of a "Service Quality Initiative"[7] management strategy in an institution that I call Dogwood Villa. Using one story from several months of observational fieldwork, I argue that this particular management initiative had the capacity to alter staff-client relations at the most intimate level. Contrary to the democratic-sounding explanations of the strategy, it attempted to enforce a different and more rule-bound kind of practice, as it also revised the hospital's ideology of care that previously had been organized around being "homelike." The new ideological accomplishment of the quality improvement strategy, I concluded, would be a creeping colonization of the minds and hearts of the caregivers with the goals and values of the market—in which competitiveness, productivity, and cost efficiency, etc., are paramount. Here, the methodology of that analysis is discussed, and I argue that experiential data offer a secure and methodical basis for my conclusions about the quality improvement strategy. Of course, as a demonstration of methodology, I am dealing with only a fragment of data to illustrate "social relations" in this context, and how they provide for the account that I am making.

Dogwood Villa's Service Quality Initiative is one of the family of Total Quality Management techniques that is altering the health care system significantly. This study gave me an opportunity to examine the dailiness of organizational change processes to discover how such efforts—to improve management and make decisions more rationally—affect caregivers and their clients. Elsewhere, (Campbell 1988, 1992a, 1992b; and Campbell and Jackson 1992; Rankin and Campbell, 2006) I have studied and written critically about the methods that organizations implement to try to make more efficient and effective use of caring labor and other costly resources. These undertakings are urged on health care managers by the difficult fiscal constraints under which health care is provided. I've watched with concern as a managerialist approach to service provision spreads with little critical appraisal throughout the health and social service sector in Canada. So in looking at what was actually happening in this research site, I was not entering it as a naive observer working in naturalist mode, nor was I looking for theory to arise out of the data, as a grounded theorist might. As an institutional ethnographer, I was informed by prior analysis of the Canadian health care system and its increasingly rationalist stance towards management. I was also informed by a social organization of knowledge approach, about which I need to say a bit more now.

Social Organization of Knowledge and Research Assumptions

Dorothy Smith's (1987, 1990a, 1990b) writings on the social organization of knowledge provide the conceptual framework of this study and its grounding assumptions about how my research assistants[8] and I would think about what we were seeing in our fieldwork. Our first working assumption was that organizational knowledge is text-mediated in contemporary organizations in industrial and postindustrial society and that the nursing work that we were observing and hearing about was organized through text-based practices that coordinated it, made it accountable, and so on.[9] We knew that those practices build their own textual realities. This meant that as we gathered observational and interview data, we operated on the assumption that we would find different versions of what was understood, even of what was actually happening, as people we talked to spoke from different ways of knowing the workplace and the work.[10] Implicit in this assumption is our understanding of the discursively organized character of everyday life in organizations (Smith 1990b: 209–224).[11] However, we also accepted that while people understand their experiences in organizations through discursive mediations, they remain bodily present and are active experiencers of the everyday/everynight world from their various locations in it. Indeed, where one stands determines what one experiences, shaping to an important extent what can be known.[12] "A setting known through special texts may appear to be different from how it is known experientially, and . . . this may create problems" (Campbell and Manicom 1995: 11) both for managers who rely heavily on textual accounts and for nursing personnel, whose work keeps them tied to local settings where knowing has a kind of bodily immediacy that also affects it. Managers who rely on texts for their knowing also experience their work, their human interactions, their environment, etc., but in this paper I draw out for research attention, the experiences of frontline workers. I want to attend in my analysis to differences in the possibility of knowing that relate to the knower's location and everyday/everynight work as well as to how such local experiences are ruled, discursively, and thus constructed ideologically as the same across knowers.[13]

The notion of bifurcated consciousness that Smith (1987: 6) discusses with reference to herself as a mother and an academic seems helpful here. She notes how, as a graduate student, it was possible and necessary to learn how to move between the world of babies and tending their bodies and the discursively organized university, entering each in its own (distinctive) terms. She made the move in both space and time—daytime here, nighttime there—and noted the disjuncture between the two. For nurses who work in a similarly bifurcated mode on the job, things are not so clearly demarcated spacially. In the workplace, they are immersed in the everyday/everynight world of bodies and at the same time their own work of recording and translating their nursing into organizational texts articulates those bodily concerns and tasks to the conceptual order of the institution (Campbell 1984, 1988; Campbell and Jackson 1992; Rankin and Campbell, 2006). They construct their knowing of bodies into discursive mode, bifurcating their own consciousness. In other words, they know their patients in two distinctive, and often contradictory, ways—as real people with bodily needs and as text-based objects of professional attention. The latter may and under modern managerial technologies often does mean that the bodily knowing is subordinated to the text-based or discursive.

This brings me to the next grounding assumption that my research team and I carried into the research setting: that the power of subordinating local experiential knowing to the discursive is the basis of textually mediated management and of what Smith calls ruling. As researchers, my team was always being attentive in our fieldwork to how the written word organizes what gets known and how it authorizes that version of it. We accepted that in those kinds of text-mediated procedures in the nursing setting, management works as a ruling practice.[14] These are intrinsic features of Smith's social organization of knowledge that are also the premises of institutional ethnography and without which institutional ethnographic procedures and analyses don't make sense. Given these premises that Smith (1987: 117–135) argues are not theoretical in the ordinary sense, but are conceptual reflections of *actual relations* among people, the researcher goes into any new setting to see "how it works." It is not to test a hypothesis but to examine the way that the social organization is put together such that people experience it as they do. In this approach, the researcher learns the standpoint or "takes the side" of those being ruled. The research is committed to exploring and exposing for consideration how ruling affects people whose everyday/everynight lives come under the influence of specific ruling practice. One cannot know about their lives without their showing or telling it in one way or another. Thus, the researcher's attention is to their voices.[15]

To carry out such an inquiry, the researcher begins with actual people involved actively in a social process, speaking from their experience. Writing field notes is always a located social practice. Both the informant's account and eventually the researcher's are methodical in that they both rely on their relation to the located social process to discipline what is (can be) said. Insofar as the informant is speaking with the terms and relevances of her own life, she brings into the researcher's presence the actual social organization of that experience.[16]

Similarly to interview data, observations of everyday life, where the researcher captures the language used by participants, can be used to gain entry for analytic purposes into its social organization. The researcher is searching for traces of how the participants' actions and talk are conditioned. The researcher relies on the methodical nature of participants' behavior. Drawing on ethnomethodology, Smith (1987: 161–167) has written about people performing their everyday activities as "work" that they sensibly and expertly organize, coordinated in relation to the local social organization and also coordinating it. Experiential data, whether from interviews or observations, thus inform a method, allowing researchers an entry to social organization for the purpose of explicating the experiences; by explication I mean to write back into the account of experiences the social organization that is immanent, but invisible, in them.

"Harmonie Briefs": The Story

For an instance of the kind of explicative analysis I am referring to, I want to turn now to a story from my study—an incident observed at Dogwood Villa involving nursing staff. I use it to analyze and illustrate the social relations of the Service Quality Initiative operating in the hospital and altering the care of the residents. Here I want to show how the voices of nurses in this story (their methodical telling of their experiences) allowed me to recover and display the meaning of this management strategy and make the argument about it that I have made. I also illustrate how to make analytic use of people's speaking of their everyday lives in ways that have the social relations "in" the talk. This is not rehearsed practice with some people knowing better than others how to do it. It is a way of ordinary talking where the speaker is making sense of the setting, for herself and for the listener. According to Smith, it is impossible to speak sensibly without speaking the social relations.

We now go back to Dogwood Villa and to some excerpts of observational data collected by a research assistant as she observed, on different days, the work of two nurses, one a clinical teacher, the other a nurse manager. The topic that the data excerpts address is the nursing staff's use of disposable diapers (called by their trade name Harmonie Briefs), for residents who are incontinent of urine, especially at night. The field notes are presented with a minimum of explanatory comment (in square brackets). In the data we see people in the setting talking about and puzzling over some questions about costs, the hospital's money, nursing plans, etc., as the researcher observed it; this provides the empirical ground for the analysis that follows.

> A Clinical Resource Nurse [a nurse employed as a teacher within the hospital] was presenting an in-service education class on the use of the Harmonie Brief to a group of nursing assistants. [These are the staff who actually change people's beds, make the decisions about diapering people and using cotton pads under them, repair the damage done by a leaking brief, etc.] The class was being held because concern about recent stats [information] on laundry costs had been brought to the educator's attention by her immediate supervisor.

> The problem was that instead of reducing their linen [laundry] costs . . . many units were actually increasing these costs in spite of the use of the disposable product. The Harmonie Brief policy had been in place for about six months when the Clinical Resource Nurse reported that on [the] unit [in question], the cost of Harmonie Briefs was $651.00 per month. She explained [in her class to the nursing assistants] that the organization had budgeted $60,000 for costs of Harmonie Briefs across the whole hospital for the period in question and therefore, there was a need to recover $60,000 from the linen budget in the same period. She wrote these figures on a flipchart for the staff to see.
>
> The nursing assistants then discussed what this was going to mean to them. They saw that they either had to use less linen for bed changes, or they had to keep the bed linens from being so soaked since the cost of the contracted-out laundry service was calculated by weight. (field notes)

This rather muddled explanation of the management concern about Harmonie Brief usage was not the end of the story. Next we have the researcher's field notes of the Director of Resident Care's (a nurse manager) meeting with Nursing Team Leaders (registered nurses) on the same unit a week later. We see them deciding how the nursing assistants who do the hands-on care are going to be required to manage the laundry cost problem.

> One of the items discussed [at the Team Leaders' meeting] was linens and diapering. The general focus was on how it is "necessary to break even," according to the Director of Resident Care. Hence, she and the Team Leaders discussed cutting back on pads that are used underneath the resident at night. It was decided that those residents with Harmonie Briefs on should not require more than one pad underneath them. A Team Leader was concerned that if the brief were put on too early [in the evening shift] that more than one [of the disposable products] might be used at night. It was decided that only one Harmonie Brief should be used per night. If a wet brief were discovered during the night, the resident should be padded, as using two briefs per night per resident would escalate costs.
>
> It is important to note that this discussion is taking place among Team Leaders who work days and who will be leaving messages for evening and night staff. (field notes)

Analysis: Social Relations as Method

I begin analyzing these data by assuming that a specific social organization coordinates what the participant observer saw and heard happening and what she made notes on. Through her notes, we see these nurses engaged in bringing that social organization into new sites—through the class where nursing assistants are told about the impact on the hospital budget of the expenditures on the new disposable briefs, how that relates to the laundry budget, and specifically that this is *the nursing assistants'* problem to solve. And, later, we see the nurse manager and RN Team Leaders developing new rules that will hold other nurses to the same routines that offer more economical use of the disposable briefs. My analysis begins in those experiences.

It is my task as institutional ethnographer to search out, come to understand, and describe the connections among these sites of experience and social organization. My sense-making is not just insightful interpretation. Nor am I looking for it to be an instance of a theory. Rather, it is disciplined by the relations that organize or coordinate what actually happens among those involved—what they experience. The procedure is to make problematic (or a topic for inquiry) those everyday experiences to which the observer makes us privy. Being able to count on using social relations to discover the concerting of action across time and space is what makes the inquiry methodical. The researcher relies on the embeddedness of social relations in the talk and action of the participants to direct the inquiry. The question to be explored is "What are the social relations coordinating those experiences?" I needed to discover, for instance, how ideas about "breaking even" and "recovering $60,000 from the linen budget" had made their way into a clinical teaching session for nursing assistants and how, or if, those ideas were related to the hospital's Service Quality Initiative. What was concerting all these actions?

Authority Relations Reorganized through the Service Quality Initiative

The authority relations operating among the nurses in this setting are easily identifiable in the field notes. Hospitals rely on a distinctive mode of managing in which authority is vested in certain categories of employees. In the field notes we catch glimpses of traditional authority relations in the Clinical Resource Nurse teaching the nursing assistants about their role in "breaking even." It appears that she has been instructed by her superior to make this a topic for the nursing assistants. Nursing assistants take heed because they are required to, as part of their jobs. Another authority relation has the Director of Resident Services involving the Team Leaders, who are RNs, in planning how to pass on a new set of rules to their subordinates, the evening and night nurses. The nursing assistants, while occupying the lowest rung on the nursing authority ladder, still have power over the residents. They exercise a certain kind of authority with regard to caring work, and that is why these employees are being instructed in the economics of disposable briefs. These are all matters that can be empirically substantiated.

An interview I conducted with a Clinical Nurse Specialist (a master's prepared nurse with a part-time university faculty appointment) showed that beyond the official authority relations, action in the hospital was being coordinated in a new manner. Her account of the work that went into the decision to purchase Harmonie Briefs offers a glimpse into the background of the experiences described in the field notes. My research task at this point was to inquire into the discursive organization of these events. I was looking for the practical basis of (what I came to see as) the restructuring of relations among managers, nurses, and residents at Dogwood Villa. According to the Clinical Nurse Specialist the decision to use Harmonie Briefs to supplement or replace entirely the use of washable cotton pads had been made through a new process encouraging managers to work together across traditional department and disciplinary boundaries. According to her, this was the first time she had ever been part of such a multidisciplinary decision-making team. She was very proud of her own involvement, which had been to conduct clinical trials of a range of competing products and recommend one to the cross-department project group. This (Harmonie Brief) group also included the managers who made the hospital's purchasing and laundry decisions and were responsible for the budgets in these areas. The Clinical Nurse Specialist's clinical trials had identified which product would keep residents drier and thus protect their skin from breaking down. She had wanted to see if the disposable briefs made the residents more comfortable at night; there was some suggestion that changing wet beds during the night upset the residents and sometimes resulted in residents hitting nurses. The Harmonie Brief project thus brought her interest in resident comfort and staff safety together with other group members' different responsibilities. Working together influenced everybody's practices. For instance, she told me that she was surprised to learn that the manager of the Purchasing Department, as a result of her clinical trials, had had to alter his regular public sector (equity-oriented across-the-board) purchasing practices, in order to buy the product she recommended.

The Clinical Nurse Specialist's story of the Harmonie Brief project contained recursive elements (see G. W. Smith, 1990) that I now want to highlight, to illustrate the textual coordination of the organizational action of interest in this inquiry. Recurring in the interview were some of the Service Quality Initiative principles that I had previously seen in the management documents describing the project. When I returned to the management documents, I found these phrases: "managers were instructed to change their values as managers, to value and trust their staff, whose intelligence is to be incorporated, as well as their caring; . . . managers were expected to focus on process (how people interact to get the work done) and to work across departments, providing the social system and resources for employees to do their jobs." The idea was to bypass customary management practices where authority to act was entrenched in traditional practices of public sector hospital management and supervision. If we look at the Harmonie Brief project as the Clinical Nurse Specialist described it, we can see that the way that this project group worked was consistent with new principles being taught to members of the Dogwood staff in Service Quality workshops, etc. For example, the Clinical Nurse Specialist spoke enthusiastically about how a "communication workshop" she had attended as part of the Service Quality Initiative had helped her to work across the hospital's traditional disciplinary boundaries, avoiding barriers of status, hierarchy, and discipline that interfered with discussing and implementing better solutions.

The new authority, according to the Service Quality Initiative documents, was to be found in reference to meeting the customer's needs. Before I could understand how that idea was translated into nurses' action in different hospital sites, I needed to explore further the notion of "customer" as it was being introduced through the Service Quality Initiative.

Customers and Suppliers: Meeting Each Others' Needs = Quality

The new system, an internal Service Quality Initiative document explains, requires staff to act as "suppliers of service as well as customers receiving service." The implementers of the Service Quality Initiative put great emphasis on everyone using the term *customer* at Dogwood Villa. This training began with the formal definition of the Service Quality Initiative emphasizing customer, as follows:

> Service Quality determines the way we work. It is achieved through processes that meet or exceed the expectations of our internal and external customers. The Service Quality processes focus on identifying customer-supplier needs and expectations, meeting these expectations, teamwork, doing the right things the right way, continuous review of our performance and feedback to customer-supplier. (internal memo, April 15, 1993)

It seemed that talking about a "customer" was supposed to engage employees' involvement in thinking about their work differently, following the new principles. But "customer" was a contested notion. In meetings and discussions at Dogwood Villa, staff interpreted "customer" to mean "the resident" and some found the new language uncomfortable and pretentious. Some felt their professionalism was offended and refused to talk about the people they cared for as customers. But by and large, the caregiving staff did not take very seriously either the language or the whole Service Quality Initiative, seeing it as "just the latest fad, which will pass." Management staff were more faithful in using the language, perhaps because they felt more accountable for the project's success, and perhaps because modeling the new principles was part of their management performance for which they were held accountable.

I began to see that how people were talking about the project was itself part of the process of reconstructing the authority relations in line with the new ideal. As I came to understood this shifting form of authority, I was able to reflect back to how strenuously the hospital's CEO had objected when I had referred to the Service Quality Initiative as a management technology in my research proposal (minutes of December 13, 1993, IAS committee meeting). It was, he told me, not to be talked about in those terms. It must be seen (and promoted) as a participatory project, never as a management initiative. While this account, at the time, seemed to defy the facts of the matter, it begins to make sense, when we see the Service Quality Initiative as reconstituting authority relations.

In retrospect, I see that there were two incongruent and competing formulations of "customer" in use; the one was defined in the internal document, where employees were to be suppliers of service as well as customers receiving service, and the other was the commonsense one that staff operated with, where the resident was the customer. In practice, the distinctions were often blurred. The latter, the resident as customer, held positive implications for the nursing staff, even when they objected to the language, because it was in line with well-established values of the hospital. In this interpretation what was good for the resident was an acceptable rationale for any change in work processes. Staff liked the suggestion (set out, for instance, by the CEO to the management group, January 4, 1994) that "those most closely involved with a particular work process would be empowered to help design the work system to be used"; and staff could identify with changes where the customer (the resident) was to be considered first. This came to be understood as "decision-making pushed down in the organization to those most closely involved with the work being done," which became a popular slogan used by Service Quality implementers. The slogan made the initiative seem to be a method of democratizing decision-making, allowing workers more individual discretion, in the name of resident satisfaction. And yet, in the Harmonie Brief story, we saw a high-profile project in which the suggested changes in the work processes were not designed by those closest to where the work was being done. Nor were they straightforwardly "good for the resident."

As the fieldwork progressed, I saw that the flexible or squishy interpretations of *customer* were not simply a different choice of words. Rather, the Service Quality Initiative introduced a new ruling relation. "Employees as customers of each others' work," the version of customer that competed with "the resident as customer," legitimated an officially sanctioned approach to the work that organized employees' discretion in line with new organizational priorities. The new practices that the Service Quality Initiative legitimizes found their authority, not in established management hierarchies and professional practices, but in being consistent with the hospital's economic priorities. (At the time of the study, cutbacks, restructuring, and budget deficits were anxiously on everybody's minds.) The new social relations that coordinate work practices carry values organized around budget and cost efficiency. In the field notes that we are examining, we see one moment in which these changing values penetrate nursing work plans. This is an important moment because it lets us in on how individual caregivers are incorporated into a changing value system, in an enforceable way. The clinical teaching session introduced a new kind of thinking about what was important in nurses' caring work.

Much has been written on "quality management" strategies about which J. M. Price (1994) says, "Consent to market values (is) strongly reproduced throughout the workplace" (p. 69). The critique made is that group discussion and input into redesign of work processes aims at intensifying individual worker commitment to the work group, to the productive task, and to the product. Central to Total Quality Management and other quality management strategies is the idea of employees being part of a chain of suppliers of products to both internal and external customers with everybody's attention being focused on how each can satisfy his or her own customer's needs. (*Products* are here being understood as whatever it is that their work produces, even if, as in a hospital, it is changing bed linens.) Employees are asked to think about themselves as a link in this chain of relations extending throughout the whole work process. This strategy and the work organization that supports it is supposed to make individually relevant the issues of quality and productivity standards that each worker must be responsible for, to facilitate just-in-time delivery of products, satisfied customers, maximum valued added to the product, etc. In my analysis, the hospital's Service Quality Initiative attempts to bring these features of the hospital's problems with budgets (or the capacity to compete) to the individual worker and into his or her local decision-making and action.

Service Quality Initiative and the Reorganization of Caring Work

Using my conceptual framework, I see the Harmonie Brief story as an extension of the social relations of ruling into the individual effort of caregivers in the hospital workplace.[17] I now want to discuss briefly some effects of this new form of authority on those being ruled, especially the nursing assistants and the residents they care for. Returning to the fragments of data examined, we begin to see how the cost-benefit plan that justifies the purchase of the disposable product is organizing actions that will be taken by nursing assistants.

The requirement to "break even" on this project means not just that use of the Harmonie Briefs are to be rationed to match what would have been spent on laundry, but that decisions about how to nurse, decisions normally taken at the bedside on the basis of empirical evidence (and nursing knowledge), are to be replaced by general rules that relate nursing decisions directly to the hospital's fiscal concerns. While efficient management of resources is, of course, an important goal here as in all organizations, I contend that it is being accomplished in a process that fundamentally alters the caregiving.

That is why to make sense of the Harmonie Brief situation, we must see it not commonsensically—not as an instance where the nursing assistants are working for the resident as customer. This story is clearly not an instance where everyone focuses on how best to serve the resident. Nursing assistants, in the instance examined, stand in a particular consumer or customer relation to suppliers of other hospital services—those who are responsible for the contracted-out laundry services paid for by weight, others who purchase disposable briefs, and still others who must balance budgets. Nursing assistants' work creates varying levels of demand for those services and products. Because the overall goal for the Harmonie Brief project within the new competitive environment is to "break even," the officially legitimized customer-supplier response is for nurses to curtail their use of the (scarce) services and resources. The analysis that began in the nurses' experience of a clinical in-service class where the budget for disposal diapers was related to a need to reduce the laundry costs thus comes back to illuminate and make sense of that experience.

These nurses are learning how to carry out their work in terms of its cost efficiency, learning how to make clinical decisions that are coordinated in relation to the hospital's budget. Their own everyday/everynight thinking is dominated by the market relations that are penetrating the long-term care hospital and the caring relation. To hospital managers, this is the successful outcome of the Service Quality Initiative. But the story has deeper implications. Given the delicate balance nurses must maintain between adequacy of care for the hospitalized elderly and the conservation of hospital supplies, moving decision-making over the use of disposable briefs further away from the bedside is a matter with serious clinical consequences. We learned that decisions about the use of the Harmonie Brief are being established by people several levels above the nursing assistants in the organizational hierarchy. The new rules that are meaningful within the context discursively organized by the Harmonie Brief group (e.g., clinical trials, cost-benefit analysis of disposable versus washable pads) will look completely arbitrary in the context of the night nurses' experiential knowledge. Nurses are left in an ambiguous position regarding caregiving. It seems that the hospital is sanctioning a less stringent attention to resident care. Should caregivers try to work around these rules for the good of the resident?

Checking back a year later, I found that the nursing staff, left with the responsibility of keeping the residents' skin intact within the constraints set by the new rules for use of resources have learned how to adjust their efforts to the new demands. They are happy with the nursing results of using the disposable product. However, most interesting for this analysis is how this hospital has adapted to its concerns about "breaking even": it finances the extra costs of the disposable briefs by asking individual families to pay for them. When a resident's sensitive skin requires nurses to use more briefs then the rules allow, they must be paid for privately. Of course, not all residents have families nor the money to pay extra charges; this is how inequity creeps into long-term care.

Conclusion

My analytic interest in this incident is of two kinds. I have examined how management strategies are helping health care institutions accommodate the demands of fiscal restraint in a globalizing economy (J. Price 1994), and I have demonstrated a method of analysis that moves from particular (experiences) to a general analysis. In regards to the former, I have shown how a strategy of "quality improvement" works as a means of transforming institutional governance, making nurses' individual professional action accountable to a set of goals and objectives formulated externally to it, in this case a cost-benefit calculation. Nurses are being taught to see the good sense of these rules and to bring their thinking and actions into line with them. They are being expected to take up the ruling actions and perpetuate them. This, I argue, is much more than training in economical use of resources. The new relations undermine the integrity of caregiving and professional practice.

The Service Quality strategy examined helps to organize the authority relations that preempt local nursing expertise, suggesting how organizational action in a long-term care facility can be made accountable to a political agenda of deficit reduction and reduced social spending. Here, we are seeing (a piece of) the very complex business of bringing a new cost awareness into everyday decision-making of health care workers. This Service Quality Initiative helps to insinuate ruling ideas into local settings where workers themselves will carry them forward.

The paper also makes a methodological argument about the use of people's experiences as data. Responding to the voices of nurses as they go about their work, I explicated the social relations that organize these nurses' thinking and acting. This is the way that institutional ethnography "makes sense" of people's experiences and draws broader implications from methodical analysis of local experiences. I can claim that what was happening among the nurses was part of something generalizable about "quality management" in that setting and indeed in the management of health care more broadly. This facility's Service Quality principles, the need to "break even," and so on, apply across the organization, not just to the nurses observed and interviewed. To enlarge the claim even further, we would look for similar features of health care organization in other hospitals. So, while this incident may be specific to one time and place, and one set of actors and their experiences, the relations that organize those experiences can be demonstrated to be general.

Understanding how a management technology "works" as a ruling practice to influence nurses and nursing care helps to demystify this management practice, showing some of the ways that market forces penetrate the consciousness of caregivers. Here I made the empirical discovery that "customer" is a concept that operates in different and contradictory ways, its effects being to subordinate nurses' caring to concerns related to the market. This kind of knowledge may be crucial to the struggles that will need to take place over health care in Canada as public policy shifts to subtly incorporate a market orientation.

The relations of ruling do not disappear by learning about them, however, nor can they be shaken off by individuals themselves. They are ever-present in our lives, like the water that fish swim in. Knowing more about how our lives are tangled in ruling relations can help to reduce the frustration we feel about living and working in societies such as ours where things seem to get decided behind our backs, or at least outside of our control. For health care workers who find themselves in these kinds of situations, knowing how one's work setting and one's own decisions are being influenced may help people make useful choices about how to act.

But what does this article say about experience? It is certainly not that experience is authoritative. And it is not "pure" in any essential way; we can see how nursing assistants' lives (at least those experiences to which we are privy through field observations) are being discursively organized. In the analysis that I have attempted, those rather puzzling observations (of events that were perhaps just as puzzling to the participants) were the "way in" to understand the manner in which a particular management discourse rules the nurses' work lives. What was done and said in that work setting offered the clues, the traces of the social relations, that could be followed by the researcher, to be fleshed out and related back to the original field setting. Only then could that moment's experiences be read as the concerting by organizational actors of their local everyday work lives with ruling institutional arrangements. In the setting where this study was conducted, there were many contending versions of what was happening: some people said that the Service Quality Initiative was a participatory project to improve care; others said it was simply a management fad; others disagreed about whether or not it was a money-saving scheme. My analysis relies on accounts of particular experiences to anchor what can be said about them to the actualities of nursing assistants' lives. Theirs is the standpoint from which the analysis is made. It is trustworthy to the extent that it accounts for their experiences. Perhaps the most important thing about experience as data is that, in institutional ethnography, it makes an analysis accountable to the everyday/everynight world as people live in it.

Notes

1. Earlier versions of this paper were presented at the 13th Qualitative Analysis Conference "Studying Social Life Ethnographically," McMaster University May 28–31, 1996; and at the Society for Studies in Social Problems Conference, New York, August 17–19, 1996. It was published originally as "Institutional Ethnography and Experience as Data," in *Qualitative Sociology* 21(1) 1998: 55–73. Support for the research is gratefully acknowledged from Industrial Adjustment Services, Human Resources Management Canada, on a cost-sharing basis with the research hospital, September 1993–March 1995; and from Social Sciences and Humanities Research Council of Canada Grant #816-94-0003 funding a research network, "Understanding and Changing the Conditions of Caring Labour," 1993–1997.

2. For example, Canning (1994) in social history; Code (1991) in philosophy; Nicholson (1990) in literary criticism, among many others.

3. See Smith (1999, chapter 6, "Telling the Truth after Postmodernism" specifically).

4. For some lively examples of published institutional ethnography, see Ng (1996), Diamond (1992), Walker (1990), and Swift (1995).

5. The research was funded through a joint agreement between the hospital, three health care unions, and the Canadian government's Industrial Adjustment Services (IAS) in the Ministry of Human Resources Development. The goal of the IAS program is to help Canadian firms and their labor forces adjust to changes in the production environment. The hospital qualified because of its implementation of the Service Quality Initiative. The specific project for which funding was obtained was a formative evaluation of the initiative. The author was both the chair of the joint IAS committee and the principal investigator of the evaluation research conducted in 1993–1994. One researcher worked half-time on the site during the nine-month study period and was involved as a member of all IAS committees. All three researchers conducted participant observation in work sites. Field notes were supplemented by interviews with informants from all levels of the organization. Activities and documents associated with the Service Quality Initiative were analyzed. Periodic research reports were circulated to all staff, the hospital executive, and the board of directors. As befits

a formative evaluation, discussion was encouraged and feedback incorporated into the data collection. A final report (submitted to IAS, the hospital, and the unions in 1995) is available from the author.

6. Readers from the United States may be more familiar with the term *nursing home* used to describe the same kind of facility.

7. The Service Quality Initiative was a locally developed and implemented strategy that owed much to the ideas and literature of Total Quality Management. Total Quality Management and Continuous Quality Improvement are popular management strategies employed in both industrial and human service organizations to improve organizational functioning. For a strongly optimistic account of how quality improvement strategies work in health care agencies, see Phillip Hassen's *Rx for Hospitals* (1993).

8. Bev Miller, MSW, and Pat Larson, MN, were research assistants on this project and conducted with great sensitivity and attention to detail much of the field research.

9. Ng (1996) shows how accountability relations influence an organization's goals and activities.

10. Diamond (1992) shows "reality" experienced and understood differently, from different sites in an organization.

11. A good deal of the work in any organization consists of turning events, experiences, and transactions of the people whose lives are its concerns into text and acting on the basis of those textual accounts. Smith (1990b) has argued that this form of text-based interaction is ubiquitous in contemporary Western societies, discursively organizing social relations in ways that can be investigated as practical activities.

12. De Montigny (1995b) provides a dramatic illustration and analysis of how this happens.

13. In Walker (1990), "discursive organization" is shown to be practical activities of policymaking and governing.

14. For a fuller discussion of this, see Campbell (1988 or 1995).

15. As one reviewer of this article points out, the residents are also being ruled and the study might have used their voices, as Diamond's (1992) research did. It should be noted that the social relations organizing any setting are consistent, no matter whose standpoint is used to explicate them.

16. This paragraph paraphrases an e-mail communication between Dorothy Smith and Bethan Lloyd. The responsibility for its interpretation here is mine.

17. For Canadian readers, this analysis has special implications. The Canadian public health care system has not until recently been directly subject to competitive capitalism. This paper shows how, within the nonprofit (publicly funded and administered) Canadian hospital system, market relations are being established and are becoming the legitimate basis of caregiving decisions.

6

Keeping the Institution in View: Working with Interview Accounts of Everyday Experience[1]

Liza McCoy

INSTITUTIONAL ETHNOGRAPHIC RESEARCH often begins by interviewing people, singly or in focus groups, about their everyday experience, in a way that brings into view the interface between their individual lives and some set of institutional relations.[2] In this kind of interview individuals are asked about their experience as, for example, gay students in high school (G. W. Smith 1998), mothers of children in elementary school (Griffith and Smith 2005), or people living with disability who use home care services (Campbell, Copeland, and Tate 1998). A panel of informants like this gathers together individuals whose standpoint the research takes, whose experience generates the problematic to be investigated and provides the entry point into a set of institutional relations. The analytic goal is to make visible the ways the institutional order creates the conditions of individual experience. What happens to people? What shapes or constrains the possibilities open to them, including the possibilities for knowing and telling their experience? From this initial exploration of people's descriptions of their experience, the researcher can identify specific institutional sites, work processes, or discourses for further investigation.

That is the idea: the challenge is finding a way to analyze the interviews that will keep the institution in view. In my own research and in my work with students I've learned that the period of data analysis is a time of vulnerability in an institutional ethnographic project. A kind of unintended analytic drift can occur, in which the analytic focus shifts from the institution to the informants. For example, the researcher might generate descriptions of the informants' meanings and perspective or develop typologies of their strategies and orientations. This work may be done with much sensitivity and ethnographic skill, but it will be about the informants rather than the institution. Sometimes the researcher gets caught up in conflict among the different informants' stories, and takes sides, while missing the institutional order that gives rise to the conflict and the available understandings of it in the first place. Or the researcher succumbs to what Smith calls "institutional capture" (Smith 2005) and begins converting informants' accounts of their experience into the terms of an institutional discourse that constitutes people and their activities as the objects of professional or managerial knowledge. In all of these cases, institutional relations and the social organization of experience have slipped from view.

In this chapter, I offer some strategies for working with interview accounts of everyday experience in a way that maintains an institutional focus and lays the groundwork for further research and analysis. To illustrate my points I draw on examples from a collaborative research project[3] where we interviewed seventy-nine people living with HIV infection about their experience of looking after their health (see McCoy 2005; Mykhalovskiy and McCoy 2002; Mykhalovskiy, McCoy, and Bresalier 2004).

The Helpful Notion of Work

The notion of "work" serves as an orienting concept in institutional ethnography, and it is particularly useful both in conducting and analyzing interviews about everyday experience. It directs the researcher's attention toward precisely that interface between embodied individuals and institutional relations, which is the object of interest in institutional ethnographic research. In its grounded concreteness it renders securely graspable what is otherwise slippery and elusive.

As used in institutional ethnography, work simply refers to "what people do that requires some effort, that they mean to do, and that involves some acquired competence" (Smith 1987: 165). This sense of work is, for me, also informed by Schutz's (1964) notion of "the everyday world of working"[4] in which we are located, in our bodies, and which we "gear into" through our purposive actions (pp. 226–227). "The notion of work directs us to its anchorage in material conditions and means and that it is done in 'real time'—all of which are consequential for how the individual can proceed" (Smith 1987: 165). Used in this way, *work* is an empirically empty term; it does not define types of work or identify some activities as work in contrast with other activities that are found not to be work. Its value lies in directing analytic attention to the practical activities of everyday life in a way that begins to make visible how those activities gear into, are called out by, shape and are shaped by, extended translocal relations of large-scale coordination (what Smith calls relations of ruling).

Viewed in this way, work happens at (gears into) the interface between the individual, embodied subject and the physical and social worlds, the worlds of time and things and weather and other people. These spaces of everyday life (including the mental space of consciousness) are in contemporary society also sites of interface between individuals and a vast network of institutional relations, discourses, and work processes. You get out of bed, turn on the tap, make coffee, read the newspaper you collected from your front step—and you are participating in institutional relations (municipal water systems, international trade, the mass media). A good institutional ethnographic interview elicits detailed descriptions of work that make visible the institutional hooks and traces, as well as the lived experience of the teller. (For more on this kind of interviewing see DeVault and McCoy, this book). Once the interview is transcribed, the next step is to read the interview, or collections of excerpts from multiple interviews, in a way that finds and explores the accounts of work, while maintaining the analytic focus on the institutional interface.

What's the Work? How Is It Evoked by and Articulated to the Institutional Order?

Working with interview data is a bit like doing another interview, this time with the data. I find it helpful actually to pose explicit questions, such as the following: What is the work that these informants are describing or alluding to? What does it involve for them? How is their work connected with the work of other people? What particular skills or knowledge seems to be required? What does it feel like to do this work? What are the troubles or successes that arise for people doing this work? What evokes the work? How is the work articulated to institutional work processes and the institutional order?

For example, in our research with people living with HIV, we asked people about their doctors. Most informants reported having both a general practice (GP) or primary care physician and an HIV specialist. In interviews and focus groups we explored how people used their different doctors. Here is an excerpt:

> I: What do you see [the GP] for?[5]
>
> P: If I get a cold and cannot shake it off. But I really do not need to see her for anything. Like I had a stone and that was while I was taking the Crixivan and I went to see her about that.

I: So do you see her for anything that has to do with HIV?

P: No. I go to the clinic every month, and I usually wait until I get there if I have some sort of problem. Like these rashes. I do not know if it is some illness or not, but I think it is something more than a GP can handle. I think it is either drug-related or nerve-related.

This is a fairly obvious description of a form of work. The speaker is talking about how he uses the medical resources available to him, his GP, and the HIV clinic where he consults an HIV specialist. He explains the sort of health problem he takes to his GP (a cold, a stone). He gives an example of some rashes he is having, and in his discussion of that we can see that he does mental work considering the possible cause of the problem and relating that to the expertise available to him, in order to decide whom to consult and whether to wait for his monthly visit or make a special appointment.

The next analytic step is considering why his work takes this form. Addressing that question prompts the explicit recognition of what is common knowledge: that the delivery of medical care in North America is structured by a division of labor based on parts of the body, bodily systems, and types of malady, with a hierarchical distinction between generalists and specialists. Some informants described how they had had to learn about this organization—about types of doctors, how to access them, and when to consult them. This was especially the case for research participants who had been healthy young people before getting their HIV diagnosis, with very little experience of medical services. As I studied these and other comments from other informants, I named the work they were describing the "patient's triage work," borrowing the term used in emergency medicine to indicate the work of sorting patients by the nature of their complaint (allocation of medical resources is organized on the basis of this sorting). The notion of the patient's triage work recognizes that, in most cases of accessing outpatient medical services, patients gear consciously and actively into the system, matching whatever trouble they seem to have with the professional expertise available to them; they also take into consideration the interactive styles of individual doctors and organizational features of the health care setting (difficulty getting appointments, expected wait times). The notion of the patients' triage work thus focuses the researcher's attention right at the interface between individuals and the institutional organization of medical expertise and health care delivery.

It is possible to pick out the subtle traces of two other sets of institutional relations that are shaping the speaker's triage work. Notice his reference to consulting his GP when he had a stone while he was taking Crixivan. Crixivan is one of the antiretroviral drugs that are used in combination therapy to reduce the activity of HIV. For many people, antiretroviral drugs provoke a sweep of side effects, from nausea and diarrhea to nerve and liver problems. Later on the speaker mentions the rashes he is having that he thinks might be drug- or nerve-related. Both of these examples suggest that some of his trips to the doctor and some of the topics he raises when he goes for his monthly appointment are occasioned by his participation in pharmaceutical treatment. Taking antiretroviral therapy brings people into a particular kind of relationship with health care services, involving regular monitoring through blood tests, making adjustments or changes to the medication regimen, and treatment of side effects. Thus we can see in this person's account of his triage work an interface between his embodied experience and the complex of work processes through which pharmaceutical products are designed, tested, marketed, prescribed, and distributed.

Then there are his references to the rash and the thinking work he has been doing, considering if it is the sign of an illness or drug- or nerve-related. Here he is clearly drawing on a working knowledge of typical side effects of antiretroviral medication and common opportunistic infections that beset people infected with HIV. The circulation of information about HIV-related illnesses and HIV treatments is a significant set of practices in the institutional field surrounding people living with HIV. Many community-based AIDS service organizations are active in this area, producing fact sheets and newsletters and setting up information-sharing meetings. We don't have here an account of how this man gets his information (although other parts of the interview did explore the work he does around information), but we can see that his triage work necessarily draws on the information he has been able to gather and build into a working knowledge. Here therefore is another point of interface.

Obviously, in producing this discussion, which fills out some oblique references, I am drawing on my own working knowledge about how health services are organized, about biomedical treatment of HIV, reported side effects of antiretroviral therapy, and the production and circulation of treatment information. Picking out the institutional traces in people's accounts and seeing how their work takes shape at the institutional interface involves a hermeneutic process of reading, in which prior knowledge of institutional sites and processes informs the reading of the accounts, and the reading of the accounts raises questions that prompt further exploration of the institutional field, which then informs repeat readings of the interviews. The objective is a kind of analytic mapping that locates individuals and their experience within a complex institutional field. At this initial stage the goal is primarily to identify what is going on in the field (as it becomes visible in the informants' accounts). Only some parts of that field, some institutional sites and processes, will be explored through further investigation in later stages of the research.

Look toward the Institutional Complex Rather than the Individuals

There is a form of analytic drift that occurs when the focus on work veers into a classificatory interest in the different ways people describe doing the work, with an emphasis on the apparent beliefs, motivations, or competencies that underlie their different approaches. Creating typologies or typifications, identifying this sort of person or that sort of approach, is a common method of understanding, in everyday life (cf. Berger and Luckmann 1966) and in research (see for example, Lofland and Lofland 1995). The mind, it would seem, eagerly moves in such a way, so that the researcher who has interviewed a number of people starts grouping them mentally into distinctive types. In an institutional ethnography, however, if this ordinary mental process is extended into systematic analysis, the focus begins to shift to the individuals, in a descriptive, explanatory way, and away from the institutional field that is shaping their experience.

For example, here are four accounts from the HIV study, all by different speakers, all referencing some aspect of the work of obtaining medical care.

1. Every time I go to any doctor or whatever, I got my book out here, or I've written, I always know what I'm going for. So I have a piece of paper, one to ten or twenty and I make sure every single thing is covered as possible.
2. If I'm ringing the bell and doing everything and . . . I'm going by the hospital rules, and I know that I'm in pain and I keep hushing it down . . . and I'm not getting any better, I'm sorry the nasty part of me is going to come out. I'm starting to get more aggressive, like, "Hello? I'm here, I'm in pain, I need something here to calm me down." . . . And even when the doctor comes, it still takes ten years to come with the medication, so you still have to constantly go on in the same way until you get the medication.
3. For me there are days I am timid and there are other days I can be a bit more assertive. If I have a problem I will try to solve it in my head because he is not going to listen anyway.
4. I have got to know him and rather trust him and he does not steer me wrong. He does not wait for me to ask questions; he explains everything and I like that and then I do not have to be thinking for a week before I get there everything I need to ask him because he is going to explain it all anyway.

One way to approach such comments analytically is to read them as revealing different positions on a continuum of passivity-assertiveness. Thus we see the first two speakers being assertive—the first in a rationalized, efficient way, the second (describing a visit to the emergency room) more emotional and rebellious. The third and fourth speakers both describe forms of passivity, with the third speaker holding back in his dealing with the doctor, and the fourth happy he doesn't have to ask questions or do much thinking before his appointments. Analysis along these lines might construct a systematic typology of patient orientations. In contrast, the notion of work at the institutional interface prompts us to seek the institutional organization that provides for the sense of the stories being told, that shapes the activities and situations described.

When these four accounts are read looking toward the institutional order and work processes they reference, the social organization of health care delivery begins to come into view. Notice that the excerpts are all describing situations that take place after the work of patient's triage discussed previously. These are descriptions about what happens after the person has gone to a site where medical consultation or treatment is to be had; in the situations they describe they are in some kind of contact with health professionals. Why would these people feel the need to do what they describe doing, organizing the doctor, demanding treatment, or stifling disagreement? This is not a question about individual motivation but about the institutional context in which such strategies make sense and go to work. Why is it important that the doctor provides information without being prompted? What are the institutional processes that evoke this work, these concerns?

When I was working with this data and asked these questions, my attention shifted toward a consideration of the medical visit as a social form. I drew on what informants said, on my own experience as a person who consults doctors (through which I could initially make sense of their stories), and I turned to research on doctor-patient communication that examines transcripts of actual medical consultations (e.g., Fisher and Todd 1983; Makoul, Arntson, and Schofield 1995; Waitzkin 1991). What you can see in all of the excerpts are accounts of people's work gearing into, sometimes actively intervening in, the organization of the medical visit. For example, the work described by the first two speakers is shaped by and oriented toward the scheduling of the medical consultation and the distribution of medical resources (the doctor's attention and time, medication). There is a work organization here, and patients don't control it. They don't decide when the doctor will enter their cubicle or how long the consultation will last; they don't control the sequence or shape of the medical interview. Nonetheless, some people gear into this work process in a way that attempts to influence the timing and content in their favor, as a way of looking out for their own health needs. In an institutional ethnographic analysis, it is certainly relevant to take note of different strategies for engaging with health services, but these should be located in relation to the institutional work process that evokes them and to which they are directed.

The third and fourth comments highlight the doctor's interactional style as it calls out typical forms of work for the individuals speaking (note that they are not describing single events, but describing general, repeated aspects of their relationship with the doctor). Both reference the doctor as a potential source of information or problem-solving advice, although in one account the doctor does not come through and in the other he does. Earlier I mentioned the importance of treatment information for people living with HIV. Although there are extensive community-based resources that make up-to-date treatment information freely available to HIV positive people, some individuals find it difficult to draw usable information from print sources and say that what works best for them is to talk with someone knowledgeable. Other people feel overwhelmed by the amount of information and the fact that HIV treatment is in a constant state of development, with new information coming out all the time. For various reasons, people see a role for the doctor in providing understandable information about HIV treatment and keeping their patients informed about new developments. Looking toward the institutional order, then, we might ask, How well do doctors do this work? What is it about their professional training and the organization of health care delivery that facilitates or hinders the extent to which they have the time, the inclination, and the skill to provide sufficient and usable information to their patients? These are questions that point the way to further research, which might involve interviewing doctors and reviewing the content of medical education.

Let me offer one other set of contrasting readings to illustrate the difference between studying the informants and studying the institution. Two of the accounts quoted above contain clearly or implicitly evaluative statements about doctors. One doctor is being criticized (for not listening, not helping) and one doctor is being praised (for generously providing information and trustworthy advice). Much of the talk people do about their doctors has a strong evaluative dimension. Here again, the typologizing, classifying mind goes into action. It is interesting to talk about the data in terms of what people liked and disliked, identifying what they look for in their relationship with their doctor. This is, in fact, a received approach. There is a literature on patients' perspectives and lay evaluations of health care. For example, Calnan and Williams (1996) report on a study where female informants were asked in semistructured interviews to evaluate their doctor's performance. The analysis focuses on the evaluative criteria used by informants, and it further notes some class differences. Middle-class and professional women (designated as social classes I and II) evaluated the doctor's willingness and promptness in making referrals to specialists; they also were concerned about the extent to which the doctor treated their complaints as trivial or took them seriously. Working-class women (social classes III and IV), on the other hand, emphasized the doctor's manner with children and, more generally, the extent to which the doctor was rude and abrupt. The analysis goes no further than this. These differences in preference are treated simply as emanating from different class locations, but how they do so and why is left unexamined. Whether the different groups of women (who were grouped by the researchers according to a standard method for assigning research subjects to class categories) had different experiences at the doctor's office, which understandably would influence their evaluative criteria, also goes unexamined. Although the women are talking about the organization of health care delivery as it enters their individual lives, the analysis keeps the focus squarely on the women, their preferences, and their evaluative criteria.

From an advocacy perspective, systematically presenting people's assessments of their medical care can be a good way to inform health providers about the preferences and concerns of patients. What an institutional ethnographic approach contributes to that advocacy project is an institutional focus that keeps attention oriented toward the organization of health service delivery (what is being evaluated) and prevents it from stalling at a typology of evaluative criteria (studying the patients). For example, in our research, we discovered some differences not unlike those reported by Calnan and Williams. Although we did not group our research participants into formalized social class categories, we had recruited people living in a range of social and economic circumstances, from well-off middle-class professionals to people living in poverty and social marginality. Among the latter, we heard stories about troubled relationships with doctors, along with areas of concern not often articulated by middle-class or highly educated participants, such as unwelcome pressure from doctors to take antiretroviral medication and inability or unwillingness of doctors to provide sufficient or clear information about treatments. Examining that data we asked, what is it about the delivery of outpatient health services that causes more problems for people who gear into the health care system from life circumstances of poverty and social marginality? (See McCoy 2005.) Here again is a question, generated from the standpoint of patients, that can be carried forward into interviews with doctors and health professionals.

In summary, analyzing informants' stories and accounts through the notion of work has two related goals. One is to develop an understanding and appreciation of individuals' embodied experience—what happens to them, what they do, what it feels like. The second goal is to use those stories and accounts to bring into view the institutional field in which the individual and her or his experience are located for the purpose of identifying institutional sites and processes for further investigation.

How Are People Able to Talk about Their Experiences? Spot the Institutional Discourses

In the previous section the focus was on *what* people are talking about—their work and the work processes of other people they gear into. But we can also begin to see important features of the institution and the institutional interface if we attend to the *how*: how it is that people can talk about their experience. How does it come to be available to them to know and tell their experience in that way? Here particular attention is addressed to institutional or ruling discourses as these are taken up by the research informants. In addition to the interface that happens when a person gears bodily into institutional work processes (for example, by seeking medical care or participating in pharmaceutical therapy), this sort of interface happens conceptually and linguistically.

Language is, essentially, a phenomenon of interface—partly in and constituent of individual consciousness, but also shared. "[L]anguage, for the individual consciousness, lies on the borderline between oneself and the other. The word in language is half someone else's" (Bakhtin 1981: 293). But language, in the sense of "English," is not a unitary phenomenon. Within what we treat as the shared language of English, there are various discourses, speech genres, registers, vocabularies, ways of talking and getting things done. And language is a key constituent of institutional relations: in contemporary society, large-scale coordination is effected primarily through text-based forms of objectified knowledge (see Smith 1990a). What institutional ethnographers refer to as an institutional discourse is, therefore, any widely shared professional, managerial, scientific, or authoritative way of knowing (measuring, naming, describing) states of affairs that render them actionable within institutional relations of purpose and accountability. Far more than "jargon," these are conceptual systems, forms of knowledge that carry institutional purposes and reflect a standpoint within relations of ruling.

In contemporary society, many institutional discourses are not esoteric or exclusive to trained insiders; they are moved into wider circulation through the mass media and popularizing literatures. Some are transmitted through formal education or picked up through frequent encounters with institutional work processes. Indeed we can recognize a kind of classing process that occurs through participation in or exclusion from forms of authoritative knowledge and dominant discourses.[6] For example, Griffith and Smith (2005) identify the ways the middle-class mothers they interviewed participated in a child development discourse they had learned sometimes through their own formal education but also through a committed engagement with parenting books and magazines. This showed up not only in the way they talked about their children, but in the kinds of work they described doing with their children, implementing projects informed by the child development discourse and aimed at producing children who could be successful in its terms.

Taking up once again the example of the research with people living with HIV, we can recognize that the main institutional discourse organizing the field of HIV research, HIV treatment, and health care delivery is that of biomedicine. (Indeed, knowing oneself as a person infected with HIV is already to take up a position within institutional discourse.) Biomedicine is one of the widely circulated institutional discourses. Most people participate in it to some extent when they are recipients of biomedical health services, but they also do so through their lay knowledge of types of disease, causes of infections, and forms of treatment. Some of this knowledge is so generalized throughout the population as to be viewed as common sense—for example, that washing hands reduces the spread of germs that cause disease—while other forms of biomedical knowledge are more specialized and acquired on an as-needed basis, usually related to the personal or familial health problems of the knowing individual.

The extent to which people participate in the discourse varies. Those who can appropriate the institutional discourse can often move with greater ease through its processes; they know what to expect, they can imagine how things work, and they have the language to advocate for themselves and their families (cf. Darville 1995, on organizational literacy). At the same time, acquiring this level of expertise usually means that they assimilate the institutional gaze; they come to know themselves and their families as objects of institutional attention. They work on themselves; they produce their actions in ways that more tightly articulate the institutional processes. Learning the discourse carries the intentionality of the discourse into the personal spaces of people's lives. This is, in the terms I am using here, another kind of individual-institution interface. You can see all this happening, see the traces of it, in interviews.

Here is an excerpt from our data that illustrates what I mean. The speaker is talking about a time in his life when he had trouble keeping up with his antiretroviral medication regimen.

> I struggled with this compliance issue for a while and then finally, it was actually one of the residents, she said to me . . . "I do not think we should start you on a new cocktail until we get your head around this problem that you are having because you could screw that up and you are running out of options." So I went to a psychiatrist briefly and worked my way around the issues with compliance and then I started on a new cocktail last July which was Crixivan, delavirdine, and [d4T] and then everything since then has had amazing results I never dreamed of. And compliance is almost perfect, almost.

In this account, the speaker formulates his problem using the institutional term *compliance*, which expresses a medico-managerial/public health interest in whether and how well patients carry out the doctor's instructions and take medication as prescribed. The way he uses the term and the story he tells are consistent with current institutional discourses on compliance that view compliance failures as arising from psychological or mental states (health beliefs, attitudes, habits of mind) that can be adjusted through therapeutic intervention involving self-examination and behavior modification (see Mykhalovskiy, McCoy, and Bresalier 2004). We see this discourse operating in the reported work of the resident and the psychiatrist. The resident formulates the matter as requiring the patient to "get his head around" the reasons for his failure to take all his pills as scheduled, and the psychiatrist provides the professional expertise to help him do that. But we also see the discourse in the narrator's introduction and conclusion in which he takes up compliance language and the conceptual frame it carries as his own.

By contrast, here is an account about quitting antiretroviral medication that neither references nor draws on the compliance discourse or, more broadly, biomedical discourse:

> I did take it and it didn't agree with me. . . . [I was] moody, cranky. . . didn't want to be around people. . . . I couldn't handle it, so I just took myself off of it.

This speaker assesses the medication with respect to how it makes him feel emotionally and how it affects his relationships with the people in his life. He does not reference objectified, scientific forms of assessment of the drugs' less visible effects on HIV, such as CD4 and viral load counts. He does not represent his quitting the drugs as any kind of failure. The drugs did not agree with him. The failure is not his.

When considering the accounts of participants who don't do institutional discourse, I find it helpful to distinguish between extra-institutional talk and oppositional talk. By the former I mean accounts that are structured by other relevancies, not explicitly in opposition, just different, such as the account of quitting medication quoted above. Oppositional or critical talk takes a stance that highlights the differences between the institutional discourse and the forms of knowing and being the speaker feels to be preferable; it does not necessarily imply ignorance of the dominant discourse. For example, when speaking about treatment information, one participant pointed to other women in the focus group and said, "I would rather hear her story, her story, or her story than read the stats, because the stats don't mean shit." Yet the wise researcher will avoid making incautious assumptions about what people think or know based on how they talk about their experience in an interview. Most people have linguistic repertoires that allow them to vary the language, the register, the emphasis, even the narrative frames of the accounts they provide in order to fit their verbal contributions to the emerging conversation or to achieve particular ends. For some people this involves an ability to do both institutional talk and extra-institutional or even oppositional talk.

I must stress that the analytic interest in identifying different levels of participation in institutional discourses is not about slotting informants into a typology, assessing whether participants are sufficiently knowledgeable in appropriate ways, or celebrating the resistance of those who don't do institutional talk. The analytic interest lies in discovering how the discourse operates in people's lives and what difference it makes for people to participate or not to participate in the discourse in various ways. Here the focus is not only on their movements through and engagement with institutional work processes, but also in their experience of self-understanding and critique, their worries, their projects of self-improvement, and their feelings of success or failure. As well, taking a broader view, the analytic interest goes beyond what people know and how they participate in institutional discourse, to consider what routes are available to them for learning the discourse or the ways in which individuals are targeted for information transfer and public education campaigns.

Of course, you have to be doing research into the professional discourses that organize the institutional relations you are studying in order to recognize when they are surfacing in people's accounts. This approach to working with interview data constantly refers the researcher beyond the transcript, to other sources, other informants, and other texts in order to investigate what is organizing those aspects of the discourse or institution that are visible in people's accounts. In some cases, the researcher may come to the study already familiar with the key professional discourses. In the HIV study, for example, most members of the research team had worked in community-based AIDS service organizations; they had been involved in writing and disseminating HIV treatment information and influencing public policy. I was one of two people on the team who didn't have that background. So in addition to learning from my colleagues, I read HIV treatment information materials, health consumer activist literature, HIV research reports, and health policy documents.

Be Alert to Your Own Allegiance to Institutional Discourse

As you attend to the way your research informants use and participate in institutional discourses, it behooves you to attend to your own participation, as a researcher, in the same discourses. A maxim of institutional ethnography is that research should begin outside of institutional discourse. Institutional language organizes ways of knowing the world in institutionally actionable ways. Despite your intentions, if you are conceptually beholden to the institutional discourse, if you treat the institutional language as merely descriptive and attempt to use it that way in analytic writing, the opportunity to investigate the institution has been abrogated. To continue with the example of the compliance discourse in biomedicine: we couldn't fully study the way that discourse operated in people's lives if we adopted that language ourselves, discussing whether our informants were compliant or noncompliant or grouping them according to their reported success with medication. Michael Mulkay (1981) writes about the "intellectual vassalage" of researchers in the sociology of science whose analyses are derived from scientists' narratives about good and bad science, leaving unexamined the institutional discourses and language practices through which these distinctions are produced. Mulkay's term *vassalage* suggests sociologists who uncritically privilege the standpoint of a high-status group. Smith's notion of "institutional capture," on the other hand, suggests the researcher who is unwittingly trapped in institutional language. Indeed, researchers who take a critical perspective on relations of ruling are not immune to institutional capture. Many linguistic forms that organize knowledge in institutionally relevant ways have spread so far into common speech that we are not always aware how they are operating. (See for example Smith's argument that "No One Commits Suicide" [1990c].)

Researchers embarking on institutional ethnographies usually attempt to gather data in ways that begin outside institutional relevancies. Still, it often happens that it is only as the research progresses that the researcher is able to identify all the ways her thinking about the matter at hand is drawing on institutional discourses. Therefore, just as it helps bring the institution into view to spot the discourse in the way research participants talk about their lives, it is also helpful at the data analysis stage to watch out for the ways the discourse frames the researcher's own work.[7] Here is another kind of dialogue with the data. Paying attention to what people say calls into question the way the researcher has been thinking and prompts a rethinking.

For example, we initially identified one of our interview topics as "making treatment decisions." We knew there was a research discourse around treatment decision-making, involving various models and studies, and with a basis in rational choice theory. We expected that our data would suggest that the work of making treatment decisions was rather more and other than what was accounted for in the model—and we did find that. But we still talked about "making treatment decisions," and we used the same wording as a sorting category to group chunks of transcript data for analysis. However, in the midst of the work of locating and assembling interview excerpts about "making treatment decisions," we recognized that while some research participants spoke a language of decision-making, others did not. They talked about starting treatment but never in a way that characterized themselves as having made a decision. They spoke about doing whatever their doctor recommended. They talked about feeling forced to take medicine or giving in under pressure from their doctors or family members. It would have been inaccurate to categorize those stories—even provisionally—as instances of "making treatment decisions"; used in that way, the sorting label turned into an analytic category that subsumed rather than merely indexed what people said. In part these different accounts reflect the different circumstances under which people started treatment and the relationships they could have with their doctors. But they also reflect the ways people did or did not take up the health consumer discourse with its emphasis on the informed and assertive patient who makes treatment decisions based on good information and a careful assessment of advantages and disadvantages. Until we stepped completely out of that discourse ourselves, however, we couldn't see the way it operated among our participants. We renamed the sorting category "coming to be on treatment," a wider and more empirically open term. Through this move, we brought the treatment decision-making discourse out from the shadows of unexamined linguistic affiliations and into the analytic spotlight. (See Mykhalovskiy 2004.)

The Next Step—Move the Investigation into the Sites and Processes of the Institution

In institutional ethnographic research, the primary function of the sort of interviews I have been describing is to make the researcher acquainted with the work and concerns of some group of people (who are often constituted as a distinct group by their relationship to some institution—e.g., people diagnosed as infected with HIV who come into the health care system as patients). Initial published analysis may present a description of their experience, highlighting the institutional interface as I have shown here, but this is not the *final* analytic goal of institutional ethnography. That goal is to develop a detailed, descriptive analysis of some portion of the institutional relations that have been identified as consequential, in order to show how these institutional work processes are organized and how they shape the ground of people's everyday experiences. Doing this requires additional research. Therefore, in working with the accounts provided in the interviews, the task is to glean good ethnographic understanding of the informants' lived experience and circumstances in a way that brings into view the institutional hooks and traces, identifying sites and processes for further investigation.

One way to pursue this project is through a two-stage model of institutional ethnography. The research starts with interviews or focus groups. These are transcribed and then analyzed along the lines described above. Further research questions are generated and specific institutional processes are identified as important for further study. The second stage of the research addresses these questions through interviews with institutional functionaries, observation of institutional work processes, or examination of key institutional texts. This is a good workable model and one that has the advantage of making sense to people unfamiliar with institutional ethnography, such as funding bodies or edgy ethical review boards. But institutional ethnographic research doesn't have to progress in orderly and distinct stages. It is quite possible to work back and forth, in parallel, to be talking with institutional functionaries, for example, at the same time you are talking with people at the receiving end of institutional work processes, with information gained through one avenue of inquiry informing the questions you explore in the other. This latter approach is most appropriate when the researcher already has a good working knowledge of the institutional field and is adept at recognizing institutional hooks and traces in people's accounts. But whether the examination of key institutional processes happens in tandem or at a later stage, what is crucial is a way of working systematically with the interview data to bring the institution into view and to raise questions that will open an exploration of institutional processes.

Notes

1. This chapter first took shape as two different papers: "Keeping Social Organization in View: Data Analysis in Institutional Ethnography," presented at the annual meeting of the Canadian Sociology and Anthropology Association in Quebec City in June 2001; and "Interview Accounts of Everyday Experience," presented at the annual meeting of the Society for the Study of Social Problems in San Francisco in August 2004. The helpful comments of Marjorie DeVault, Kamini Maraj Grahame, Peter Grahame, Paul Luken, Karen MacKinnon, Eric Mykhalovskiy, Susan Turner, Dorothy Smith, and Suzanne Vaughan are gratefully acknowledged. I remain, in the customary way, solely responsible for the chapter's shortcomings.
2. In institutional ethnography, the concept of institution directs attention to clusters of ruling or administrative relations organized around specific functions, such as health care, law, finance, social services, or municipal government.
3. Members of the research team were Darien Taylor, Eric Mykhalovskiy, Craig McClure, Michelle Webber, Loralee Gillis, Michael Bresalier, and Liza McCoy. All members of the team shared in the work of conducting interviews and developing a preliminary analysis of the data. The research was funded by a grant from the Glaxo-Wellcome Positive Action Program.

4. Schutz's notion of work comes from a typology of action and excludes mental work or what he calls covert action. This Cartesian distinction is unhelpful. But the image of work as gearing into the physical and social world is splendidly apposite and worth expanding to include—as it does in institutional ethnography—thought work and emotion work and any other intended actions of the conscious, embodied self.

5. "I" refers to the Interviewer and "P" to Participant. Ellipses indicate that some content has been omitted to make the quotations easier to read by eliminating digressions, repeated phrases, and extraneous material.

6. There are resonances here with Bourdieu's metaphor of "cultural capital." (See Bourdieu and Passeron 1977).

7. Suzanne Vaughan, in a personal communication, suggests that researchers can develop their familiarity with institutional discourses—and spot their own allegiance to these—by reading historically and comparatively on their topic. Seeing how the institutional framing shifts over time or varies in different world regions makes current institutional framings more visible; they stand revealed as historical and contingent.

7

Constructing Single Parent Families for Schooling: Discovering an Institutional Discourse

Alison I. Griffith

Introduction

ONCE UPON A TIME, my children and I were a single parent family. There are many phrases used to identify families like ours was—"broken family," "lone parent family," and "one parent family." The concept "single parent family" and its synonyms coordinate our participation in a text-mediated discourse[1] that designates some families as different and then reads back from the child's participation in society to identify their single parent family as the source of the identified problems. The single parent family discourse can be found in policy documents, in newspaper stories, and in research particularly in the disciplines of education, social work, psychology, and psychiatry and in the ordinary talk about students done by teachers, school administrators, school social workers, and school psychologists.

In this chapter, I will trace some of these text-mediated practices as I describe the institutional ethnographic research process through which I explored the topic of single parent families and schools.[2] The problematic of the research was to discover the ways that single parent families are constructed as different from other family forms. In other words, the focus of my research was not on single parent families, *but rather on the textually mediated, discursive practices that constructed us as different.* I begin this chapter in my experience as a single parent and then discuss the research process through which I became aware of the how the concept coordinates our understandings of single parent families as different from other family forms.

Single Parent Family Experiences

As single parents, we rarely see ourselves as socially deviant. Rather, our concerns are often about money, how our children are growing and maturing, the kind of adults they are becoming, and so on. Our children's experiences of schools are always a hot topic. We are often puzzled by some of the difficulties our children encounter in school. We speak about school problems with other single parents without necessarily being able to understand or resolve the issues.

During most of the time I was a single parent, I was attending university. I had realized that the only employment available to me was dead-end jobs, and I hoped I could manage the costs of university through student loans and part-time work. Of course, university was more expensive than I had expected and even with my parents' help I was unable to make ends meet. At that time, it was possible to attend university full-time and to receive welfare benefits. So I applied and the monthly income, although small, was enough. We were very poor but, with my parents' help and scholarships, we managed.

Applying for and collecting welfare was my first recognizable encounter with the textually mediated processes that structured our family as different. A social worker was assigned to my case and together we filled out the application form based on information from birth certificates, my marriage certificate, and letters from the children's school attesting that they were enrolled. In order to be eligible for welfare payments, I had to sue my husband through the provincial family court for nonpayment of child support. The court process required many of the same documents—birth certificates, marriage certificate, and school attendance records. These texts were part of the process of identifying our family as indigent, as single, and as deserving of welfare benefits. Once the forms were processed, we became a certified single parent family.

One of the benefits of receiving welfare is that in British Columbia all medical and drug expenses are covered. A medical card was issued that was (almost) identical to those issued to all provincial residents. Often, when I went to the pharmacy, I noted that one pharmacist would begin our interaction with a smile and a welcome nod. But soon his demeanor changed: he stopped smiling, became distant, and treated me in a brusque manner. One day, another pharmacist was on duty and he said (in what seemed to me to be a very a loud voice), "I see you have a *W* on your card. When you are on welfare, you don't have to pay for your prescriptions." The medical card was coded to let the pharmacist and other medical practitioners know that our family was different. In the medical system of the province, the coded card was (necessarily) a feature of the textual processes that coordinated our medical coverage and professional payment for services. The card identified us as a family receiving welfare. In the pharmacy, this had interpersonal consequences as well as being part of text-mediated social relations.

In K–12 education, teachers and administrators speak un-self-consciously about the "problem" of children from single parent families. During my PhD research, a school principal told me, "You can always tell if a child comes from a single parent family." A teacher in one of my graduate school courses said, "Boys from single parent families tend to draw on their writing books." Recently, one of my students said, "That school is really difficult to teach in. Many of the children come from broken families."

What is it about a household of a mother and two sons that calls forth such ordinary and unthinking references to social deviancy from educators, psychologists, and social workers?

Researching Single Parent Families

The experience of being a single parent family, then, has its defining moments both inside *and* outside the family. In order to address some of the issues that had been so unclear to me and other single parents, I focused my research (Griffith 1984) on the socially organized processes that structure some families as different, particularly in the context of schooling. My research was designed to track the sites within the Board of Education where the "single parent family" made a difference to the everyday work of educators.

Thus, and in contrast to most other research on single parent families, I treated each text I encountered as data. While this is an ordinary strategy when working with interviews and other field data, it rarely extends to the research literature, the media stories, or the ordinary documents that pronounce a family as an indigent single parent family. But these texts and the interactions they mediate are a fundamental part of the social construction of single parent family difference. The research literature on single parent families[3] is focused on this family form as a social problem and, typically, takes two different approaches to the topic. The majority of the studies focus on the impact of the single parent family on children's emotional development and long-term behavior. Single parent families are usually depicted as dysfunctional or as producing damaged children. The second approach addresses the social matrix in which the single parent family lives. This theme is typically found in social work journals and focuses on the social issues of poverty, housing, crime, and so on. In the twenty years since my original research, these themes still dominate the research literature, continuing to focus on difficulties inherent in the single parent family experience (Golombok 2000; Hanson 1995; Hardey and Crowe 1992; Hudson 1993; Jenson and McKee

2003; Offord et al. 1979; Rae-Grant 1976; Rankin 1983; Rowlingson and McKay 2002; Smart, Neale, and Wade 2001; Walters and Walters 1980). Regardless of research interest, the research literature assumes a normatively organized conception of the family, often eliding the nuclear family with the conceptions of a normal family.

Smith (1993a) has identified text-mediated discourses—such as the Standard North American Family (SNAF)—that permeate the sociological research literature on families.[4] In education, the curriculum and the child development discourse that underpins the curriculum are SNAF-infused and textually coordinated with the mothering discourse (Griffith 1995) constructing the nuclear family as the "norm" and other family forms as "different." Lareau (2003) notes that the mothering discourse is situated in the work activities of particular professional groups:

> Professionals who work with children, such as teachers, doctors and counsellors, generally agree about how children should be raised. . . . Because these guidelines are so generally accepted, and because they focus on a set of practices concerning how parents should raise children, they form a *dominant set of cultural repertoires* about how children should be raised. (p. 4)

Lareau's cultural repertoires about children's raising are what Smith and I (Griffith and Smith 1987) have identified as the mothering discourse. The mothering discourse was developed out of the early initiatives for public schooling (Chamboredon and Prevot 1975) through the advice literature for mothers in the psychological literature and the hygiene movement in the early 1900s (Richardson 1989). Although the particulars of this discourse change, the assumptions about the gendered family work organization do not. The research and professional literature and practice is coordinated around the notion of single parent families as different.

Media Stories

During my research, I paid attention to media reports about single parent families, collecting a clipping file that included articles from across Canada, the United States, and the United Kingdom. These articles cite the findings from research studies as well as reporting the anecdotal comments of professionals who are experts in the field of family research, education, social work, psychiatry, and so on. As with the research literature, the majority of the articles focus on the negative impact on single parent family members, particularly children (Griffith 1984). In the twenty years since my original research was done, media articles continue to identify single parent family membership with social deviance. A typical example is a *Globe and Mail* newspaper story about the DNA identification of the twenty-third victim of Robert Picton, a man charged with murdering a number of women whose bodily remains have been found on his pig farm near Vancouver in British Columbia. The DNA traces are of a woman named Dawn Crey, who had been a heroin addict and prostitute in Vancouver's East Side. The article states: "Ms. Crey was 43 when she disappeared and her life was punctuated by the same tragic themes that marked the lives of many of the other missing women: *broken families*, childhood abuse and drug dependence" (Armstrong 2004: A9, emphasis added).

Media stories also draw from the research literature on families for many stories. When a study is released that is determined to be newsworthy, an article that summarizes the study for popular consumption will appear in the newspaper or be reported on television. For example, a recent Swedish study (Weitoft et al. 2003) was first published in the *Lancet*, a prestigious medical journal, and was reported within the week by newspapers in the United States and Canada. The newspaper reports in four media outlets on Friday, January 24, 2003, read: "One-parent children at higher risk, study finds. Twice as likely to develop addiction, schizophrenia. Research followed 1 million youths over 10 years" (Ross, *Toronto Star*); "Children of single parents suffer poorer health: study. Eight years of research" (Evenson, *National Post*); "Swedish study: Kids of single parents more likely to suffer mental health problems" (McAlary, *Voice of America News*); and "Depression twice as high among single-parent kids: study" (*ABCNews*). The news stories claim their veracity from the research study.

In this article, I am not interested in arguing about the veracity of the research and media claims. Others (e.g., Popay, Rimmer, and Rossiter 1983) have addressed the systematic bias that permeates the media stories about single parent families (see also Smith 1998). Rather, I am interested in the way that the concept "single parent family" is used by the media to signal social difference across national boundaries, social contexts, and varieties of family situations. This conceptual practice plays off socially normative conceptions about families—the textually mediated Standard North American Family (Smith 1993a). Media stories, and the research on which they draw, generalize single parent families' problems that may include addiction, mental illness, and schizophrenia as the risks for *all* single parent families. The research, and the popularized media versions, locate the problem of children's mental health as *a feature or effect of the single parent family.* The textually mediated coordination between the research literature and the popularized media stories are fundamental to the ongoing construction of single parent family difference.

However, the complexity of the social construction of single parent families as deviant families becomes more visible as we move away from the flat textual surfaces of research studies and media stories. In education, for example, following the story of single parent family difference begins to illuminate the contributions of social class and gender to the way the concept operates.

The View from Education

In an earlier section of this chapter, I noted the ordinary talk about single parent families that I encountered in my research, in my graduate courses, and in my university teaching. The previous section shows that these notions of single parent family difference are also a feature of the research literature and the media stories that report on the research. In this section, I want to shift our focus to education where similar notions about single parent families appear in educational policy documents as well as in schools and classrooms.

One of the educational areas where the concept "single parent family" made a difference at the time of the research was in the development of the inner city policy (Griffith 1984, 1992).[5] I interviewed a superintendent at the central office of the Board of Education who was responsible for the department that administratively supported the dispersal of extra funding to those schools who were designated "inner-city schools,"

The inner-city policy provided the administrative basis for differential funding between schools in the Board of Education—schools designated as inner-city schools received extra funds based on the identified level of student need. Principals in low-income schools were encouraged to demonstrate that their schools were different from most schools in that the student population included a sufficient number of children who fit into the administrative criteria for an inner-city school. One of the criteria for extra funding was that of "single parent family." A teacher said:

> A couple of years ago . . . we [the principal and the teacher] were speaking about how the society was changing in this school population. At that time, I mentioned to him that there seemed to be more single parent families, at least in the kindergarten. The year before that, in a class of twenty-one, I had had seven children from single parent families. Then he began looking at other aspects and that's when he started considering that we should be in one of the categories of an inner-city school.

Student records were checked, and students were counted by both the school staff and the auditors from central office. Those schools who had enough children in the designated categories received extra funds to support more teachers, lower class size, social and psychological supports, and increased out-of-school events. However, this apparently straightforward process of counting children who fit into several social categories has some interesting and unexpected corners.

In my original research, I wanted to discover whether single parent family membership actually made a difference to the everyday work of schooling; I interviewed teachers of primary students, principals of elementary schools, central office administrators, social workers, and school psychologists in two schools in the Greater Toronto Area.[6] One school, Valley School, is located in an upper-middle-class area of large homes on tree-lined streets. Primary level students are often walked to school by a Filipino or Afro-Caribbean nanny. The other school, Woodson School,[7] is located close to a large Ontario housing project and several busy, commercial streets. Children walked to school with other children, with parents or babysitters, or by themselves. The interviews told a complex story of who became a single parent family and who didn't; living arrangements were not the only definition.

Woodson School

The number of children from single parent families who attended Woodson School was estimated by the superintendent, Mr. Taylor, as close to 80 percent. In contrast, a classroom teacher, Ms. Ellis, estimated the numbers of single parent families as between 40 percent and 50 percent. The difference in the estimates is embedded in two work knowledges about Woodson School students—administrative knowledge and pedagogical knowledge. The school had been designated as one of the neediest schools and had received the highest amount of funding possible through the Inner City Department. Mr. Taylor's knowledge about how many of the children in Woodson School were from single parent families was generated through the data-collecting procedures coordinated by the inner-city policy. Nontraditional or informal family arrangements did not count for the purposes of Board of Education funding.

Ms. Ellis had been teaching in the "inner city" for most of her career. In her view, and in the view of the other teachers I interviewed, the inner-city statistics were an inaccurate snapshot that didn't capture the complexity of her students' lives. She noted, "I'm not sure if it is true, but I think that the office doesn't recognize any other than the standard relationship on the Ontario Record Cards." Ms Ellis knew her students' immediate family circumstances through the relationships she had established between her students, their classroom work, and their families. For her, the issue of single parenting was not an administrative category, but a pedagogical one in which her students' families were fundamental to the child's participation in the classroom (Griffith and Smith 2005).

The teachers and other educational professionals I spoke with had extensive experience teaching in inner-city schools. While some were having a "hard year" with a "difficult class," they did not expect, nor want, to leave the school. Educators and other professionals at Woodson School consistently described their work with children as "a different kind of teaching" (Ms. Ellis), or requiring extensive professional intervention into families (Ms. Baker). Indeed, the majority of the students in Woodson School have lives that are different from students in middle-class schools. Individual student problems—having had no breakfast, being cognitively unprepared for educational tasks, living in difficult family circumstances—are not uncommon in this school context.

It is in this context that my interview questions that asked educators what difference children from single parent families made to their work drew the response, "None." Ms. Ford, a grade two teacher, said, "Since you came to talk to us, I've been cudgeling myself to isolate what I do around single parent kids that's different. But the kids here have so many other problems that are vital." At Woodson School, the term *single parent family* does not have pedagogical currency, although it is administratively relevant for purposes of inner-city funding. Single parent family organization was seen as merely one more feature of a troubled school population. Nor was it the most consequential factor according to the teachers. "Poverty," "depression," and the "parents' lack of education" were cited as the most important issues for Woodson School students.

The numbers of children from single parent families attending Woodson School and the organization of the family-school relation in this working-class area means that the normative differentiations between families that underpins research in the social science and educational discourse, including the compensatory funding policies of the Inner City Department of the Board of Education, do not organize the single parent family's relation to the school as deviant from other families. *Rather, the whole school population is seen as a deviant population, that is, inner-city.* The single parent family becomes just one of the many problems in the inner-city school—one that can be identified but which has little currency in an educational setting that, by definition, deviates from "ordinary" schools.

Valley School

Valley School is an "ordinary" school that provides a vivid contrasting example to Woodson School. Valley School is located in an upper-middle-class neighborhood. The families were described as upwardly mobile business and professional class families with extensive social and economic resources. Most families are Canadian-born, and few are members of visible minorities. On most levels, there are dramatic differences between the Woodson and Valley Schools. Thus, the family-school relation is different. Valley School educators spoke of high parental expectations for their children and for the teachers. As the principal Mr. Morris said: "It's two different jobs entirely. You're a social worker down there [Woodson School] whereas here you're strictly an academic dealing with the frustrations of trying to get the wishes of the parents satisfied over and above the system. You work for the children downtown; here you work for parents."

At Valley School, the relation between the family and the school is a careful articulation of the work processes of the home, the classroom, and the professional and administrative organization of the school system. The parents, typically the mother, place educational work, family resources, and time in the service of their children's participation in the school. Many mothers volunteer in the school in classrooms, tutoring, and in after-school programs. Family activities often fit well with school curriculum. As Ms. Norton said, "They [the children] lead such exciting lives. They go to the ballet. They go to the symphony. They go to everything, so naturally they're going to do well." The family activities offer a wide range of experiences that can be used as curriculum resources. Indeed, it may be assumed that many family activities are organized with educational relevancies in mind. The child is constructed as a pedagogical subject (Chamboredon and Prevot 1975; Lareau 1989, 2003; Walkerdine 1984), as the focus of teaching and learning by both the family and the school. *Given the coordination of the educational work of the family and the school, the child's family background is rarely used as a rhetorical device for identifying educational problems.*

At Valley School, the description of a family as a single parent family is situated in a family-school relation that is different from the one I encountered at Woodson School. If a family does not or cannot participate fully in the coordinative relationship between the family and the school, then the family is identified as requiring special resources. At that point, that a child comes from a single parent family is sufficient explanation for her or his behavior. Contrast, for example,

Mr. Parton: I have children from single parent homes who are very well adjusted, and children from two parent families who are basket cases, depending on their home life.

Ms. Loring: The single parents who live in this area have determined that they will not stick out, and they don't. The ones who do are those who have very severe behavior problems. That happens to a small percentage of single parent families.

Ms. Norton described one single parent mother who didn't "stick out":

> I don't know how this woman does it. She's just such a loving, sharing, warm person. She does everything: trips to Florida and just gives him all kinds of experiences. She has a lot of kids over on the weekend and you know that's hard when you teach kids full-time all week. She's a teacher. She's a wonderful woman. She does so many things around the school. . . . I wasn't really too worried about her child when the parents separated.

The striking feature of this single parent (and others like her who don't "stick out") is her ability to construct her family's relation to the school in ways that fit with what the other parents do, and with what Ms. Norton approves of as parental work. For this family, single parent status does not make a difference to the relationship between the family and the school. To be a "regular parent" (Ms. Parton) at Valley School is to be able to construct the family-school relation in normative ways.

If the family work process is seen to be inadequate to the requirements of this family-school relation, then these families are identified in the terms provided by the social science and educational research. Explanations of differences in children's participation at Valley School focused particularly on their emotional well-being. For example, Mr. Morris said, "It doesn't matter the age, and it happens at any time in the child's life and affects them. . . . They still seem to be feeling the absence of the other parent and they become aggressive for quite a number of years; three or four or five years at times." Then, the concept "single parent family" works to identify a child's behavior and a family-school relation that is different.

Concluding Comments

In this chapter, I have tried to make transparent the institutional ethnographic work of uncovering the institutional processes that construct our commonsense notions of single parent families. I began in my experience as a single parent, in the moments of discomfort and disjuncture that are an ordinary feature of the lives of single parents. Why and for whom are single parent families a problem? Why did the teachers say such things as "Boys from single parent families tend to draw in their exercise books" and infer that drawing is a problem? One way to understand this kind of problem talk is to treat it as an individual problem. However, collecting instances of single parent family talk—botanizing as Dorothy Smith called this collecting process—showed that single parent family talk is not limited to educators but rather is an ordinary way of distinguishing between families. In other words, the talk pointed to knowledge about single parent families that extended beyond our individual experience of it.

As any good graduate student would, I turned to the literature to discover what had been written about single parent families. Here, again, I found the problem of the single parent family. Perhaps these researchers knew better than I did about single parent families. Or perhaps they had all made the assumption that single parent families are different, and then looked to discover the problems that single parent families caused. Drawing from Smith's notion of ideological practices—ways of acting in the world that are coordinated by the textually organized relations of ruling and that subordinate our everyday experiences—I treated the research literature as data. That is, I began to view the research and professional literature ethnographically. How does the literature construct single parent families as a research topic? What notions of "truth" about single parent families are embedded in the literature? The one "truth" on which the research rests is that single parent families are different from nuclear families. This conception of difference coordinated the work of researchers through the academic and professional discourse about families.

Not surprisingly, the notion of single parent family difference identified in the literature is also present in the media, in educational policy, and in the talk of administrators, social workers, and teachers. Some media stories are written from research reports (Ibrahim 2004), and the background research for educational policy draws extensively on the research and professional literature. As educators and other professionals involved in schooling work with policy-based administrative documents, their conceptions about single parent family difference are reaffirmed and, in some instances, contested.

Notably, the themes of single parent family difference are textually mediated through academic journals, newspapers and magazines, and policy documents. They coordinate the work of teachers, administrators, social workers, and those who write research articles or popular media stories. The concept, then, not only coordinates the work of professionals; it shapes our everyday language as we agree with and contest conceptions of families and difference. Through our diverse experiences as single parent families, as educators, as consumers of popular media, we reflect on and use the concept that speaks the discourse of difference.

Notes

1. Smith (1993a) defines text-mediated discourses ". . . not as culture, meanings, significations or chains of significations, or texts without located readers, but as skeins of social relations, mediated and organized textually, connecting and coordinating the

activities of actual individuals whose local historical sites of reading/hearing/viewing may be geographically and temporally dispersed and institutionally various" (p. 51).

2. The original research was done for my PhD dissertation (1984). Since then, I have continued to "botanize" those moments when others refer to single parent families. As a professor in a faculty of education, my collection of the uses of the concept has become quite large.

3. I reviewed the major journals in the disciplines of psychology, psychiatry, social work, and sociology.

4. Smith's article also analyzes the ways that we imported SNAF into our research on mothering work for schooling.

5. A fuller description of this aspect of the research can be found in A. Griffith (1992), "Educational Policy as Text and Action," *Educational Policy* 6(4): 415–428.

6. Descriptions that would be made of these schools today would be very similar except that, in both schools, issues of diversity (language, culture, (im)migration) are now coordinated with those of class.

7. The school names are pseudonyms. So, too, are the names of those interviewees cited.

8

Mapping Institutions as Work and Texts[1]

Susan Marie Turner

MAPPING ACTUAL SEQUENCES of work and texts extends ethnography from people's experience and accounts of their experience into the work processes of institutions and institutional action. It is a formulation and application of institutional ethnography that treats quite literally its central concepts of text-based social relations and texts as essential coordinators of institutions. It recognizes the extraordinary capacity of texts to produce and to organize people's activities and extended and general relations in local and particular sites. Mapping institutions as work and texts is unlike other forms of graphical mapping of organizations and institutions. It does not produce, for example, a chart of organizational structure, map of job descriptions, work flow analysis, or diagram of a social network. Rather, the analytic procedure results in an account of the day-to-day text-based work and local discourse practices that produce and shape the dynamic ongoing activities of an institution. Such an account extends from the accounts and observable work of people engaged in it who may not be aware of just how their routine textual work puts together the large-scale institution and its outcomes. Texts (as reiterated by Dorothy Smith in this book) are the material forms of words, images, and sound that we can see, hear, and touch. At the same time that they are integral to local practices, they connect what individuals are doing to processes going on and organized elsewhere. I began mapping text-based work processes as a resident wanting to understand just how municipal planning organizes land development and sidelines residents' and other environmental interventions (Turner 1995, 2003). How planning texts operated in decision-making was particularly of concern for novices who wanted to intervene in governing and policy processes. The problematic for ethnographic inquiry emerged as residents including myself were drawn into these routine activities. In order to understand how governing and policy work, we had to track the work people do with texts that is generally understood to put "policy" into action and that produces what happens as "routine."

As part of my ethnography of municipal planning, land development, and environmental interventions (Turner 2003), I mapped a coordinated complex of institutional sequences of work and texts into which multiple actors, including developers, lawyers, banks, real estate agents, residents, government officials, and land surveyors are drawn to participate. What became visible were the standardized working relations and forms of language and text-based sequences of action through which democratic planning and governing processes operate. Ethnography draws on people's actions in specific settings in time and space, in such places as a public city council meeting where texts or talk alone can seem powerful, and controversial things are said and done (Turner 1995). But, unlike conventional accounts of politics, public policy, and governing, these moments are not the focus. Nor are the texts or talk alone. Institutional ethnography broadens its view to the replicable forms of social action that actual situated textual activities produce. When they are put together, they *are* the acts *of* the institution.

The focus of institution mapping is first on individuals' observable activities with texts in particular settings. One can begin with a particular text—such as a report, memo, letter, or legislation—but the analytic goal is to situate the text back into the action in which it is produced, circulated, and read, and where it has consequences in time and space. Observing what people do with the text is next. The focus of inquiry and analytic description is on how individuals take up the text in unique yet standardized ways, reading, writing, and speaking—doing something. The work is to see these textual practices as temporally located in *sequences of action* that are happening, so the text is made present in a setting, and *occurs*. It is also to see how individuals produce their acts as standard—located in and constituent of *the sequence* and accountable in *its* terms. The focus of the research is always the institutional, so it is how individuals take up texts and coordinate their actions so they produce *the particular institution's standard sequences*, its decisions, policies, and outcomes. In land use planning as other large-scale institutions, these are complex sequences that coordinate individuals' diverse consciousnesses and activities into *institutional action*. They go on in surprisingly ordinary ways. They can be mapped graphically.

In this chapter, I describe the kind of discoveries mapping can make and illustrate ways I've opened up settings and texts into translocal *text-based work sequences* to map coordinated institutional action. The illustrations are drawn from my study of planning that began with a developer's plan to build in a wooded ravine near where I lived. Mapping produced a working knowledge of these forms of activities as they were going on. I was not mapping these processes based on my own experience alone. I learned from participant observation in several settings where city work goes on: talking with city officials, planners, engineers, developers, agency and ministry officials, clerks and others, and examining the texts they were reading and using routinely. I wanted to produce an account that was useful to anyone to grasp what people do routinely when "doing planning" and that would make visible how those activities produced the "planning system" as people talked about it.

Analyzing Institutional Texts

I mapped what came to hand in the course of participating in a municipal planning process. The Notice of Public Meetings (Notice), circulated to property owners near the site, presented a peculiar "municipally known" world and organized how the reader could think to act next (Turner 2001). Analysis was oriented to how it operated in an ongoing course of action with seemingly inevitable results. The text implied that the significant event for what happened on the land would be the city council's "decision." In this sequence the Staff Report was the text occurring in the setting that the Notice announced—located in the action where elected members of councils read and talk about what is in it when they make decisions in public. I thought at the time as other neighbors did, that the problem was the planners and politicians. Then I talked to planners and councillors who shared residents' concerns and wanted to make good decisions for the city. But things were going on outside their purview. I asked questions about their work with texts and began to track and map the sequences of action and texts embedded in them that connect the work people, in multiple positions and physical locations, do day to day. I did not undertake formal interviews or focus groups as many institutional ethnographers do. Rather, I talked to each person as a resident—in such public processes a "concerned citizen," "ratepayer," or "neighbor" and legitimate "stakeholder"—who is interested in how the process goes on and its outcomes. I wanted to discover people's work and how the process was put together in what each did. The resulting mapped sequences were not visible in the official accounts of the planning process, including how texts represented it and how planners and the news media talked about and described what went on. But these sequences shape the ground for individual actions and how participants can develop and display competence in the "system."[2]

Institutional ethnography views the social act as an extended dialogic sequence among actual people.[3] Doing so enables the kind of "micro" level analysis of text-talk-text activity within settings that can display the articulation of local language practices to "macro" processes. This view of extended social acts also enables us to take analysis outside of a particular setting and across settings so the organization of *translocal work processes can come into view.* Examined as an actual sequence of activities coordinating people's mind, text and talk, events that are the focus of scholarly and activists' attention like a government's "decision" or "policy," appear as they are—actions in which people prepare and read texts, talk, rework or reword them, and/or produce new texts that build upon prior texts. My ethnography aimed at creating an accurate map of the textual practices and local sequences *as they went on* that produced land development *decisions* and brought the institution—the so-called land-use planning system—into existence. While analysis of a public hearing or decision as an extended work sequence can be done the way conversation analysis and studies of representational practices do so beautifully,[4] I wanted to also make visible the work going on outside the public setting that seemed to make the council's approval so inevitable. I wanted to understand just how something happened textually. I mapped the texts and what people did with them, the bits of texts people activated and what they said that was of consequence. This is a shift from viewing the text itself as doing something or as powerful in a situated text-reading to analytic description of its coordinative power translocally. Residents wanted answers to their questions—"what happens next?" "where?" and "who does it?"—and to see just what "it" was they would be doing and did. I also wanted to see just how and what texts or parts of texts could be activated, how and by whom, to produce the characteristic power in these relations, and move "the process" along so inevitably.

Locating Textual Practices in Translocal Work Processes

Tracking and mapping actual text-based sequences avoids the analytic trap of categorizing or typologizing events such as "government decisions"—common analytic strategies that close down the analysis. As standard ways of working, speaking, and hearing, the mapped connected sequences of action are the actual conditions of people's work, the "context" that constrains their actions. This conceptualization of institutional forms of action is based on how institutions actually operate. Their discovery via ethnographic mapping stands apart from such notions as "institutional arrangements" or "formal organizations and the environments in which they act." As people read, write, and speak with others in their work routines, they produce their actions as accountable in the terms of the particular process and institution. How they produce the particular "context" and orient to it in setting-specific local practices is discoverable. Ethnography of institutions is possible because people's actual practices that put institutions together—the daily replicable textual work practices that produce routine, standard, repeatable, and teachable procedures—are observable. How you would utilize such an account is dialogic, working with others to extend one's own and others' situated work knowledge that is produced and operates in different sites.

Multiple forms of texts are produced and read in sequences that organize a particular institutional function. How the function is carried on, the institution's social existence and its organizational change, rely on specialized mundane textual practices often taken for granted by those who work with them. My study of planning processes analyzed these observable aspects of organization:

1. the work an individual reader does to activate a standard text (Notice of Public Meetings) in order to orient to the institutional process;
2. the coordination of several individuals' work in talk and text in a setting (the council meeting) that produces an authorized body ("the city") and its accountable decision;

From these settings where institutional textual practices are available to experience and observation, I mapped the translocal sequences in which they are located, identifying the discursive forms associated with the text-based work that accomplish them:

3. the local practices linking multiple individual acts via texts across settings in a legislated institutional process (consulting with agencies and boards) that connect organizations and public and private spheres of work (figure 8.3);
4. the specialized local discourse practices or speech genre (Bakhtin 1986) practices that sequentially produce such recognized steps of a planning or governing process as "consultation" (figure 8.4)

Carrying out these analyses of coordinative organization relies on the concepts of texts and work specific to institutional ethnography's social ontology (see Smith 1999, 2001) and the conception of *text-based work processes* (Turner 2003) that is central to this mapping method. I tracked sequences of text-based work and local discourse practices and indicated graphically different aspects of standardized textual organization thus:

- Solid lines indicate a direct connection of activity taking place in time and space. The lines generally indicate a chronological and temporal sequence and organized relation left to right. Where texts and circles of activity stack vertically they occur relatively at the same time in different locations.

- Curved, horizontal oblong shapes with bottom shadow indicate the numbered steps identified in the official government brochure.
- Tinted boxes indicate texts that are produced in the action, are the product of previous work, are present in the setting, present physically in some form for the work to be done as part of the process, and are the basis of the next sequences.
- Broken line boxes indicate texts that are activated, talked about, and oriented to by speakers, writers, and readers in their work activities. Not physically present in the local work settings I focus on, they are *made present* by the work that people do in talk and texts as individuals refer to them or sections of them. They include legislation, policy texts, sections of official plans, and so on.
- Clear circles indicate the activity performed as people take up and do something with texts. These are moments where different parties are at work with the texts.

Mapping's Discoveries and Analytic Description: Figures 8.1 and 8.2

The Notice of Public Meetings—the initial text that drew me into a particular zoning process for a particular piece of land—occurs prior to the council meeting where the Notice says "a decision will be made." I discovered in the course of my ethnography that by the time the Notice had arrived and council's discussion of the development was scheduled, the developer, planners, engineers, and agencies had already done significant work preparing the multiple documents that accompany the developer's application. When you go to a municipal office or look online at the provincial Ministry of Municipal Affairs and Housing brochure *The Subdivision Process*, you see the official representation of what goes on as a sequence of steps: "before applying," "the application," "consideration-consultation," "draft approval/refusal," "final approval and registration," and "sale of lots." Residents are drawn into a moment where "consideration-consultation" takes place.

My map, figure 8.1 "Processing Development Applications: The Residents' Participation" illustrates the actual extended work processes that accomplish the six steps represented in the brochure and locates the residents' experience of the public process in them.

The longer I was involved in planning activities for the ravine site project, the further I got into planning relations and the more complicated I saw "the process" actually to be. The developer's application is a standardized simple

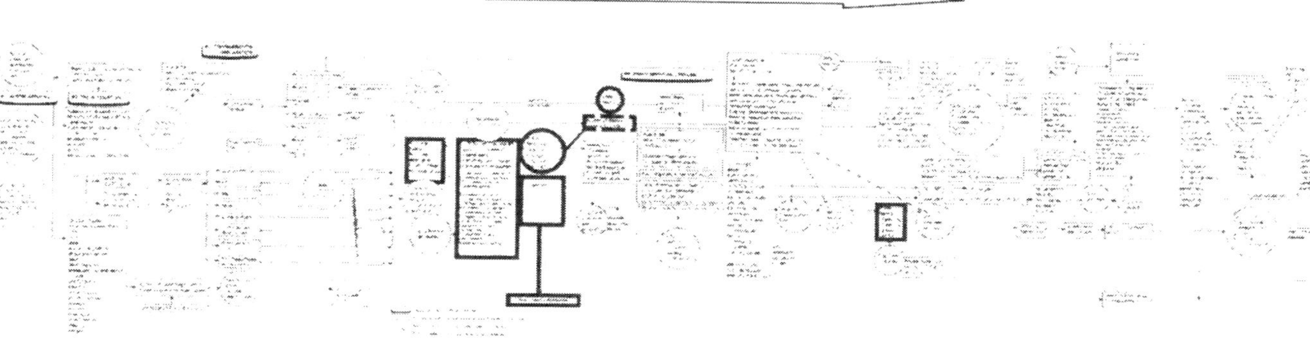

FIGURE 8.1.
Processing Development Applications: The Residents' Participation

form, but several texts are required by the provincial Planning Act to accompany it. *Its* "submission"—a municipal and provincial file made for it and a number assigned to it—formally activates the complex of work procedures constituting "the public process." For residents entering the process only when they receive the Notice and attend the council meeting, it is difficult to find out and follow what is going on and to anticipate, and prepare to engage with, the texts and activities that actually produce the consequences to the land.

I originally did the mapping work by hand. I taped together large sheets from newsprint drawing pads and taped them to the wall in my living room. I added texts, activities, syntactical moves, and phrases as I encountered them—as planners, councillors, developers, and others talked about them, they were read or at hand in public settings, or they were referred to in some other text and so on—and as they went on in time. I included texts people talked about, produced, read, and wrote. The map was approximately twelve feet long by five feet high. Reducing it to book page size makes it virtually unreadable, but I want you to be able to see the complexities that mapping can explore and represent as well as how much had gone before and occurred after the point at which the residents intervened.

This diagram is of course not exhaustive. There is always more that goes on than we can see and make visible in this kind of textual representation. This map is based on ethnography of the rezoning, condominium, then subdivision processes for one piece of land. But in the processes governing land use planning these mapped sequences are standard sequences of action in which people's experience is located and they bring their activities into relation. They are required by legislation. Even those who do the work badly or with different intentions or motives must reproduce the textually standardized outcomes and operate in the same text-based work processes. "Good" and "bad" planning, so-called "green," "sustainable," and otherwise, all must produce the textually standardized sequences of action and outcomes in intertextual work in order for what is done to be counted as doing "planning." The standardized texts mapped are the essential regulatory devices that bring into existence the activities constituting and organizing the multisite institution of land use planning. They organize standardized forms of action and procedures of an institution that transcend the local activities of individuals.

We can treat the complex of work processes that figure 8.1 makes visible as an institutional field of action that is organized and reproduced in these multiple coordinated work processes. Figure 8.2 "Institutional Texts and the Social Relations of Planning" could then be produced. It shows key consequential moments where texts operate outside public settings and view. Governing and ruling relations come into view as specialized translocal sequences of action involving multiple actors in multiple settings sometimes unknown to each other. The map makes visible the work processes of these diverse actors whose

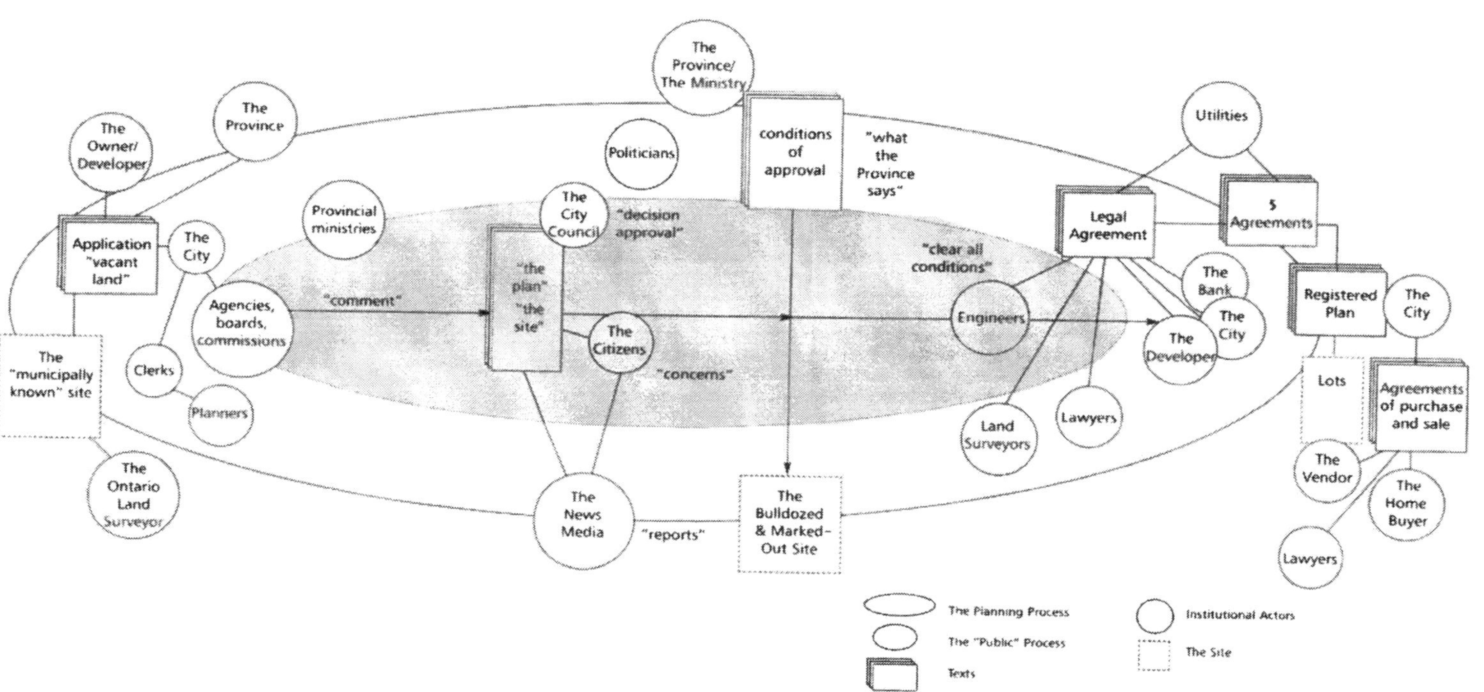

FIGURE 8.2.
Institutional Texts and the Social Relations of Planning

diverse interests are coordinated through, and in, the language practices and textual products of their work.

In figure 8.2, the larger clear oval indicates schematically the extensive complex of institutional work processes explored and mapped in figure 8.1. The shaded smaller oval indicates the public process that draws provincial government ministries, agencies, boards, residents, and other actors into these relations as part of a democratic governing. Governing land development is carried out primarily at the municipal level. While local governing bodies have been given the responsibility for planning land use within their boundaries and for "balancing interests" in land, the work of provincial ministries plays a part and legislation is a participant in these relations. But just how is to be discovered in local text-based sequences of work.

Figure 8.2 maps the sphere of relations in which its key texts—replicated across the province and its municipalities—sequentially operate to pull in certain individuals to do certain kinds of work with texts and to standardize those activities in text-based sequences of work. The gray-tinted, layered oblong shapes indicate key texts that draw in particular institutional actors. The texts are produced in people's activities in the sequences. Their titles reflect how they are spoken of by practitioners in the process. Small clear circles indicate institutional actors doing something with the texts. There is a temporal sequence of activities that is coordinated, recognizable, and reproducible as "the planning process."

Sequentially a variety of texts stand in for the objectified "site." Institutional actors, rather than individuals, are *positions* that are produced in the action and texts as separate from the individuals that occupy them. The "owner"/developer or his hired planner who works on his behalf works with city employees who act as "the city." Clerks, engineers, planners, and others work up "the developer's application" that activates the temporal, legislated process which is this complex of text-based sequences. The application can be seen to standardize data collection and application procedures in municipal offices across the province. It draws in the prior work procedures of land surveyors, land registry, and municipal clerks that constitute the physical land as the "site" as it is "municipally known" for the process that follows. The textual reality of "the site" stands in for the physical land. In the application to develop the wooded Howitt Park ravine, the physical land is described as "vacant land." The forms of "municipal knowing" already exist, are already constituted, and have their peculiar textual technologies. The forms are activated and reproduced each and every time, in every site development planning process. The land is described and becomes known in language, by numbers and mathematically drawn lines that stand in for the size and shape and contours of the physical land. This textual reality makes present the work of the licensed Ontario land surveyor who has measured and made visible the property with its boundaries.

The application pulls in the property owner, staff for the city, clerks, surveyor, ministry officials, and planners and engineers in agencies and boards, among others in producing the required texts. The Staff Report, a text standing in for "the plan" and "the site," hooks participants including those who work as reporters in the news media into the public setting of the council meeting. In a next significant "step," what is in local discourse practice spoken of as "what the Province says" about a particular application, is produced in a text called "the Minister's conditions." That text relies on prior work in several sites that produces legal clauses called "conditions." This local textual work is consequential to what happens on the land. "Minister's conditions" in the municipal planner's file stand in for provincial oversight and "draft" approval that allows the site to be bulldozed and lots marked out.

On the right in the figure is the "legal agreement" that is required by legislation. In local practice it is called the development agreement. Practitioners talk about it as "ensuring the conditions." Local discourse practices observably operate the notion that legal agreements act as a mechanism to constrain developers' private interest to profit through use of land. The development agreement, when signed and filed in the Land Registry Office, is said to register the plan and conditions "on title," that is, attach them through the legal title or deed of ownership to what happens on the property. Having the "registered plan" in hand allows a municipal official to issue building permits to the developer for each of the lots that are "for sale." A closer look at the general development agreement reveals that one of its clauses requires the developer to enter into further agreements with different city departments, utilities, and banks. Clauses can be seen to specifically authorize and activate work processes of building contractors, accountants, solicitors, and so on. All along the way in the process, the development agreement is the prospective text to which experienced participants orient. All prior activities can be seen to project into and be building the particulars of the legal agreements. Municipal land use planning is a powerful form of governing, and it is not to be thought of as simply "local government." Nor should it be thought of as a specialized professional activity.

Mapping's description of the organization of institutions and institutional action via their actual text-based work sequences is analytically powerful. A process that would usually be treated as a "case" dealing with an individual site rather is opened up to map *the institution's work practices.* Since development agreements are a standard textual product, reproduced across the province by the hundreds in each municipality, standard wordings of clauses are produced and kept on file and inserted into agreements routinely by clerks in municipal offices. These routine forms of action are the unseen power of large-scale organization. Descriptive particulars for each individual piece of land as a site to be developed are inserted at the planner's request to clerks. But the particulars connecting each piece of land to its textual reality are subsumed to the operation of the sequences and forms of action. The legislated legal development agreement preauthorizes prior particular courses of action in which they are constituted, and not others. It preauthorizes, for example, the negotiation of the wordings of legal condition clauses with agencies, the negotiation of costs and legal liability with ministries and municipal departments, and the negotiation of agreements with banks and not with residents. It is the operative prescriptive text, routinizing the production of its legal clauses as what gets done and is negotiated and put together in the planning process. The text's format—a set of numbered legal clauses with prefatory directional statements—organizes planners' and agency representatives' work, and the work of Ontario land surveyors, lawyers, and Land Registry Office clerks to produce the registered plan. Thus the function of the process and the institution is realized. The legal agreement coordinates and shapes *institutional relations* via the processes and procedures for building up the text.

Mapping makes a significant finding. Where residents and agencies are drawn into a public process, the negotiation of this private agreement and its contents goes on elsewhere, outside the public view. Preliminary versions of the text's contents—legal clauses—are present in the public council meeting in the Staff Report. They pass through the public setting on the way to becoming component parts of the developer's agreement with the city. They cannot be changed or rewritten by residents here. Compiled by the municipal planner and inserted into the Staff Report for reading and decision in the council setting, the council may amend them but would rarely do so. They are *the city's* clauses.[5] The clauses approved by council in the Staff Report are reworked by a Ministry official, compiled with others into a text, and sent back to the municipality as "Minister's conditions."[6] Back in the municipal offices, these "conditions of draft approval" hook directly into and organize the work of public employees into the subsequent production of private developers' for-profit business.

This finding is politically significant and powerful as well. The text-based moments of action identified within the shaded oval area in figure 8.2 hook institutional actors into the development of a local economy. The activities are required by law as part of the public land use planning process. But the legal development agreement—that so powerfully coordinates the work of lawyers, clerks, people representing the banks, utilities, and land surveyor with the work of the developer and his private consultants—is primarily a textual product of extensive work by municipal planners.[7] Tracking how texts operate in local practices and organize diverse actors' working relations can make visible the private processes that are invisible in the public process. On the right in figure 8.2 are financial agreements, the registered plan, agreements of purchase and sale—legal texts that are required to be produced in the process. There is often speculation about how private land "deals" are made. Mapping brings to view how the legally required texts order and link the productive work practices of diverse institutional actors. My study focused on the work practices of planners, councillors, agencies, and residents. Among others, institutional actors include the banks, lawyers, real estate agents, and the vendor of the land, as well as a category of actors who are indirectly implicated—the future home buyers of the houses that are one of the products of a development process.

The broken-lined boxes in figure 8.2 indicate what is happening to the land known as "the site." At application we see the municipally known site made visible as text. Appropriately worded and formatted texts shape and order the talk-text practices. An institutional functional complex is put together. It is reproduced in people's activities in the routines of "the planning process." These are the generalized relations that are activated in individuals' actual local practices. They are represented in official discourse as neutral and as driven by publicly produced and sanctioned policy. Mapping the text-based work that productively moves the process along shows how individuals' routine local textual practices produce a powerful coordinated complex of work sequences and the *acts of* a large-scale *institution* with irrevocable consequences on the land.

We begin mapping text-based work processes in text or talk that is observable, available to experience. Institutional text or talk operates at the intersection of the translocal institutional work organization and everyday experience. The focus on text-based work can begin in the observation of talk—in conversation or interviews. (See McCoy in this book for illustration of identifying the institutional in experiential accounts.) This is the situated point of entry into the institutional relations. Attention is directed to the language that is central to social organization here. Language practices carry out the organization of the social. Language practices—oral and in text—give direct evidence of the organization that is happening and how to go forward with inquiry. We analyze the text at this intersection. For example, my analysis of the Notice of Public Meetings was undertaken some time after we residents had gone way past it in our rush to go to council. We read it "for information," unaware of how it had organized our own action. Later I located it in the institutional processes in which it is required by law, situating the text in a sequence of action and analyzing how it organizes a readers' attention to municipal processes and how residents formulate their intervention strategies in them (Turner 2001). This is how I've opened up local sites via individual text-reader interaction. In the next sections I describe mapping from texts in institutional work sequences.

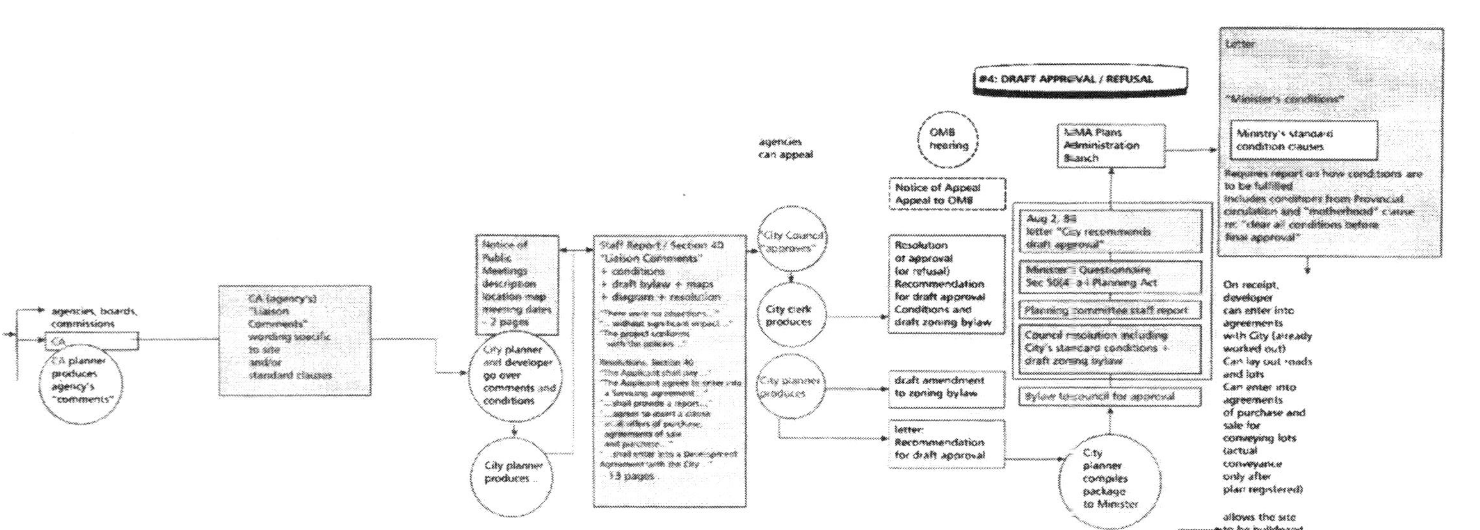

FIGURE 8.3.
Consultation Sequence, Layer 1: Work and Texts "Resolving Concerns through Conditions"

Tracking a Governing Work Process via the Texts: Figure 8.3[8]

An analytic strategy in institutional ethnography is to take up how a text organizes an in-common object of knowledge and the consciousnesses of individuals in a setting through their talk-text interaction. For example, I've analyzed diverse individuals' readings of a diagram called a *site plan* that is part of the Staff Report and the talk-text interaction that produces the accomplishment of the council's "act" constituting *its* decision.[9] I am illustrating a different analytic strategy here, tracking the conservation agency's *comments* and what happens to them in a text-based work process that coordinates diverse actors' work into institutional action. Tracking text to next text in a governing sequence involves making visible people's activities with texts as they project to next settings and the work of particular actors. Planning processes are often talked about by practitioners as a *conversation* or *consultation* where different actors *have something to say. Consultation* is a peculiar governing work process. In land-use planning consultation sequences, agencies acting "in the public interest" are asked to comment on developers' plans and their concerns taken up and resolved in the process. These sequences go on outside public view. Texts stand in for what a formal body *has to say* in the process. The residents thought the conservation agency could protect the ravine and looked for what the conservation agency *had to say* and how it could have an effect in the public process. In a city council meeting the Staff Report is the text that stands in for *the developer's plan* and includes *the city's conditions* for the council's approval of the plan. As a product of municipal staff it is a product of complex work, including that of agencies who've commented on the developer's plan.

Figure 8.3 illustrates the standard sequence of text-based interchanges required between the municipal and agency planners that accomplish commenting and conditions produced from consultation in a planning process. Different kinds of textual entities are treated as comments. A municipal planner receives diversely formatted texts from numerous agencies, city departments, and so on. Following a work sequence internal to the conservation agency, the agency planner produced a letter on agency letterhead containing these statements:

> There is a ravine running along the rear of the Lots 1 through 7, and Lots 4 through 7 (inclusive) have slopes greater than 1:2.
>
> Based on the above, we would recommend that this plan not receive draft approval until such time as the applicant *submits a satisfactory grading plan which shows the proposed building envelopes, proposed slopes and methods of controlling erosion of these slopes.*
>
> Upon receipt of satisfactory plans, we may be in the position to recommend draft approval subject to certain conditions.

Such *comments* that diverse agencies send in various forms to the city planner hold details pertaining to the physical land as well as negotiative terms in an ongoing conversation between the agency and the city. These are not present as such in the text that elected councillors read. How the councillors "consider" a plan and are made aware in-text of the particulars of agencies' comments, can be identified as a site for potential change in textual practice. Here, the conservation agency's recommendation to hold back approval until a satisfactory grading plan is in hand, for example, made based on its professional expertise and provincially delegated mandate to regulate steep slopes, is not present in its original textual form in the council meeting. It thus cannot readily be visible to councillors nor be treated by them as at issue.

What produces the issue I'm pointing out is the seeming "sameness" of the texts. "Submitting a satisfactory grading plan," a future-projected act by the developer, is present in both texts and appears to be the main focus. Left out is the indication of timing of the submission in the sequence of events (the agency would have it prior to their recommending draft approval, which should come prior to the council's approving the plan), and at the same time, to whom the grading plan must be satisfactory becomes ambiguous. The text of this clause renders invisible its power: to shift the assessment of the grading plan from the public conservation agency and outside public purview to a private engineering consultant hired by the developer; and to move the timing of its submission and approval to later on in the process, after draft approval and after bulldozers are in the ravine (Turner 2003). In the council meeting however, clause (p) in the Staff Report compiled by the city's planner seems to address the conservation agency requirements:

> (p) The Subdivider shall meet all requirements of the [. . .] Conservation Authority including *submission of a satisfactory grading plan which shows the proposed slopes and methods of controlling erosion on the slopes and ravine*, and shall receive a full clearance for these requirements from the [. . .] CA, prior to registration of the plan.

A closer look at how the clause operates within the text in this setting and in a translocal sequence gives us a different view. Clause (p)'s insertion in the Staff Report is consequential. Its inclusion authorizes the entire wording to be treated as a *condition*. In the council meeting, as well as in multiple future texts and settings, the clauses can be read as *the city's* conditions. Selection and insertion is the work of the municipal planner, who has extracted the phrase I've italicized from the conservation agency's letter and embedded it into the (p) format. This work is done with each letter received from "liaison circulation," producing thirty or more clauses for the Staff Report. The clause stands in for what the agency *said*. But operating in the organization of municipal economic development, they are *the city's clauses*; they orient to and anticipate the city's future work processes with the developer.

In this process and similar municipal processes the developer, in this case "the subdivider," is the active agent. The phrases "... shall meet" and "shall receive" projects into future activities of the developer and the city. In particular, "... receive full clearance" is a private work process called "clearing the conditions" that involves the city clerk or solicitor and the developer or his representative who agree via a checklist, matching the Minister's list of conditions but not yet produced, that listed requirements are met. The standard format of the Staff Report enables the completion of the council's task in the meeting in which the text is read—councillors will perhaps not in fact actually read it in its entirety—and thus enable the process to move along via a particular textual mechanism. The legal clauses themselves are subsumed under the formal language of a *resolution*—recognizable as such and selectively read by councillors as what they can take up and upon which they can act *as a council*:

> THAT the application... *be approved and recommended* to the Minister of Municipal Affairs, subject to the following conditions: ... (emphasis in original)

The Staff Report to council regarding the ravine project—three legal-size pages plus a diagram titled "... PLAN OF SUBDIVISION"—has the resolution, *the city's standard conditions* for subdivisions, and the diagram. The typeface of clauses is uniform. They can be treated uniformly, as standard, and as "covering" diverse *agencies' requirements* and *the city's standard requirements.*[10]

In textual analysis, we attend to both what is in the text and what individuals can be seen to do with it. Residents oriented to clauses (i) and (j), and (p), previously listed, that seem to orient to, and be able to produce, outcomes on the actual physical contours of the ravine:

> (i) The Subdivider shall grade the subdivision to the satisfaction of the City Engineer and shall ensure that sideyard slopes on each lot do not exceed 2 to 1 and that rear yard slopes do not exceed 4 to 1, to the satisfaction of the City Engineer.
>
> (j) The Subdivider shall retain a Professional Engineer to design and supervise the construction of any retaining wall deemed necessary by the City Engineer, and shall build any required retaining wall in the subdivisions, to the satisfaction of the City Engineer, prior to the issuance of any building permits for any of the lots in the plan.

These city clauses seem to attend to the entities "slopes" and "ravine." However there is nothing that attends to their protection as physical terrain intrinsically. Even where councillors agree in the public council meeting that protecting the physical ravine is a valid concern (Turner 1995), "guaranteeing" environmental protection gains cogency not in terms of the actual physical features of land that the residents are orienting to, but in the terms of these other projected sequences and relations which go on outside public view and in which we see the conservation agency's intervention is limited and diverted.

The agency's intervention *to protect slopes of the ravine*, represented as the produced condition clause (p), is *incorporated into* the business of building structures, not environmental protection. The shift made in the text from steep ravine slopes with contours to "side yard slopes" and "rear yard slopes" of a residential lot held up by a professionally designed retaining wall, is not just a shift from one text to another order of texts. The text provides a sufficiently standardized format and wording that makes further organizational action possible. Here, it allows the council to make decisions, passing a resolution enfolding clauses that give the appearance of providing the local government a semblance of control over what happens on the land. At the same time the move from the text to courses of action outside the setting is built into this text. Figure 8.3 also illustrates the limited action of the elected council.

Council's approval of the resolution in the Staff Report authorizes the lifting of decision and authority out of council's public hands and inserts it, legally, into what is preserved in governing discourse as a private relation—that between the developer and the city. *The city's conditions* can be treated in multiple connected settings as "the same" interactional objects. Treated as "the same," clauses can coordinate the work of people in multiple sites and move an institutional sequence along. Indeed, in the talk in the public meeting, the city engineer can assure the council—his employer—that, as clauses (i) and (j) state, what happens on the land will be "to *his* satisfaction." The work of the city clerk subsequent to a council meeting produces on city letterhead a text of "the city's approval" and "the city's conditions." Circulated to settings of its reading outside the municipal office, the clerk's letter enables these clauses to be treated as institutional entities, as the recognizable products of the city's consideration, consultation, and decision. *The council's act* and *its conditions* can be thus taken up by others in other sites such as: the developer's consultant planner, in a sequence that goes on outside public view, faxes the text of the clerk's letter in order to pressure the conservation agency to change its comment because "the city decided"; someone in the Ministry of Municipal Affairs will receive them as the acts and products of "the city" and to be treated as what is required for producing the text that will stand in for provincial draft approval; and in subsequent municipal settings of work they will activate courses of action.

Figure 8.3 "Consultation sequence, Layer 1" maps a standard sequence tracked from the moment the agency submits a text to the city planner, through *its* insertion into the Staff Report in the council setting, to the textual modification and production of *it* in "Minister's conditions"—a text that accomplishes "draft approval with conditions." This is the text that allows the developer to proceed to bulldoze the site and mark out lots for sale while conditions are still being negotiated. Figure 8.4 "An Institutional Form of Action and Speech Genre,"[11] illustrates the text-based discourse sequence and the forms of language that operate in the legal agreement that links the work of the city to the private business of the developer in the subdivision agreement and, as utterances that when present in-text and read and "heard," enable the next action and move the process along.

These are specialized local practices of the land use planning discourse. The multiple processes hooking the work of the city into that of the developer's private profit-making are present and projected in the text in the public meeting. So are these local discourse practices that are temporally located in the sequence. They are observable. The Staff Report orders these procedures of negotiating, accounting, and constructing and so on. The specialized discourse practices visible in this talk-text-talk sequence authorize and ensure that, according to law and planning discourse, conditions of development are imposed on developers, they are monitored, met, then cleared.

In the Staff Report in the public setting, there are several condition clauses that are requirements "to pay." They begin in a standardized way: "The subdivider shall pay to construct. . . . ," ". . . shall provide services . . . ," ". . . shall pay the actual cost of installing. . . ," ". . . shall pay the cost of erecting. . . ," ". . . shall pay the city a flat rate charge. . . ," and so on. All of these clauses are anticipated by the developer and by councillors. This is the projected work of private negotiation processes as they appear in public. Each clause will activate negotiations, and calculations of "actual costs" are central items that will be negotiated. A key clause—that projects ahead to the future general development agreement document—recommends that "the city" enter into multiple legal agreements with the developer to carry out the works listed. Readily recognizable for approval by a council, this standard clause authorizes and activates sequences of negotiations involving staff in several municipal departments with outside bodies including utilities. These negotiations and financial dealings are routine matters that are already going ahead and that link the developer's investment and the internal financial management of the municipality. They establish ongoing working relations. Mapped as actual text-based work processes, planning processes for formulating conditions of development approval and inserting them into legal agreements can be seen to tie individual developers' business into municipal management and sideline environmental interventions.

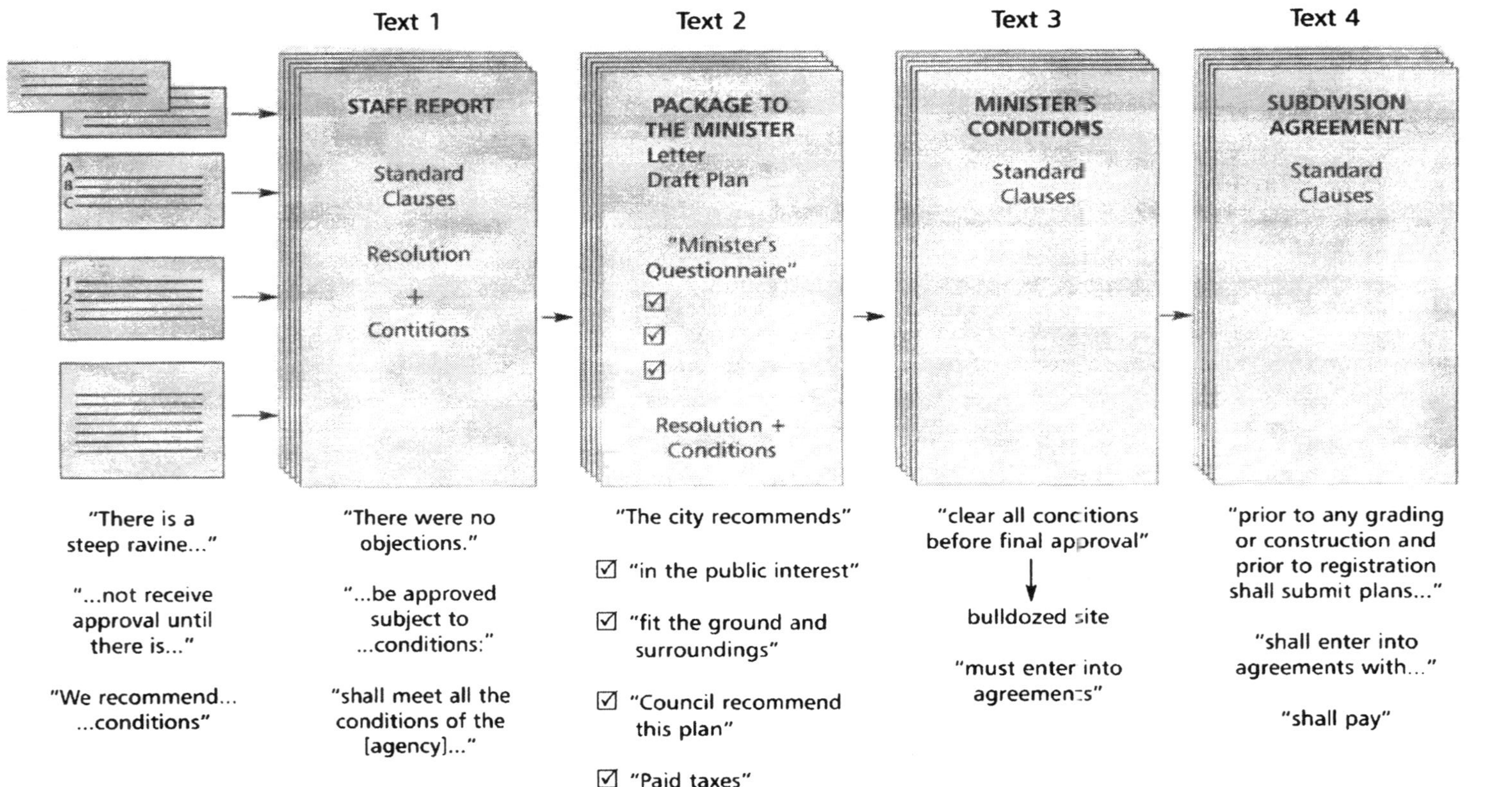

FIGURE 8.4.
An Institutional Form of Action and Speech Genre: Layer 3

Conclusion

Operationalizing in inquiry the conception of the significance of texts in the organization of standardized sequences of work and institutions is central to institutional ethnography. It is a move that cannot be overemphasized. Tracking a sequence of text-based work gives us a way to not just map position locations within an institution but to make visible the power of texts to organize what is getting done and how. We sociologists would ordinarily begin with a concept of an institution—such as a notion of "the planning system" or "the economy" or "political decisions" and their actors, sites, and policies that may be known to us. We would take for granted what we know about governments, resident groups, and developers and what happens in development or policy processes. Or we would engage with land planning discourse in such a way that its mundane local practices, as they go on and residents would encounter them in public settings, would not appear.

Institutional ethnographers, however, bring into question what is commonly known, and examine the conceptual and textual work that in actual local practices bring commonly known institutional entities into existence and coordinate large-scale organization. "Work" is a concept that orients us to the action as it goes on and to texts as situated constituents in and of that action, *occurring* as part of actual local practices. The illustrations I've given of the examination of institutional texts and their operation in text-based work sequences were extracted from a larger study and its accounts of how an institution works as people's observable practices in talk and text in multiple sites. Opening up inquiry into governing processes via texts situated in the actual action as it goes on, and mapping what one discovers as *text-based work sequences*, can make visible the current dynamic forms of institutional action and their discourse practices so that we may anticipate them and better develop intervention strategies that can work in them. I've presented an overview of what mapping translocal processes looks like and how texts are examined in an ethnographic practice that understands them as integral to the action and coordination of diverse work across settings and in time.

The maps, as accounts of how texts are integral to institutional action as the particular organization of text-based work processes, are useful for those whose work is organized in these work processes and for others who intervene in them. The dialogic process of working with the maps to account for large-scale work organization and local policy consequences engages various participants in inquiry and exploration of their work knowledge and its constraints on activities. In the context of economic and political restructuring, and their concomitant reorganization of specialized work processes, collaborative institution mapping may bring into view the specific aspects of institutional changes that are being planned and are taking place and their consequences for people's work and institutional outcomes. It is the particular forms of institutional action and how they carry out in observable ways the institutional function across localities with multiple peculiar, and sometimes devastating, consequences that demand our attention as inquirers.

Notes

1. This work was originally presented as a plenary talk entitled "Mapping an Institutional Field of Action" to the Annual Institutional Ethnography Conference at the Maxwell School of Citizenship and Public Affairs, Syracuse University, June 1–3, 2001. Thanks to Marjorie DeVault for the opportunity and to those who have commented on this work. It is also part of a larger study (Turner 2003). Many thanks to Dorothy Smith and Tim Diamond who read an earlier version of this chapter and provided helpful editorial suggestions.

2. A city planning director told me that one of the biggest problems in municipalities was that new graduates of planning schools did not have a grasp of the essential work required of municipal land use planners—processing developers' applications.

3. This view follows and extends the theoretical work of George Herbert Mead (1962), M. M. Bakhtin (1986) and V. I. Volosinov (1973), whose work develops a social ontology at the level of individual interaction, where we can observe, and thus examine and make visible, people's actual temporal coordination of consciousnesses and other practices. This social ontology is advanced through the posing of a distinctive *interindividual territory.*

4. See Bogen and Lynch (1989) and Lynch and Bogen (1996) for excellent examples; also see Lynch's (1983) analysis of the textual practices and graphic technologies that take up and measure natural phenomena and produce them through a series of graphical renderings as scientific objects; and Lucy Suchman's (1988) treatment of whiteboards in the constitution of an in-common scientific knowledge, and as embedded in a network of activities. My 1995 work is an ethnographic analysis of the decision-making process in a city council meeting that aims to open up the setting beyond the boundaries of analyzing the accomplishment of discourse and social order within it.

5. Municipalities and agencies commonly have a database of legal clauses from which appropriate clauses can be selected and inserted into reports. They will be readily accessible to planners and planning clerks for their compilation and clerical work, and recognizable by councillors and others who must "consider" and activate them as part of their routine work.

6. In Ontario this process has been severely streamlined by the delegation of responsibility for draft approval to independent cities and municipalities. At the same time, the number of municipalities has been reduced through amalgamations.

7. The restructuring of municipalities in Ontario continues to shift the burden of work in these processes and their successful approval to the municipal planning staff. At the same time as the provincial government guidelines require that the municipali-

ties assist developers by providing "early consultation" to "ensure . . . early dispute resolution" with agencies (http://www.mmah.gov.on.ca/business/plansys/chap-03-e.asp), municipalities themselves set out their own forms of being "open for business" and providing "streamlined" services and incentives to developers, industry, and businesses.

8. The figure 8.3 and 8.4 titles mention a "layer"—1 and 3 respectively. This was relevant in a longer analysis (Turner 2003), where the consultation sequence is mapped in three layers. Layer 1, figure 8.3, maps the sequence of activities known in planning discourse as "resolving concerns through conditions." Layer 2, whose representation I have not included in this chapter, shows the actual textual formats and work that transforms the agency's "comments" into texts that are treated as "conditions." Layer 3, figure 8.4, begins to map the discourse moves, as in-text utterances, that comprise an institutional form of action and practices of a specialized speech genre.

9. I have analyzed this accomplishment as an extended sequence of coordinated work-text-work that has a standard form, drawing on some of the conventions of conversation analysis in order to analyze selected portions of a transcript of a city council meeting discussion. I placed emphasis on the operation of the text in coordinating the diverse participants' consciousnesses and utterances into the single action of "the council." This included the accomplishment of *its* act via a vote and other clerical practices constituting *its* decision, as well as the particular language practices that connect the present action to a larger active discourse of planning and to simultaneous and future activities happening outside the council setting (Turner 1995, 2003).

10. The description offered here is a much abbreviated version. (See Turner 2003, chapter 8 for a full treatment.)

11. This illustrates how we might observe practices that have been addressed by V. I. Volosinov's concept of *reported speech* and the problem of *hybrid utterances* according to M. M. Bakhtin. Dorothy Smith addresses the dynamics of *hierarchical intertextuality* in this volume. All three highlight for us the power of complex, organized everyday language practices that subsume, while making present, the "voices" and "utterances" of others. Each theorizes and emphasizes the necessity for social researchers to inquire into the particularity of these forms of action in different social, or institutional, spheres of action.

Part III

INQUIRY, PROJECTED AND ACCOMPLISHED

THIS SECTION IS INTENDED to do two things: one is to give a sense of institutional ethnographic studies at various moments in their creation. Thus Smith, Mykhavlovskiy, and Weatherbee's proposal, as it was developed for the then Department of Health and Welfare in Canada, shows what an institutional ethnographic project proposal might look like (it was funded); Eastwood's chapter was written at a stage when she was just entering into a new project; Wilson and Pence, however, write of a project already completed.

In including these three chapters, I have also wanted to expand the reader's sense of the range of exploration that institutional ethnography opens up. Of course in preceding chapters, we have already had instances of ethnographies in a senior citizens' residence, a long-term care hospital, the health care work contexts of people with AIDS, an educational discourse, and municipal government. These three final chapters, however, expand our sense of institutional ethnographic possibilities.

9

A Research Proposal

George W. Smith, Eric Mykhalovskiy, and Douglas Weatherbee

INTRODUCTORY NOTE from Dorothy E. Smith:

This is a project proposal that was made to the National Welfare Grants, Health & Welfare Canada, around 1990. It was funded; the research proceeded; and a final report, Getting "Hooked Up": A Report on the Barriers People Living with HIV/AIDS Face Accessing Social Services, *was submitted in 1994. George Smith participated actively in the research process but was unable to share in the preparation of the final report. He died of AIDS in the fall of 1994.*

Much will have changed both in the treatment of AIDS and in the health and social service institutions to which it refers—though not necessarily, in the latter cases, for the better. The project description is presented here not for its substance, but for the remarkable intellectual clarity and practicality with which institutional ethnography is translated into a research project.

Getting "Hooked Up" An Organizational Study of the Problems People with HIV/AIDS Have Accessing Social Services

A Research Proposal Prepared for

National Welfare Grants, Health & Welfare Canada

George W. Smith,
Eric Mykhalovskiy,
and
Douglas Weatherbee

December 1990

PROJECT DESCRIPTION

Statement of Objectives

People who are HIV positive or who have AIDS experience distinctive problems because of their infection. The impairment of their health is long-term; if AIDS has developed, it is a terminal disease. They may be well for long periods of time or suffer from long periods of low energy interspersed with episodes of more or less serious illness. In spite of a changing public opinion, they are likely to be stigmatized. There are still irrational fears of contagion. If a man is identified as HIV positive or as having AIDS, he is likely to also be identified as homosexual and hence experience the widespread homophobia typical of our society. People with HIV/AIDS may find friends and relatives unable or unwilling to sustain support, either material or emotional. They may be unable to sustain employment at their former level or at all: coworkers may be unwilling to associate with them. They can experience emotional trauma as a result of any combination of these factors.

People who are HIV positive or who have AIDS have radically to revise their lives and expectations. They are forced to live differently. How people reorganize their everyday lives under conditions of HIV/AIDS, consequently, can be viewed (as "Wages for Housework" theorists have viewed it) as work. For example, they may well have to change their lives if they are to maximize their chances of not progressing to frank AIDS by seeking sources of health care, information, and support. If they have AIDS, illness commits them to ongoing participation in the health care system on a chronic basis. This is particularly so during periods of severe illness. In addition, those close to them who choose to become involved in their support are also absorbed into this work regime, contributing resources of time and effort. What we are interested in, in the first instance, is the organization and reorganization of this kind of personal work regime necessitated by HIV/AIDS. We call this the "lifework" of people because it is critical to their efforts to extend their lives. It is the organization of this "lifework" and its necessary linkages to the health care system that distinguishes people with HIV/AIDS from the majority of recipients of social services.

For the most part, the main business of AIDS is addressed from the standpoint of the health care and social services systems—e.g., the problems they confront in providing care, public health information, and education, and in providing welfare supports, and so forth. This study takes a different approach. It begins from the standpoint of those who are HIV positive or have AIDS: it examines the social services system from this standpoint. This procedure is not concerned, however, with the subjective feelings or perspectives of these people. Nor is it intended to indict or to criticize social service agencies or the "attitudes" of their workers. Rather, it is focused on how the interface between the two gets organized as a matter of the everyday encounters between individuals who are HIV positive or who have AIDS and social service workers. For this reason, we have conceptualized the issues for people with HIV/AIDS in terms of the everyday ongoing organization and reorganization of their "lifework." We want to insist that people with HIV/AIDS put time, thought, and energy into the daily living that they depend on.

On the one hand are the distinctive configuration of everyday problems and working solutions these people put together, and on the other, the institutionalized practices of agencies organized by legislation, administrative regulations and practices, professional philosophies, etc. Our questions are these: How is this relation actually organized? In particular we want to examine the legislation, regulations, policy directives, and standard paperwork practices that organize the interface between people with HIV/AIDS and social agencies from the institutional side. What characteristic problems emerge? How are such problems generated by the interplay between the HIV/AIDS configuration of life problems and the institutional structure within which social service agency employees work? How do the conditions of the everyday work of living with HIV/AIDS, the organization of that work, and its relation to social service agencies vary with the different social locations (e.g., class, gender, injection drug use, ethnicity, race, etc.) of these people? And, lastly, what effect does the stage of someone's illness have on this organizational matrix?

In preparation for this project, we interviewed advocates for people with HIV/AIDS who described this interface as a process of "hooking up" individuals to the services to which they are entitled. It is this "hooking up" of the everyday "lifework" of people living with HIV/AIDS with the institutional structure of social service agencies that is the focus of our study.

Background Information

Establishing the Problematic

Our problematic arises out of the everyday experiences of people with HIV infection as they encounter the organization of social service agencies. Within the HIV community, stories constantly circulate about the problems people have getting the social services to which they are entitled. Here are some examples:

> **There were the problems a mother encountered last summer trying to secure home care for her son who was in the terminal stages of AIDS. She wanted to take care of him at home rather than leave him in the hospital. He was a single

person in his late thirties who had lived on his own for many years. When she took him from the hospital to her home, her income rather than his became the basis for determining the services to which he was entitled. Because hers was a middle-class family that was entitled to very limited social services, his home care became a burden on the family's financial resources, even though these arrangements saved the government the cost of hospital care.

**An eighteen-year-old woman with HIV infection is attempting to return to high school in January of 1991. She had been living on and off with her mother in northern Toronto: the high school she is able to attend is in central Toronto. She intended to move into an apartment near her new school at the beginning of November. Her living arrangements with her mother have been precarious because of her HIV infection. She also wants to establish herself in her own home before school begins. She expected that Student Welfare would cover her living costs for November and December. However, she found out at the beginning of November that she would not be eligible for Student Welfare until she actually begins school. This news came as a complete surprise to her. She then applied for General Welfare but was told it would take at least one and a half months before she would receive any money. She approached a community-based group in Toronto for assistance. But it too was unable to help. She is now trying to raise enough money to live on her own for two months until her schooling and Student Welfare begins.

These two stories illustrate the disjunctures between the way people with HIV/AIDS and their supporters organize their "lifework" and the institutionalized responses of social service agencies. These organizational disjunctures can take many forms. What we are particularly interested in is how the "lifework" of people with HIV/AIDS is impacted by both the stigma and stage of their illness in relation to the operations of social service agencies.

Another, quite different, example comes from the group interview we conducted with benefits counselors working with people with HIV/AIDS.

In my experience there's a difference between the people who for what ever reasons in their lives were previously hooked into social services, they've been on welfare, they know the ropes, they know what they can expect. . . . So people who've been users of those services ahead of time . . . [o]nce they've been diagnosed with HIV, it's easier for them. They've adjusted to poverty, it's not a good thing but they can live on it. They know what that cheque means . . . It's the family or the individual, whether gay or not, who suddenly realizes that this cheque is what they've got to make do with. This is it. There is no more out there. So we (counselors) can say, "You need to adjust to living within this amount." But Family Benefits is a joke! What's much harder is their friendship network may not realize that living in poverty is a real problem . . . . You know, they can go ask for a winter coat. Well, you know what it's like to go sit down there at the [welfare] office and have to wait there and ask for something. The shock of this, what this is (is?) a class crisis . . .

Here the organizational disjuncture between a person's everyday life and the institutionalized work processes of social service agencies can be seen as one of class. This kind of problem has also been described by Kaetz (1989). What is ordinarily not visible to middle-class people applying for welfare is the work the welfare system does to help manage the labor market (Hick 1991). If at nothing else than an intuitive level, this condition is understood by the poor because it is integral to the official treatment meted out to make sure they are not merely poor but are the "deserving poor" before providing financial relief. People living in poverty, consequently, often know how to organize their lives more easily to fit the constraints imposed by dependence on social services. For middle-class people with HIV/AIDS who have never been unemployed and who now can no longer be employed, the work welfare agencies do managing the labor market creates organizational problems for them in their efforts to get general welfare or family benefits. The work social agencies do to ferret out "freeloaders" is the bane to people with HIV/AIDS. They are, in this respect, a feature of the social organization of class in our society.

The organizational disjuncture, presupposed by the metaphor of "hooking up," is the focus of counselors in community-based organizations who see their work as helping to bridge this gap. They do this primarily by being advocates for people with HIV/AIDS.

> Well, I know when I have a woman who comes in, an immigrant woman or a woman who speaks Portuguese, English as a second language, and [she has] AIDS. It really is about . . . *empower* is such a nifty word these days . . . but it's how to very carefully go through, "You have a right to ask for these things." "Can I partner with you." Being an advocate for somebody. That tends to be our role in these kinds of community-based agencies.

From our preliminary inquiries it appears that the organizational disjuncture that we have identified as existing between the everyday, commonsense organization of people's lives and the institutionalized work processes of social service agencies is what needs to be understood if the barriers affecting the delivery of social services to persons living with HIV/AIDS are to be identified and modified.

Review of the Literature

The Study of the Relation between People with HIV/AIDS and Social Service Agencies

Literature that addresses social services with regards to people with HIV infection is scant. Some articles have as a focus the attitudes and perceptions of social service practitioners and society as a whole as they relate to social services for HIV positive people (Dhooper, Royse, and Tran 1987/1988; Fraser 1987). There is also literature which concentrates on the education and training of social service practitioners as it relates to people with HIV infection (Bourgon and Renaud 1989: Canadian Association of Schools of Social Work 1988) and on the community response to AIDS in Canada (Clausson 1989; Ryan 1989). There are researchers who have made use of a needs assessment methodology to ascertain the perceived needs of social workers and HIV positive service users (Clark et al. 1989; Mathews, Radford, and Weatherbee 1991) and others who have measured the attitudes, knowledge, and behaviors of uninfected Canadian youth (Radford et al. 1989).

In a review of the available literature, we have found that study of the social organization of the social services from the standpoint of people with HIV whose "lifework" includes accessing these services has not taken place. The accounts of HIV positive people on their daily work of accessing social services remains absent from the literature with one exception (Kaetz 1989); however, this article remains only an introduction to this subject. The kind of organizational study we propose of social services as they relate to the organization of the "lifework" of people with HIV and AIDS has thus far not been undertaken.

There are, however, some studies of social service agencies and of the delivery of social services that have both a substantive and methodological connection to the research proposed here. The 1979 study by Bodnar and Reimer on "The Organization of Social Services and Its Implications for the Mental Health of Immigrant Women" is a good example. This study investigated the accessibility and relevance of social services to immigrant women experiencing "mental health" problems. The work was taken up from the standpoint of immigrant women. Two other studies by Ng (1981) and Cassin and Griffith (1981) have a close methodological relation to this work. Two studies of social work by de Montigny (1989) and Hick (1991) are particularly useful ethnographies of social service agencies that are methodologically similar to the research design put forward in this proposal.

The Study of Textually Mediated Organization

The study of the organizational significance of texts and documents originates in Max Weber's early-twentieth-century studies of bureaucratic forms of authority (Weber 1978). He gives considerable emphasis to the importance of files and records, an example that was followed by years where this aspect of administrative and managerial practice was neglected. The production of forms, instructions, factual data, etc., is a specialized, technical matter. The organization of systems of corporate "memory" in files was already highly sophisticated before the generalization of the computer and the advent of computer-based systems of data management. Studies of the formal organizational significance of texts and documents are relatively sparse and recent. These include Zimmerman's (1974) pioneering study of facts as practical accomplishment showing the facticity of welfare claims as a routine organizational product; Atkinson's (1978) extensive study of the social construction of suicide, in which he elucidates coroners' methods of transposing lay accounts of a death into the forms required for official records; a study by Silverman and Jones (1976) of the language practices involved in promotions' procedures in a corporation; two excellent Canadian studies of bureaucratic "ideologies-in-practice," one by Don Handelman on legal and professional definitions of child abuse, the other by Eliot Leyton on the local operation of the Workmen's Compensation Board (Handelman and Leyton 1978); Burton and Carlen's (1979) study of the language of a parliamentary commission; Chua's (1979b) valuable contributions to an analysis of textually mediated discourse as a component of democratic process; Green's (1983) highly innovative study of the textual organization of the British Poor Law Commissions of 1834 and 1909; and Campbell's (1984) analysis of documentary practices of accountability in the context of hospital nursing.

Design of the Study

The design of this study takes the form of an institutional ethnography (Smith 1987). This is a method of research which investigates, ethnographically, a "section" of the social world from the standpoint of the organization of the work of those who in various ways are involved in its production. This kind of ethnography takes as its problematic the complex of relations in which this local world is embedded. In this sense, the ethnographic enterprise is not confined to what can be directly observed, or to what informants have directly observed. Rather, it seeks to reveal the extended bureaucratic, professional, legislative, and economic, as well as other social relations involved in the production of local events and activities.

Various methodologies are used in institutional ethnographies, including in-depth interviews, archival research, and textual analysis. The choice of methodology depends on the social organizational properties of the phenomena under investigation. In this study, the methodologies to be used are in-depth interviewing and the analysis of documents. The focus of research is the forms of social organization coordinating relations between the "lifework" of people with HIV infection and social service agencies. Three main sites have been identified: the social locations of individuals with HIV infection, the location of community-based people who act as advocates for them vis-à-vis social agencies, and the location of social service agencies themselves.

Starting from the Standpoint of HIV-Infected Individuals

The design of this study starts from the standpoint of HIV-infected individuals. What this means is that conceptually the study is designed to take up the problems people with HIV infection face in accessing social services. It is their experiences that define this starting point and not the legislative, bureaucratic, or professional requirements governing the workings of social service agencies. In this respect, the study is neither one of the attitudes of social service workers (Dhooper et al. 1987/1988) (e.g., homophobia, AIDS phobia), for example, nor a needs assessment survey of HIV-infected people (Mathews at al. 1991). Rather it is a study of social organization—first, in terms of the "lifework" of people with HIV infection, and secondly, in terms of the social organization of the delivery of social services. In this context, the problem HIV positive individuals face in accessing social services is taken up in terms of the ways in which the managerial organization and everyday practices of social agencies connect or fail to connect with their lives.

The Reflexive Basis of Our Understanding of the Give-and-Take World of Social Services

The research is to be carried out in a reflexive fashion from inside the social organization of not only our own world as researchers but, by extension, the social worlds we intend to investigate. The point of doing interviews and of perusing the relevant documents is to extend the everyday, commonsense understandings we have of our own world to understanding other people's lives—in this case to the "lifework" of people living with HIV/AIDS and to the everyday work processes of social service agencies. Three additional strategies are relevant to this reflexive orientation:

1. Informants are to be treated as knowledgeable about the social organization of the local settings in which they conduct their affairs. Informants are taken to be competent practitioners within the context of their everyday world. The point of interviews is to have them share these competencies, thereby extending them to the interviewer.
2. The social world under investigation is not taken to be truncated at the boundary of local settings but to be treated as extending in a contiguous fashion beyond the purview of the everyday. These extended courses of

action are taken up as social relations organized as a series of moments that are dependent upon one another and articulated to one another not functionally, but reflexively, as temporal sequences in which the foregoing intends the subsequent and in which the subsequent "realizes" or accomplishes the social character of the preceding.

3. Texts and documents are investigated as active constituents of social relations. We want, in this respect, to see how they operate as extra-local determinants coordinating and concerting the organization of local settings.

Interviews

The interview procedure will be open-ended. Tape recordings will be made for transcription. Tape-recording and transcribing interviews is essential to be able to develop detailed and systematic interpretations of the data. Making interpretations as part of in situ notetaking makes it more difficult later on to explicate the social organization of the relations in which informants' descriptions are embedded. These procedures, consequently, provide for a more rigorous approach to data collection and analysis. The interviews, themselves, will address the organizational knowledge of those who are active participants in relevant settings. Interviewing will involve two main strategies:

1. Investigating with respondents their own working knowledge of the organizational processes they are part of. Interviewing a series of respondents positioned differently in the "hooking up" process enables us to assemble a picture of relevant organizational sequences as actual courses of action. In particular we will be concerned with informants' normally explicated and practical knowledge of "how things work."
2. Previous work in the area of textually mediated social organization has led us to see organizational documents as significant constituents of organizational processes. Interviews will also try to uncover what respondents can tell us about how documents enter practically into the routine ordering of their work.

The recruitment of informants will be organized through community-based AIDS organizations and social service agencies. To begin with we intend to set up focus groups of clients from community-based organizations. On the basis of these group meetings we would then do in-depth interviews with a number of selected individuals. We will attempt to include individuals from different backgrounds and circumstances. However, we will not attempt to develop a randomized sample. The general and generalizable features of the analysis are taken to lie in the abstract, general character of the "hooking up" phenomena under investigation. For example, provincial legislation and government regulations controlling the operations of social agencies organized them "in general." Descriptions of these abstract, generalized characteristics of the society, consequently, have the same general properties as the phenomena they describe.

The Study of Social Agencies and Community-Based Organizations as Textually Mediated Social Organizations

An important feature of our society is the ability of documentary forms of organization to shape and determine events in local settings. A good example is the way legislation, passed in one location, comes to impact people's lives in other locations across time. This iterative, recursive capacity resides in its documentary or textually mediated character. This is the reason why, in addition to interviews, techniques of textual analysis are an important aspect of institutional ethnographies.

An ordinary property of textually mediated social organization is its exploitation of the capacity of texts to crystallize and preserve a definite form of words detached from particular local contexts. Texts speak in the absence of speakers; meaning is detached from local contexts of interpretation; the "same" meaning can occur simultaneously in a multiplicity of socially and temporally separated settings (cf. Smith 1984). This social character of texts is essential to their uses in organizing administrative, managerial, and professional forms of organization.

This organized character of institutions and agencies depends heavily on the various uses of texts to coordinate, order, provide continuity, monitor, and organize relations between different segments, phases, and levels of organizational courses of action. Organizational texts order and coordinate activities, which are dispersed spatially and temporally in a variety of organizational settings. In the context of this study, this theoretical framework directs investigation and analytic strategies towards the textually mediated processes, which are used to articulate the needs of people with HIV/AIDS to social service agencies. Our interest is in providing an account of organization and how it works and not in evaluation as this is ordinarily understood.

The theoretical approach which the research will, in part, make use of, consequently, is one which emphasizes the significance of texts and documents in professional organizations. This is not news to practitioners. Nonetheless, it is only recently that researchers have begun to take seriously the project of investigating just how texts and documents enter into these organizational processes. The work of Dorothy Smith (Smith 1973, 1979, 1981, 1983, and

1984) has provided both a conceptual framework and analytic strategies for investigating textually mediated social organizations. We view this textually mediated character of the "hooking up" phenomenon we intend to investigate as having special relevance to the study of how relations between institutions and people's everyday lives are structured.

Case Studies

The first six months of the proposed research will be devoted to interviewing HIV positive clients of social service agencies with a view to discovering how these individuals, with different backgrounds and located in different situations, go about organizing their "lifework" and how this ties into their access to social services as part of coping with HIV/AIDS. With the passing of social welfare legislation, it might appear that social services are simply there to be had. However, anecdotal accounts provided us in our preliminary investigations indicate that this is not the case. This discovery, in turn, directed our attention to what people have to do to get the social services they need. In studying and documenting these activities, we would not want to examine them as just a set of personal experiences, but instead take them up as work processes that make sense within the context of how these people's lives are put together. We would want to be able to provide a description of how HIV positive people go about getting access to social services so as to study the interaction between the organization of their everyday lives and the lives of their friends and families, and the institutionalized work order of social service agencies. For example, what organizational assumptions does this institutionalized work order make about the lives of people with HIV infection? Is it assumed, for example, that clients are experienced at getting on welfare? We expect that in a six-month period we would be able to do approximately sixty interviews. Because they involve individuals who do not work in institutional settings, these interviews will take a considerable amount of time both to organize and to do as we try to fit into the "lifework" of informants with HIV/AIDS. Not only will these interviews involve holding focus groups at the outset. There will be individuals who would be missed by these activities that will need to be included (e.g., individuals from minority groups—native, black, Asian, etc.,—as well as injection drug users, and hemophiliac and heterosexual groups). This will also be an intensive period of research as we learn from our informants just how things work for them, given how they organize their "lifework." Informants will be selected from a variety of backgrounds in order to study the various ways the standard practices of social service agencies (as these are shaped by legislation, etc.) come to interface with the everyday lives of people with HIV/AIDS.

The Textually Mediated Work of Community-Based AIDS Organizations and Social Service Agencies

We want to be able to study the work organization of these groups. Again, our interviews will begin, if at all possible, with focus groups that will be used to establish for our informants the relevancies of our research and to select individuals for later in-depth interviews. The hub of our investigations will be the everyday work done by social service workers in processing various applications made by people living with HIV/AIDS. An important part of these investigations, as has already been pointed out, will be the examination of documents as coordinating and concerting the work of these agencies. The range of documents to be encompassed is quite wide, from legislation to agency applications and other bureaucratic forms. The work of community-based AIDS organizations will be examined in relation to group mandates and the mandate created by specific grant applications.

We intend this part of the research to take four months and involve approximately twenty interviews. The organization of unemployment insurance, general welfare assistance, family benefits allowance, housing agencies like City Homes, co-ops, shelters, home care, homemaking, and transportation services, etc., as these are related to the needs of people with HIV/AIDS, will be studied. Interviews will also be conducted with workers at the major community-based AIDS organizations. From specific interviews with community-based and social service workers, documents will be identified and collected in relation to the work of both groups and agencies.

Analysis

The central analytic for this research project is the notion of "social relations." Within the context of this research, this notion operates as an investigational technique for locating and describing the social form of people's activities over time. It provides a method of looking at how individuals organize themselves vis-à-vis one another. The notion of "social relations" in this sense does not stand for a thing to be looked for in carrying out research; rather it is what is used to do the looking. It operates as a methodological injunction that requires the researcher to examine empirically how people's activities are reflexively/recursively knitted together into particular forms of social organization.

People's lives do not exist in a social vacuum. When individuals apply for welfare, for example, they are entered into an institutional course of action over which they have limited control. This course of action organizes them not only in relation to their families, their friends (in terms of money for socializing), their landlord (in terms of their ability to pay rent), and so on but also to social workers (in terms of determining their eligibility), and indeed to the government of the province and of Canada (in terms of providing the necessary cash allowance)—to name just a few organizational features of this form of social action. It is in identifying and describing how this institutional course of action works to shape and determine people's lives that the notion of social relations guides the analytic work of the researchers. Another example of the social organization produced by individuals with HIV/AIDS that comes to organize their lives is the organization of what we have called "lifework." This is a self-generated course of action that individuals organize for themselves as a result of testing positive for HIV antibodies. Analyzed as social relations, it is possible to see how, as a practical, everyday matter, this activity organizes people with HIV/AIDS vis-à-vis others engaged in providing emotional support, medical services, social services, and so forth. Moreover, it is also possible to see how external social courses of action such as the relations of gender or of homophobia can have a negative impact on the organization of these people's "lifework." In examining how people's lives are put together, the notion of social relations is used to carry out just such an analysis by being used to help determine where to look and how to see the coordination and concerting of social organization.

An important discovery of this method of work is the active role documents play in coordinating and organizing people's lives and hence their activities. This discovery provides for the researcher's ability to investigate and describe networks of co-ordered activities going forward simultaneously across a number of distinct sites of social action. The concept of "social relations" also operates, in this sense, to enter the social world into the text of the research report by helping researchers formulate their descriptions of it.

The notion of "social relations" is employed in a practical manner to talk about and to investigate the actual practices of individuals, articulated to one another, as constituting work processes where different moments in a course of action are dependent on one another and are articulated to one another not functionally, but reflexively. These are courses of action that, while coordinated and concerted over time in the activities of people, are neither initiated nor completed by a single individual.

Secondly, the notion of "social relations" is involved in discovering the recursive properties of spatial-temporal forms of social organization. Texts as active constituents of social relations can iterate the particular configuration of their organization in different places and at different times, thereby conceptually coordinating and temporally concerting a general form of social action. Recursion, consequently, is also discoverable in how particular, textually organized local experiences of people have the same social configuration as the experiences of others, organized extra-locally through the same text, at other times and places. The recursivity of a generalized course of action, consequently, makes it possible to go from particular events in local settings to a set of general, textually mediated social relations because they have the same social form.

Results and Their Dissemination

The results of this research will take two forms. First, there will be a detailed description of the social organization of the work of social agencies and community groups and the way these organizations are articulated to the organization of the "lifework" of people with HIV/AIDS. Secondly, this description will provide the basis for recommendations reorganizing the work of social agencies in order to provide a better organizational fit with the lives of people with HIV infection. Given that the report will feature a description of the current organizational disjuncture between social agencies and the lives of people with HIV/AIDS, it will also provide managers of social agencies and policymakers an opportunity to take initiatives on their own to make recommendations for change. They will not, in this sense, be limited to the recommendations of the report if they can see a better way to improve the situation.

The main deliverable produced by this research will come in the form of a report to the Department of Health and Welfare Canada, with permission of the Department. Journal articles will also be prepared for journals such as the *Social Worker* that are ordinarily read and used by social service agency managers and workers. The results of our study will also be disseminated to community-based AIDS organizations and to social services policymakers at the 1992 Delegate Assembly of the Canadian Association of Social Workers. And lastly, results will be made available to the academic community through the presentation of papers at the Learned Societies meetings and the publication of results in suitable Canadian academic journals. [Editor's note: the rest of the text, comprising job descriptions, budget, etc., has been omitted.]

10

Making the Institution Ethnographically Accessible: UN Document Production and the Transformation of Experience[1]

Lauren E. Eastwood

Introduction

THIS CHAPTER DEVELOPS some themes that are intended to be seen as a prelude to conducting an actual institutional ethnography. Unlike some of the work presented in this volume, I have not yet completed an institutional ethnography with the data I discuss here. Instead, I am very much in the process of "discovery" that is integral to the doing of an institutional ethnography. As Smith (2005) explicates, in conducting research informed by the ontology of institutional ethnography, the researcher deploys a discourse "that avoids imposing interpretations and elaborates with informants—or . . . with the ethnographers themselves—in *discovery*" (p. 140, italics in the original). The objective of this chapter is to talk through some of this process of discovery by using specific examples from research I've recently been conducting at United Nations–related meetings.

I entered the United Nations (UN) in 1998 with little to no understanding of the work that people do to make policy. My aim was to investigate the UN forest policy negotiations that were going on at that time. The "work knowledges" (see Smith 2005, especially chapter 7) that I developed through my original project (Eastwood 2005) are integral to my current research in that they inform my ability to engage with the policymaking processes and to make sense of the activities that I observe and in which I participate. However, I maintain the process of "discovery" that is crucial to the institutional ethnographic project, which means, for the institutional ethnographer, "not just learning what she or he did not know but disrupting either the concepts with which the research began or the preconceptions not fully formulated" (Smith 2005: 141). In light of this, in this chapter I talk through the process of keeping an institutional ethnographic eye to data collection and preliminary analysis by discussing the ways in which one can begin to make the UN "ethnographically accessible."

Making the UN Ethnographically Accessible

> Institutions exist in that strange magical realm in which social relations based on texts transform the local particularities of people, place and time into standardized, generalized, and, especially, translocal forms of coordinating people's activities. Texts perform at that key juncture between the local settings of people's everyday worlds and the ruling relations. (Smith 2005: 101)

For the institutional ethnographer, "accessibility" has a different connotation than it does in standard qualitative research projects. While gaining literal "access" to the research site is key, in Smith's discussion of "ethnographic accessibility" there is an additional factor. One is not merely gaining access to a site but is instead attempting to open spaces where one can investigate the linkages between the everyday lived experiences of practitioners and how those experiences are coordinated by larger social relations. In other words, the notion of "accessibility," as it is used by Smith, is inherently informed by the ontology of institutional ethnography. Elements of this ontology are articulated in the quote that starts this section. The institutional ethnographer approaches the research site with a view to unpacking the generalizing and abstracting mechanisms of the institution. As Smith emphasizes, this generalizing process—the abstraction of experience into the standardized language that is recognizable by the institution—happens through texts. In fact, to the institutional ethnographer, the text is recognized as being a "bridge between the actual and the discursive" (Smith 1992: 92).

It would be hard to *not* see the UN as a textually mediated organization. UN estimates place the annual production of printed pages by the UN itself at approximately 700 million pages (Deen 2005). While statistics are hard to locate, in part due to the seemingly endless interconnected chain of UN bodies that extend beyond primary UN locations, one UN document noted that the increased use of electronic technology allowed headquarters alone to reduce paper output from about 5,862,000 pounds in 1995 to about 3,975,000 pounds in 1997 (United Nations Consultative Committee on Administrative Questions 1999). This quantity is amassed through the daily production of major documents, many of which are printed in all six official UN languages.

In addition to daily documents, regular meetings of UN subsidiary bodies—at both headquarters and additional locations—produce a range of documents from successive negotiating texts to final reports.

However, note my language. "Meetings produce documents." This is the standard way of discussing the textually mediated nature of the UN system. Bringing that phrase ("meetings produce documents") under scrutiny reveals that, indeed, "meetings" don't produce documents. In fact, "the UN" doesn't use paper. The activities of a wide range of individuals are obscured in these phrases and in the final documents produced. It isn't headquarters that reduces paper output. Someone, somewhere, needs to recognize that "paper output" is a problem, and perhaps in conflict with the UN-based efforts to generate, for example, forest policies in response to global deforestation. The process of installing electronic alternatives to paper document production requires the concerted activities of multiple individuals following budgeting protocols, installing software, working on websites, cataloguing data, and far more.

In order to begin to reinstate the activities that become abstracted in phrases such as "the UN produces documents," I have attempted to gain more insight into the work that practitioners do as they attend meetings and in preparation for those meetings. Thus, I began attending various UN-based meetings that were organized around negotiating forest policies in 1998. However, as I soon discovered, attending meetings does not necessarily give a sense of how the UN as an organization works. Indeed, attempting an overall picture of the UN as an organization would be a very different project than the ones I have engaged in. The politics that inform that type of study would themselves be very different than those that drew me into the research that I have been doing through the UN. Rather than focusing on what it means for the UN to be a "paper factory," as it has been characterized in light of its voluminous document production, I was initially attracted to the UN as it represents a site where far more is being produced than simply sheer quantities of texts. In fact, those texts are the sites of key struggles that are currently taking place. These struggles are organized around practitioners' attempts to influence the meaning of terms that are integral to the making of environmental policy.

The politics of my project, which take seriously the contested terrain of the texts, require looking closely at the ways in which terminology has been taken up within what George Smith has termed "politico-administrative regimes" (G. W. Smith 1990). The larger discursive terrain serves to organize the ways in which actual people and the issues they represent get incorporated into (or disenfranchised from) the policymaking process. Under the ontology of institutional ethnography, the dynamics that have been abstracted ideologically into concepts such as "globalization" and "development," forces seemingly operating without human agency (or at least assumed to be beneficial by definition), can be reattached to actual activities being carried out by actual people. Part of the project presented here involves unveiling the ideological nature of these concepts—the ways in which the terms themselves have become abstracted in the first place, and the implications of that abstraction. It is, however, also crucial that we make the actions, activities, and actors concrete as a basis for an effective oppositional stance. In other words, it is critical to make visible the activities that have systematically been made invisible through the abstraction effected by the documentary reality of the UN. As long as the concepts remain distinct from the actualities of what is going on with and among people, the effectiveness of opposition to the on-the-ground realities of "globalization" or "development" is minimized.

The importance of language in environmental policymaking has likewise been noted by scholars who do not use institutional ethnography as a method of inquiry. For example, as David Harvey suggests, discourse is not just a matter of language and text. Harvey's point is that

> . . . discourses about nature internalize a whole range of contradictory impulses and conflictual ideas derived from all of the other moments in the social process. And from that standpoint, discussion of the discourses of nature has much to reveal, if only about how the discourses themselves conceal a concrete political agenda in the midst of highly abstract, universalizing, and frequently intensely moral argumentation. (Harvey 1996: 174)

While this view of discourse and its ability to conceal political agendas is compatible with my approach to the research site, from the perspective of institutional ethnography, it is not only important to elucidate these discourses of nature. It is crucial, also, to unpack the actual activities that get subsumed into the "universalizing, and frequently intensely moral argumentation" of which Harvey (1996) speaks.

When I originally became interested in the UN as a research site, it appeared to me that, in the "final" texts produced by the UN, the politically charged nature of the debates—the ways in which the larger discursive realm is constituted and contested—is made invisible. The texts conceal the concrete political agendas that Harvey points to above. This became apparent to me as I perused the thousands of pages of documents produced during the many processes leading up to and including the United Nations Conference on Environment and Development (UNCED) held in Brazil in 1992. I was struck by the ways in which particular terms, such as *sustainable development* stood in for a whole range of specific activities. The texts served to "suppress the presence of subjects and the local practices that produce the extra-local and objective" (Smith 2001: 159). I was fascinated by the language used in UN documents and the ways in which this suppression of actual activities is so apparent. For example, note the style of writing used in the segment of the "Non-Legally Binding Authoritative Statement of Principles for a Global Consensus on the Management, Conservation, and Sustainable Development of All Types of Forests," reproduced in figure 10.1.

This piece of text exemplifies a specific type of documentary reality that is found in UN texts. As Dorothy Smith (1973) elaborates, in institutions and organizations, "a documentary reality is fundamental to the practices of governing, managing and administration of this form of society" (p. 257). The text shown in figure 10.1 represents a segment of the outcomes of extended negotiations that took place prior to (and during) the United Nations Conference

United Nations A/CONF.151/26 (VOL III)

Distr. GENERAL
14 August 1992
Original:
ENGLISH

REPORT OF THE UNITED NATIONS CONFERENCE ON
ENVIRONMENT AND DEVELOPMENT

(Rio de Janeiro, 3-14 June 1992)

Annex III

NON-LEGALLY BINDING AUTHORITATIVE STATEMENT OF PRINCIPLES
FOR A GLOBAL CONSENSUS ON THE MANAGEMENT, CONSERVATION
AND SUSTAINABLE DEVELOPMENT OF ALL TYPES OF FORESTS

PREAMBLE

(a) The subject of forests is related to the entire range of environmental and development issues and opportunities, including the right to socio-economic development on a sustainable basis.

(b) The guiding objective of these principles is to contribute to the management, conservation and sustainable development of forests and to provide for their multiple and complementary functions and uses.

(c) Forestry issues and opportunities should be examined in a holistic and balanced manner within the overall context of environment and development, taking into consideration the multiple functions and uses of forests, including traditional uses, and the likely economic and social stress when these uses are constrained or restricted, as well as the potential for development that sustainable forest management can offer.

(d) These principles reflect a first global consensus on forests. In committing themselves to the prompt implementation of these principles, countries also decide to keep them under assessment for their adequacy with regard to further international cooperation on forest issues.

(...)

FIGURE 10.1.
Segment of the "Statement of Forest Principles"

on Environment and Development. Included in the notion of "documentary reality" is the idea that documents of this type become the effective reality of the institution in terms of what can be taken up or treated as real in subsequent workings of the organization. In fact, documents of this type extend beyond the organization in that the particular documentary reality of the UN allows the "agreements" to be taken up in a wide range of settings. In many ways, these texts are actually intended to extend beyond the workings of the institution.

It was clear, though, as I approached my previous study (Eastwood 2005), I needed to find a way of approaching the texts that didn't begin with the documentary reality itself. When Marjorie DeVault introduced me to institutional ethnography in graduate school and subsequently agreed to work with me on how one might apply such a method of inquiry to the UN as a dissertation project, my approach to the texts was radically altered. Here was a way to think about the terminology used in the documents without starting in and presupposing that abstracted documentary reality. Institutional ethnography made it clear that it was necessary to somehow gain insights into the level of "what actually happens" that is subsumed in the text of documents such as the one reproduced in figure 10.1. Thus, I gained access and attended meetings of the United Nations Intergovernmental Forum on Forests (IFF) as a representative of a nongovernmental organization (NGO). In this way, my research can be categorized in standard qualitative research terms as "participant observation." However, what I observe while I am at the meetings and how I interact with other participants is organized by the ontology of institutional ethnography. I focus on the work (broadly defined) that people do that produces "policymaking." I keep an eye to such things as the ways in which practitioners utilize insider's knowledge and the conceptual currency of the organization as documents are negotiated and produced. And I am attentive to the ways in which particular terms come to stand in for a range of actual experiences in the final texts. In investigating such dynamics as "conceptual currency" in any given organizational setting, the researcher focuses on particular concepts that both facilitate the work of the organization and serve to obscure the actual material reality represented by the concepts.[2] Conceptual currency is one way of thinking about what Dorothy Smith (2005) refers to as "institutional discourse" that I take up later in this chapter in talking through some preliminary analysis of data I'm currently collecting.

UN Texts and Institutional Discourse

As Susan Turner (this book) elucidates, the text-mediated nature of institutions draws practitioners into the processes whereby their activities are coordinated as "the work of the institution." In the case of UN policymaking processes, this dynamic is constantly at work, though it takes a somewhat different form than has been examined by some institutional ethnographers. What is different about the policymaking processes in the UN is that the majority of the work done in the meetings is not organized around activating a specific *form* that is part of a predetermined work process (for examples of this latter type of analysis, see Ridzi 2003 and Pence 1996). While individuals attending meetings at the UN itself require "documentation" and credentials to get the proper identification tags which allow them (us) to enter the UN premises and move about specified areas, the majority of the work that practitioners do once they (we) enter the UN involves producing new documents and texts.

Not only do the texts not fit in nicely with prescribed sequences of action, but it is also very challenging to see what people "do with the texts" (see Turner, this book) once they are produced. The mapping work that Turner does so effectively in terms of standardized text-based work processes is complicated in reference to UN documentary trajectories. This is not to say that UN texts do not have standardized, recognizable formats through which the institutional actions become visible. The mapping analysis becomes complicated in that UN documents do not often emerge from one site of work with definite destinations where they are to be taken up and processed as part of "what happens next." The texts take on a fairly nebulous status once they are negotiated in that they then become available to be taken up in various settings by various people who may be otherwise unconnected with one another. Exemplifying this dynamic is the segment of text reproduced in figure 10.2.

Resolution 44/228, which can be seen as constituting the official origins of the UN Conference on Environment and Development (UNCED), was adopted by the General Assembly of the United Nations in 1989. The portion of the text that is reproduced here utilizes prior documents to ensure its presence and significance for the UN. Drawing in a resolution or similar agreed-upon conclusion from a prior official text is an important device used in the sublunary political negotiations and finagling that are continually at work in the formulation of the official texts. This is a fairly clear case of how one can trace the prior texts that serve to legitimate various types of UN work. We do not, however, in the process of negotiating UN texts, often see a predetermined framework for where documents are intended to "go" after they have gone through whatever processes establishes them as "official." They do, however, appear to be significant in establishing the terms of official discourse and, indeed, to permeate public discourse in general. Since I have started researching UN-related processes, I notice UN-produced texts and "language" popping up in unexpected locations, from National Public Radio reports of human rights work to U.S. court rulings that invoke UN declarations, and to

United Nations **A/RES/44/228**

Distr. GENERAL
Original:
ENGLISH

UN General Assembly Resolution 44/228

RESOLUTION ADOPTED BY THE UNITED NATIONS GENERAL ASSEMBLY

New York, 22 December 1989

Resolution No. 44/228

United Nations Conference on Environment and Development

THE GENERAL ASSEMBLY,

RECALLING its resolution 43/196 of 20 December 1988 on a United Nations conference on environment and development,

TAKING NOTE of decision 15/3 of 25 May 1989 of the Governing Council of the United Nations Environment Programme on a United Nations conference on environment and development,

TAKING NOTE also of Economic and Social Council resolution 1989/87 of 26 July 1989 on the convening of a United Nations conference on environment and development,

TAKING NOTE further of Economic and Social Council resolution 1989/101 of 27 July 1989 on strengthening international co-operation on environment through the provision of additional financial resources to developing countries,...

MINDFUL of the views expressed by Governments in the debate held at its forty-fourth session on the convening of a United Nations conference on environment and development,

RECALLING the Declaration of the United Nations Conference on the Human Environment,

FIGURE 10.2.
Segment of the "UN General Assembly Resolution 44/228"

zoo "biodiversity" exhibits that reference UN agreements, to name a few. It is partly this translocal discursive power of UN documents that invests the negotiating process with such controversy and importance for those involved. Yet, unlike other institutional ethnographic analyses of texts, it is very difficult to map out the ways in which these texts coordinate people's actions within the context of UN-based work.

Nonetheless, the work that practitioners do in activating texts in the UN can be subjected to institutional ethnographic analysis. With institutional ethnography, ". . . the analytic procedure results in an account of the day-today text-based work and local discourse practices that produce and shape the dynamic ongoing activities of an institution" (Turner, this book). As I mentioned above, reams of documents are produced during (and prior to) each UN meeting. The policy-generating nature of the organization produces texts that have clear connections both to prior negotiating processes and larger discursive terrains. Being savvy about both of these elements (prior processes and current discursive frameworks) is imperative to being an effective participant in the process. This insider knowledge is regularly displayed as texts are activated through a process whereby practitioners read through the negotiating texts to locate terminology that might be problematic to them (see Eastwood 2005). In this way, practitioners familiar with the institutional discourses negotiate the formulations, phrasings, and concepts built into texts with the goal of ensuring that final documents incorporate their "interests," when and if they come into play in the future.

One way of influencing the process is through engaging in what I've come to think of as "intentional institutional capture"—a way that practitioners are constrained to translate their experiences and "interests" into something that is recognizable to the organization. As Smith describes, under an institutional ethnographic ontology, "rather than view institutional discourses as prescribing actions, we might see them as providing terms under which what people do becomes institutionally accountable" (Smith 2005: 113). In terms of work that is done through the UN, this also involves not only the translation of people's experiences into something that is institutionally accountable, but also something that is institutionally *recognizable.* Smith elaborates on this latter notion in her chapter on "incorporating texts into ethnographic practice" in this book. The translation of experiences into institutional discourses is indeed a function of the larger organization. In order to be effective in the organization, practitioners utilize this translation by taking up the institutional discourse in key ways. To explore how this actually works, the following section presents some specific examples from a recent set of UN-related meetings which I attended as part of my preliminary engagement with the area of my future research at the UN.

Intentional Institutional Capture: Translating Experience into "Traditional Forest-Related Knowledge"

In December of 2004, the International Alliance of Indigenous and Tribal Peoples of the Tropical Forests (IAITPTF) convened an "Expert Meeting on Traditional Forest-Related Knowledge and the Implementation of Related International Commitments" in San Jose, Costa Rica. The meeting was cosponsored by the IAITPTF and the government of Costa Rica, with funding coming from several sources (both private and governmental) that have connections to UN-related negotiating processes. The primary objective of the meeting (hereafter referred to as "the Expert Meeting") was to "identify ways to improve the national implementation of international commitments on indigenous peoples, local communities and traditional forest-related knowledge" (IAITPTF 2005: 3).

While there are several international commitments that can be seen as being related to Traditional Forest-Related Knowledge (TFRK), the "international commitments" referenced in the title of the meeting were specified as being those agreed upon during two major intergovernmental processes taking place under the auspices of the UN—those organized around forests and those organized around biological diversity. Both processes originated in agreements negotiated through the United Nations Conference on Environment and Development (UNCED), including the previously mentioned "Non-Legally Binding Authoritative Statement of Principles for a Global Consensus on the Management, Conservation, and Sustainable Development of All Types of Forests." The process organized around issues of biological diversity falls under the Convention on Biological Diversity (CBD), which is a legally binding agreement among the parties (nations) who have ratified the agreement. The UN-related forest policy process, on the other hand, as is evidenced in the title of the original UNCED "Statement of Principles" (referred to previously), has not resulted in a legally binding agreement. Instead, the forest policy negotiations have taken place through a series of different intergovernmental bodies since UNCED, resulting in a series of "proposals for action" and "recommendations" rather than a legally binding forest convention.[3]

The post-UNCED forest negotiation process began with the Intergovernmental Panel on Forests (IPF), which met four times over the course of two years from 1995–1997. The IPF established a range of proposals for action. Subsequently, the Intergovernmental Forum on Forests (IFF), which also met over a two-year period (1998–2000), was charged, in part, with taking up the implementation of the IPF's proposals for action. At the end of the IFF's stint, it was decided that a standing body, called the United Nations Forum on Forests (UNFF), would be established, under which forest policy negotiations would continue. It was the second process—the Intergovernmental Forum on Forests (IFF)—that provided a basis for my original institutional ethnography. Throughout my research, both then and later, I discovered that the various intergovernmental processes are connected in complex and fascinating ways. Thus, I was particularly interested in the Expert Meeting of the IAITPTF, as it explicitly targeted agreements formulated in both the CBD and forest policy negotiations, with the objective of feeding back into the CBD and

UNFF processes. This was, in part, to be done through the production of a "declaration" and a set of "recommendations."[4]

A similar meeting had earlier been convened, with the express purpose of contributing to the Intergovernmental Panel on Forests (IPF) process. The "International Meeting of Indigenous and Other Forest-Dependent Peoples on the Management, Conservation and Sustainable Development of All Types of Forests" was held in Leticia, Colombia, in December of 1996. The results of that meeting included a list of "Proposals for Action" as well as the "Leticia Declaration," both of which were integrated into the forest policymaking processes in various ways. Initially, the texts of both documents were submitted in the form of an "official" IPF document by being included in a letter sent to the UN secretary-general from the governments of Colombia and Denmark, who had both cosponsored the Leticia meeting. Furthermore, the Leticia Declaration was regularly referenced in subsequent documents and meeting interventions throughout the ensuing policy processes (the IFF and UNFF). Both participants and organizers of the Expert Meeting held in Costa Rica hoped that the results of the 2004 meeting would be similarly incorporated into both the UNFF and CBD processes.

The actual "Expert Meeting" (held in Costa Rica) took place on December 8th through the 10th, with an Indigenous Peoples' Preparatory Meeting taking place on the 6th and 7th. Most of the participants were present for both segments of the meeting. However, some of the participants who attended the meetings based on their expertise in the "related international commitments" (referred to in the meeting title) did not attend the Indigenous Peoples' Preparatory Meeting. I gained permission from the IAITPTF to attend both segments of the meeting as an academic researcher, and as someone who was familiar, through my prior research, with the forest policymaking process and related commitments.

Participants were split into four regional groupings (Asia-Pacific, Africa, Latin America, and Northern Countries) in order to facilitate the construction of the list of recommendations to come out of the Expert Group meeting. The working groups were all given the same set of instructions from the meeting organizers. We were to start our work with a discussion of "actual experiences and actions taken by governments in regards to international commitments." Following the discussion of actual experiences, each working group was to come up with their own list of recommendations.

Each working group had a note taker, who was charged with documenting key points and getting the notes to the meeting organizers. I was asked to be the note taker for the Northern Working Group. In addition to documenting the primary points of the conversation that working group members were having, this also eventually meant translating the conversation into something that would take the form of "recommendations." This part of the process represents one of the levels whereby what actually took place at the meetings became translated into the texts of the meeting. So, for example, a fairly general discussion of problems with the application of "community forestry" schemes as development projects, particularly in terms of the ways in which these schemes do not always recognize or uphold land tenure rights of Indigenous Peoples, became recommendation number twenty-one of the Northern Working Group, which read:

> IAF [International Arrangement on Forests] and CBD should encourage member states to develop new institutional arrangements, such as an Indigenous Peoples' forest tenure, consistent with the community forest movement, which would additionally address Indigenous Peoples' rights, and incorporate their unique forest values and interests. (Northern Working Group Draft Recommendations)

Throughout the process this translation of discussion to institutional discourse was facilitated by the group members who were more familiar with the policymaking processes. At times, group members suggested terminology or phrasing that would constitute a concrete recommendation. In terms of the institutional ethnographic accessibility of this process, I was attentive to the ways in which we were all collaborating to translate the interests of the group members into something that is both institutionally accountable and recognizable.

Additionally, after all four working groups presented their recommendations during a plenary session, a smaller "drafting group" consolidated the recommendations into a preamble and eighty-one recommendations grouped around several thematic areas. While this product had to be accepted and "adopted" as the final recommendations of the meeting by the participants, the members of the drafting group used some degree of discretion in crafting the final list of recommendations. Often, though, the recommendations were incorporated verbatim into the final text. For example, the recommendation of the Northern Working Group quoted above showed up as recommendation number fifty-six of the final list of recommendations. Between the original discussions and the final recommendations, there were several layers of work that served to translate the discussions into the texts of the Expert Meeting.

In terms of this process of translation of experience into texts, the goals and objectives of the meeting focused the process so that "Traditional Forest-Related Knowledge" (often simply referred to as TFRK) came to stand in for a whole range of actual experiences. It became apparent to me that this move was an intentional, although not articulated, objective of the meetings. Making "experience" institutionally recognizable allowed for issues that are crucial to Indigenous Peoples to find their way onto the agendas of international policymaking processes. As *TFRK* is a recognizable term within both the CBD and UNFF process, it carries considerable conceptual currency. Without the translation and abstraction of these individualized experiences into terminology that is recognizable as being part of the work of the intergovernmental bodies, the capacity to influence the work of these bodies and to get "interests" on to the agenda is minimized. At the same time, however, the institutional discourse serves to displace the particularities and local substance of people's experience.

This phenomenon, that I've come to think of as "intentional institutional capture," whereby practitioners self-consciously go through the process of translating "interests" into institutional discourse, works with the notion of "institutional capture" as it is explored in Smith's work. It speaks to the insider knowledge of the participants in the larger policymaking processes in the sense that they recognize that, in order to be effective in the process, they must work within the process and the conceptual frames of the organization. Effective participants recognize that their participation is circumscribed by the appropriate terminology, as well as their role in the process. For example, while only governments can be members of the UN and are therefore accorded primary status, the participants who are not representatives of UN member states are incorporated into the meetings in various ways. The UNCED process, for example, defined nine "major groups" of stakeholders, often referred to as "civil society" in UN documents and negotiations. These nine groups of stakeholders are defined as women, children and youth, international NGOs, Indigenous Peoples, workers and trade unions, local authorities, scientific and technical communities, business and industry, and farmers.

At the level of actual meetings, while there is some discretion on the part of participants in terms of how UN rules of procedure are applied, there are strict guidelines regarding the participation of "civil society." All NGOs sending representatives to the meetings must be accredited by the Economic and Social Council (ECOSOC) of the United Nations. The accreditation process has specific stipulations and accreditation must be reviewed through a formal procedure every three years. Within the accreditation process, NGOs are assigned a particular status based upon the relevance of the work of the NGO to the work of the Economic and Social Council. This assigned status then organizes the ways in which NGOs are allowed to contribute to the meetings.[5]

Beyond knowing when one is "allowed" to speak (make an intervention) in a meeting as a member of "civil society," the knowledge of the discursive terrain is crucial to being an effective participant in the process. A striking example of this was articulated to me by participants in the Expert Meeting who had also attended the meeting of the UNFF that had taken place in May of 2004 (UNFF 4). Apparently, during an opportunity for NGOs to make interventions, an individual took the occasion to speak without working in conjunction with other NGOs and Indigenous Peoples and without tying his comments into the salient language and terminology of that particular meeting. According to those who were present during this incident, the result was damaging to the NGO and Indigenous Peoples' Organization (IPO) community.

Of course, part of being an effective participant involves the constant efforts aimed at producing spaces for shifts in the terminology so that the actual resulting documents are more in line with the participants' interests. Regardless, the very nature of "institutional capture" results in a text that abstracts away from the actual experiences that are translated into the institutional discourse. In fact, NGOs regularly articulate frustration with this very conundrum. While recognizing that they are participating in a process that results in documents that are very distant from what they would ultimately like to see, NGO participants who do participate in the process see their activities as being organized around keeping a set of interests in the process that might otherwise be disregarded entirely. For example, NGOs fought very hard to oppose a legally binding agreement on forests. While, during the UNCED process, they had initially supported the negotiation of a forest convention "with teeth," they were concerned about the shape that the convention began to take as it was negotiated. It became apparent that the terms of the convention, while taking up the terminology of sustainable forest management, would actually support the interests of business and trade as the convention reflected neoliberal economic values. Thus, there continues to be much suspicion, on behalf of NGOs and IPOs who are familiar with the forest policy process, towards negotiating a legally binding forest convention. In fact, this was one of the issues that had to be explained to participants in the Expert Meeting who were less familiar with the politics of the international negotiations. Some of the process of bringing participants "up to speed" on the international commitments was formally integrated into the Expert Meeting, as members of the secretariats of the UNFF and CBD were asked to make presentations to the participants on relevant commitments. Other dissemination of work knowledge was done far more informally during the work of the smaller groups or over meals and in the corridors. What was happening was that people were being taught by more experienced practitioners about two (connected) levels of the process—the politics of the negotiations and the discursive language of policymaking.

As the meeting went on, I was attentive to places where the tensions between actual experience and the language of policymaking surfaced. Participants regularly expressed a critique of policymaking discourse as being detached from "on the ground" reality. The term *on the ground* was intended to encapsulate the realm of experience—where actual activities are taking place and the effects of deforestation or land tenure battles can be seen. The organizers, and others who were more familiar with the international processes, were aware that a certain degree of "institutional capture" needed to take place in order for this meeting to have any influence over the targeted policymaking processes. Thus, while the meetings were designed to get a wide range of people to bring their experiences to the table, they were also designed to mediate that experience into a form that could be recognizable by the institution.

In many ways, the subsuming of experiences into the frame of "TFRK" throughout the course of the Expert Meeting exemplifies the conundrum inherent in "institutional capture." On the one hand, in order to be recognized by the institution, one needs to be savvy as to what discourse is institutionally recognizable. Gillian Walker explores exactly this dynamic in her work on the women's movement and the ways in which activists contributed to the development of a discourse of "family violence." As Walker states,

> in order to be heard, women served on committees and task forces, shaped funding proposals to fit governmental imperatives; and scrambled to prepare briefs for professional bodies and for various government hearings and conferences. Working in this way reorganized our work into a more professional mode as pressure and lobbying groups or as service providers (Walker 1995: 77, quoted in Smith 2005: 118).

As Walker articulates, the type of analysis I'm developing in this chapter is not merely a theoretical exercise. Walker (1995) states that instead, it is "an attempt to discover what documents can show us about how feminist work is caught up, though our participation in their formation, into processes of absorption and transformation" (p. 77). While Walker speaks of her work with the women's movement, her analysis is very apt for the ways in which "Indigenous Issues" get incorporated into the politico-administrative regime. In the case of the Expert Meeting, the disparate (yet, in significant ways, common) experiences of Indigenous Peoples were intended to be "reorganized" so that they could be effectively directed toward the UNFF and CBD. The rubric of "Traditional Forest-Related Knowledge" (TFRK) served as a way of capturing and presenting this wide range of experiences. However, as is explored in Pence and Wilson's project (this volume), the language of the policymaking regime is not that of Indigenous communities. An entire worldview is encapsulated in the texts and documents. Visvanathan (1991) articulates his critique of the ways in which the policymaking world effects new measures of control in the following:

> The new epidemic of reports uses the style of concern to control: it restates certain problems to erase peoples' memory of them. . . . But note, the entire act of violence is sanitized. There is no Cortez or Shakha here. It is killing through

> concepts, through coding, by creating grammars that decide which sentence can be spoken and which cannot. It is from such a perspective that the Brundtland Report—well intentioned as it is—must be seen not as a statement of intention, but in terms of the logic of the world it seeks to create and impose. (p. 378)

In many ways, the process of translation into policy-speak shifts the original meaning of experience in important ways. As was recognized by the participants in the Expert Meeting, TFRK is, in part, important to the policymaking regime due to the possible economic benefits of that knowledge. Just as Visvanithan (1991) explores the way in which conceptualizing a "tree" as "timber" immediately brings it under the purview of capital, subsuming actual experiences under the rubric of TFRK effects this same shift. There is a particular "logic of the world," as Visvanathan would have it, which is effected by the documentary reality. In line with Turner's (2003) analysis of the ways in which texts operate to shape residents' strategies and Walker's (1990, 1995) analysis of the ways in which the larger policymaking arena shapes the activities of women trying to make social change, the discursive and procedural terrain of the intergovernmental forums (UNFF and CBD) provided an overarching framework for the activities that took place under the auspices of the Expert Meeting, with consequences for the ways in which "interests" showed up within the politico-administrative regime.

Here I have moved away from the actual activities and into the analysis that one might begin to formulate from the data. Again, I don't claim to have completed an institutional ethnography on the issues that I discuss above. I am envisioning a continuation of this project that would explore several of these themes in more depth, which involves attending UN meetings, observing practitioners, and talking to participants. I'd like to talk to organizers of the Expert Meeting to see what they thought of the process, in terms of how it fed back into the CBD and UNFF processes. I'm interested in looking more closely at the Expert Meeting declaration and recommendations to try to map out the ways in which they take up (and attempt to shift) the larger discursive terrain that ties the Expert Meeting into a range of extant negotiation processes. Additionally, I'd like to get more of an in-depth look at how some of the participants in the Expert Meeting engage in these particular spheres of strategy work, such as UN-related meetings, in order to get their interests "on the table."

However, as a preliminary project, my objective in this chapter has been to point out some of the specific characteristics of institutional ethnographic research and thread those elements through some data that I am in the process of collecting. I understand research "method" to be far more than "a collection of research techniques and procedural guidelines" (Gubrium and Holstein 1997: vii). I would agree with Gubrium and Holstein when they argue that it is instead "closer to what Thomas Kuhn . . . describes as a paradigm—a distinctive way of orienting to the world." Given this understanding of research methods as being rooted in a specific ontology, I have tried to illustrate some of the ways in which one can apply the approach provided by institutional ethnography to some data I'm in the process of collecting and thinking through. The objective in this chapter was to work back and forth between the data and the "distinctive way of orienting to the world" that is specific to institutional ethnography. I've tried to present the preliminary data in ways in which one can begin to envisage a larger project stemming from this analysis. Through these points of entry, guided by the ontology of institutional ethnography as a method of inquiry, one can begin to make institutions such as the UN "ethnographically accessible."

Notes

1. I want to thank both Susan Turner and Dorothy Smith for reading and commenting on a prior draft of this chapter. Both provided excellent feedback, for which I am very grateful.

2. For a more detailed discussion of "conceptual currency," see Kamini Grahame's analysis of the way in which "skill" operates as valuable conceptual currency within the job training enterprise (Grahame 1999).

3. For an excellent review of international forest policy processes and an analysis of some of the reasons why the negotiations have taken up particular issues and not others, see David Humphreys's *Forest Politics: The Evolution of International Cooperation* (1996).

4. Both the declaration and complete set of recommendations can be viewed at http://www.international-alliance.org/tfrk_expert_meeting.htm.

5. An NGO receives either "General consultative," "Special consultative" or "Roster" status. NGOs designated with General consultative status can propose agenda items for ECOSOC and its subsidiary bodies. They may also address ECOSOC (make interventions during meetings) and can circulate statements of up to 2,000 words at ECOSOC meetings. NGOs with Special consultative status cannot speak at ECOSOC, whereas they *are* allowed to speak at the meetings of the subsidiary bodies of ECOSOC, such as the CBD. NGOs with Special status may *not* propose agenda items and are limited to statements of 500 words for circulation at ECOSOC meetings. NGOs on the Roster have no formal rights in UN deliberations. As of 2004, there were a total of 131 NGOs with General status, 1376 with Special status, and 911 on the Roster.

11

U.S. Legal Interventions in the Lives of Battered Women: An Indigenous Assessment

Alex Wilson and Ellen Pence

Introduction

On a spring night, my brothers and I were returning to our home community from the nearest city, a six-hour drive along isolated roads. Near the midpoint of the longest, emptiest stretch of road, we stopped to clean our windshield at a gas station that had been closed for the night several hours before. That is where we saw her—a young Native woman, no more than 20, sitting hunched by the road. When she saw that we had noticed her, she crouched back into the long grass. Her face was streaked from tears. I approached her and asked if she needed a ride. We were from the same community so she accepted the ride and gingerly got into the car. After an hour or so she began to talk about what had happened. She and her family had been at the Sundance. On the way home something had set her husband off—whether it was something she said, the kids crying or whatever, she didn't know. Her husband had hit her in the face and then threw her out of the truck. She had been hiding by the side of the road afraid that he would come back and hurt her more, or that the police would find her and something worse would happen. Several of her husbands' family members worked in the tribal office, one as a social worker and others as band councillors.

FOR MANY INDIGENOUS WOMEN, the scenario described above is not shocking. This story and many others like it are about the difficulties that Indigenous women who have been the victims of domestic assault encounter when they seek protection (or simply a respite) from the violence in our communities. Like this young woman, we, the members of the Native Women's Research

Project, have asked ourselves: *Can the U.S. legal system help us? Will we find protection and support from our own communities' legal systems?* Looking for answers, we turned to the women at the side of the road, and the women and men who help them. This chapter describes this process of consultation—what we did, how we did it, and the answers we found.

Mending the Sacred Hoop (MSH) is an Indigenous group within a domestic abuse advocacy program in Duluth, Minnesota. MSH provides training assistance to tribes across the country who are organizing in cities, towns, and reservations to confront violence against Native American women by their partners.

Mending the Sacred Hoop applied for funding from the National Institute of Justice under the corporate umbrella of Minnesota Program Development Inc. (MPDI) in order to conduct an analysis of the U.S. criminal justice system's handling of domestic assault cases. While some tribes still have strong traditional systems of responding to such violence, most are in some process of developing legal responses to domestic abuse. As tribes seek financial support to build intervention systems, they are often compelled or convinced to model those interventions after the institutional responses of the U.S. legal and human service systems. The question we wanted to explore was twofold. First, can Tribal Nations look to the U.S. legal system for effective intervention strategies to protect the physical and sexual safety of Indigenous women? Second, what interventions, if any, can tribal nations adapt from the U.S. legal system that are likely to strengthen and protect the relationship between Indigenous battered women and their children?

Mending the Sacred Hoop staff organized a team consisting of four Indigenous researchers from the University of Minnesota, three elders, and thirteen community members who have either used or worked in local community-based human service agencies. MSH staff sought the assistance of a number of Indigenous experts who work in other parts of the country. Additionally, the project drew on the expertise of a sister organization, Praxis International, which conducts research on analyzing how institutions impact the lives and safety of women.

The research team was asked to conduct a research project that (a) stayed true to Indigenous ways of knowing; (b) met the scientific standards of the federal funding agency; and (c) furthered our understanding of how we could draw from the experience of the U.S. legal system in our efforts to design Indigenous intervention systems to protect battered women from continued abuse (U.S. Department of Justice 2000).

Our first task was to determine what we meant by Indigenous systems of knowing (Meyer 1998; Montour-Agnus 1995). We easily agreed on the five principles we would stand by. These principles are

1. *The communality of knowledge:* (Wilson 2001). We are the interpreters—not the originators or owners—of knowledge. The value of recognizing and honoring spiritual connections, relational accountability, reciprocity, and holism is central to our work.
2. *Recognizing spiritual connections:* (Hanohano 2001). We agreed that our work must recognize the spiritual links between people and the power of spiritual connections. We offered tobacco to practitioners in the legal system and others when we approached them for help in conducting our study. We valued and discussed our dreams after riding with police, observing court hearings, reading countless court files, and listening to women who attended our focus groups. We held a feast to welcome community participants in the study, used talking circles as the format for our focus groups, and continuously imagined ourselves in the shoes of those we encountered as victims, practitioners, and offenders (Wilson 1997; Wilson and Wilson 1999).
3. *Relational Accountability:* As researchers, we are part of our research and inseparable from it. In our interpretation of knowledge, we must be respectful and supportive of the relationships that have been established through the research process (Wilson and Wilson 1998).
4. *Reciprocity:* The notion of reciprocity and the research relationship suggest that the communities of people who are the subjects of the research should be the primary beneficiaries of the research (Steinhauer 1997). Honoring reciprocity, the central goal of the research team has been to conduct research that will improve the lives of Indigenous women who have been battered and the lives of women in Indigenous communities in general.
5. *Holism:* Holism recognizes that people are the sum (and more) of their many parts. Holism reminds us that in the research process, the spiritual, physical, cognitive, and emotional aspects of all the people participating in the research (including the researchers) must be considered. This understanding shaped questions with which we began our research process: How does the current justice system attend to the spiritual needs of Indigenous women who have been battered? The physical? The cognitive? The emotional? These questions were the starting point from which we developed the guiding questions used in interviews and focus groups.

As Indigenous investigators we wanted to find out how the U.S. legal system organized its workers to think about and act on these cases. We were not out to discover if Indigenous women fared better or worse than non-Indigenous women in the system but instead to ask, "Does the infrastructure of the U.S. legal system orient its intervention in domestic assault cases to the experiences of Indigenous women who are abused and are mothers and partners and members of an Indigenous community?" In finding answer(s) to this question, Indigenous communities can draw from where the U.S. system has succeeded and avoid where it has failed. While Indigenous Nations face huge obstacles to true sovereignty as Indigenous People, we do have the possibility of establishing interventions uniquely designed to protect women who are abused.

The notion of research itself belongs in discourses that have arisen in political and cultural regimes that take for granted the historical subjugation of Indigenous Peoples worldwide. It is not easy, perhaps not possible, to find an alternative that escapes these implicit commitments. The guidance of Indigenous ways of knowing does not guarantee that an alternative has been successful in escaping these implicit commitments (Wilson 2001). Indigenous research methodologies must be consistent with the goals, objectives, audience, values, and beliefs of Indigenous ways of knowing. This research project created an innovative solution to this problem by (a) formulating an Indigenous methodology; (b) putting that methodology in charge of the project; (c) combining it with a sociological method, institutional ethnography, that coordinates with and complements Indigenous methodology. If there is to be change or if the problems located in the non-Indigenous judicial processes are to be avoided, then we need to know just how institutional practices are organized to produce the experiences identified in the analyses developed by the Indigenous methodology. Hence, in this study, the standpoint of Indigenous ways of knowing identified in the four principles of Indigenous methodology described above was complemented by institutional ethnography as a method of inquiry (Campbell 1998b; Campbell and Gregor 2002; Currie and Wickramasinghe 1998; Devault and McCoy, this book; P. Grahame 1998; Smith 1987, 2005).

We designed our research to identify specific processes that were either problematic or helpful for women and then traced them back to how the institutional work that produce them was organized (Smith 1987). We did not try to distinguish between good workers or bad workers, but rather focused on the way all workers were coordinated to participate in institutional processes that either do or do not protect Indigenous women. We recognized from the outset that some of the processes we were investigating, though carried out locally, were organized at state, national, and even cultural levels.

The Research Process

Getting Ready

Mending the Sacred Hoop got us started by holding a feast, to which we invited those members from the community that we hoped to draw into the project. Twenty-four community members attended the feast, and thirteen committed to working with us to collect our data. Based on advice from our elders, we approached each agency director that processes criminal and civil domestic violence cases by offering tobacco and talking to them about the overall goals of our project. We asked for help. We needed access to case files and a broad range of administrative directives, rules, guidelines, and texts that coordinate workers actions on a case. We told the directors that we needed to be able to observe processes and interview workers. We wanted to observe workers at every step of the process and have the ability to interview them both individually and in groups. We explained that we did not want to make judgments about how individual workers were doing their work. Instead we wanted to talk to them about how they are organized to act on cases. Each agency director gave us the okay to interview any staff who chose to participate, to observe each process, and under certain agreements of confidentiality to have open access to their files.

Our work with the thirteen community members began by mapping each step of the criminal process in a domestic assault case and then each step in a civil protection order case. This map was quite linear. We traced each action taken on a case such as a person calling 911 to report an incident categorized by 911 as a "domestic." In each step of case processing, we further identified from our own member's knowledge and preliminary phone contact with agency supervisors, each of the substeps to performing this institutional function. And so, for example, in talking to the dispatch supervisor about what interviews and observations we would need to do we talked through some of their processes, such as the operator taking the call, the dispatcher contacting officers in squad cars to respond, the dispatcher running a records check to see if there is an active protection order in place, and the operator keeping the caller on the line in cases where the danger is escalating.

Our map became a list of sequential actions with frequent points of intersections with other institutional processes, such as the development and maintenance of a statewide database on active protection orders. As part of the mapping process, we educated ourselves on the purpose of each step, read the laws and regulations that governed them, and studied the forms used by practitioners at each step of case processing. At one point we linked our sequence-of-steps map with a second map of regulating bodies at federal, state, county, and local agency levels. With this initiation we were ready to begin reading actual case files, observing and interviewing workers, knowing full well that our beginning mapping process was neither comprehensive nor completely accurate. The mapping process would continue throughout the two-year project.

In applying for our research grant we tried to follow standard research proposal writing formats and immediately got caught up in designing hierarchical relationships among us. After a month or so of experiencing role clashes in our planning and mapping meetings, we recognized the problem and shifted from a structure of principal investigator, research director, research administrator, clerical staff, assistant researchers, and community members to a research with clearly defined roles but egalitarian decision-making relationships.

Collecting Data

After the mapping was completed, we split into two groups. Seven of us worked on the civil system, and ten of us worked on the criminal system. For each step, such as taking a 911 call or filing an initial petition for protection order, we gathered multiple sources of data. We referred to any part of the process where a worker does something to a case as "an interchange" (Pence and Lizdas 2001). First we mapped each interchange to see its connection to the whole process. We viewed each interchange as part of a sequence of institutional actions. Steps before and after this interchange helped to determine the worker's actions on a case and the reasons behind the actions taken.

Next, we observed workers at each interchange in the processing of a domestic abuse case and interviewed several workers who perform the task related to each interchange. In uncovering the action at each interchange, we wanted to see what occurred before and after to see how it affected the process. To do this we interviewed practitioners throughout the intervention process to see how their actions impacted individual interchanges or the overall outcome of a case. (See, for example, Emerson, Fretz, and Shaw 1995; Schwartzman 1993; Spradley 1979). Of course the use of the term case *outcome* was quite loaded. For the practitioners we interviewed it typically meant, Was there a conviction? Who was convicted, of what? Did she get a protection order? What were the reliefs granted to her by the court? Were some reliefs she requested denied? Most of us were community-based Indigenous women and men. Our notion of outcome was both the institutional disposition of the case but also what we could glean from the data that happened for the woman who was being abused and what we could imagine did not happen. We continued to gather and read all of the key regulatory texts: laws, policies, or directives that related to each interchange. Finally, we reviewed all of the administrative texts, such as forms and matrices that standardize a worker's actions at each of these interchanges; and we read files, reports, and case notes related to cases involving Indigenous women as victims or offenders. We weren't trying to count numbers or provide a statistical analysis of how often certain activities occurred. Rather, we read files to find out how processes generally worked.

In addition to mapping each interchange, we held focus groups with Indigenous women inviting them to describe their experiences related to each step of the process. Following all of our observations, interviews, and focus groups, we debriefed on tape, transcribed these debriefing meetings, and included the community researcher's experience of the process as part of our data. We recorded and transcribed the stories of how members experienced getting into squad cars, walking into people's homes, sitting in courtrooms, and interviewing workers in the system. Figure 11.1 below depicts the data-gathering process.[1]

We met as a group twice a month to discuss our data. We kept detailed notes of individual and collective experiences of the process. Eventually the research team began to identify themes in our discussions and started to talk about certain features of the U.S. legal system that continually manifested itself in the data. One of our goals had been to uncover ways in which the

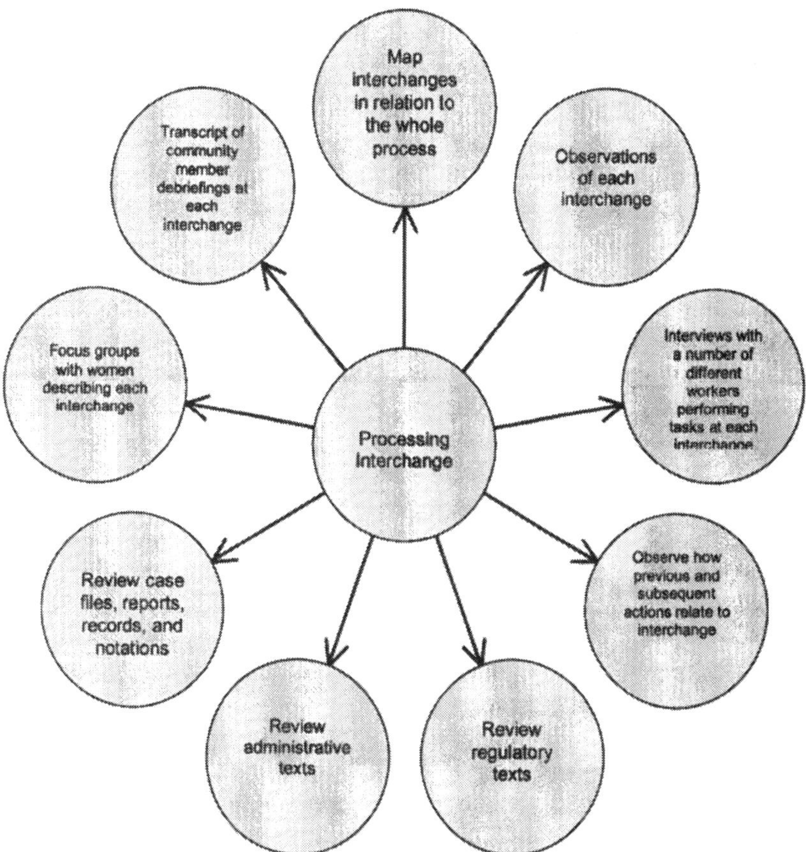

FIGURE 11.1.
Data-Gathering Process

criminal justice system and civil protection order process served to protect and enhance the relationship between Indigenous women and their children. We found, however, almost no evidence of attempts to do so in the criminal justice system and little regard for these issues in the civil protection order process. Lila George, a coinvestigator on the project, has written extensively about this absence in our full research, but we have not discussed it here (see Mending the Sacred Hoop 2000).

Data Analysis

As community members finalized their observations and interviews, they gradually stopped coming to the meetings. The interactive data collection completed, and the long road of analysis and writing ahead of us, we realized we hadn't planned a way to keep the community team involved in such a lengthy and time-intensive process. Wishing we had the team still together, we forged on with the academic research team and one of our elder advisors, Margaret Big George, and waded through our tremendous pool of data.

In sifting our data, we would locate a particular way of doing things that seemed to be problematic from an Indigenous woman's perspective or position. This we would identify it as a theme. Once we identified a theme, such as "overly specialized labor force," we systematically worked through our data to see if indeed this was a consistent feature defining the way the U.S. legal system intervened in the lives of women. To ensure a critical analysis of the most common features or themes emerging from our data collection, we decided to eliminate elements that didn't appear consistently throughout the process: if a problem seemed to be unique to only one small aspect of case-processing or one or two interchanges; to particular cases that were somehow different than others; or to a particular practitioner's unique way of handling a case. While there were a number of other features that we did and could have identified, we realized that our resources and time constraints would require us to choose a few to fully explore. We focused our written analysis and our final report on the following six: (1) problematic fragmentation and specialization of actions and workers' jobs; (2) problematic use of institutional categories; (3) the subsuming of real time into institutional time without adapting to potential harmful consequences in some cases; (4) the problematic use of texts to standardize practices; (5) the lack of ways for workers to engage in authentic communication with women who are abused and the subsequent reduction of women to data point status; and finally (6) the consistent sidetracking of violence as the cause for state intervention.

In our final research report (Mending the Sacred Hoop 2000) we fully document how these problematic features permeate case processing in the U.S.

legal system and create gaps or disjunctures between the states' intervention and how Indigenous women experience violence.[2]

Uncovering Problematic Features of the U.S. Legal System

Throughout our eighteen months of observing, interviewing, reading case files, making sense of bureaucratic case management procedures and forms, analyzing directives and laws, and talking with groups of Indigenous women and professionals in the U.S. legal system, we constantly found ourselves talking about a "they" who always eluded us in the local setting of our study. For example, we would say, "They designed this process to . . ." or, "They don't allow women to. . . ." We had expected to find "them," the ones who hold the power, at the top. Perhaps we expected "them" to be the judges or the state supreme court or the state legislature. However, in the end, we found the power we sought was not located in a position that one or more people held but in the processes and structures of the legal system.

We recognize that the Indigenous community's objections to what is "going on" in the U.S. legal system reflect more than a difference in theory, language, concepts, or priorities. They are rooted in a fundamental difference in how we see social reality in comparison to how professionals in the U.S. criminal and legal system are organized to see that reality. We want to emphasize that the differences between those of us on the outside watching the process and those on the inside carrying it out are not so much the difference of personal background, loyalties, political philosophies, or cultural experiences but a difference in where we are located.

Professionals working in the U.S. legal system are located inside a complex apparatus of social management in which, as professionals, they are coordinated to think and act within the relevancies and frameworks of that apparatus. As a group, we felt inadequate to accomplish the task of naming and fully uncovering all of the ideological practices we encountered. However, we could see what did not fit for us. We could see that integral to the legal system was a process of pulling real experience apart from the *case* to be managed. We could actually pinpoint where and how actual experiences were replaced with institutional renderings of those experiences in ways that subverted legitimate attempts to protect women. We could find, occurring in dozens of institutional interchanges, the loss of women's real experience and the replacement of it with a fabricated experience.

We continuously reminded ourselves to avoid discussions about the individual behaviors of practitioners or of their attitudes or comments. Instead, we focused on what institutional processes instructed the worker's thoughts and actions which lead to intervention that did not attend to the most cherished values of Indigenous people—a connection to our relatives, a sacredness of women and the bond between women and children, the notion of holism and the interconnectedness of all of our experiences, and the need for honesty and integrity in all of our dealings. In this painfully inadequate summary of our work we have attempted to describe and highlight a number of concrete ways we saw the U.S. legal system produce a false representation of the problem of violence that Indigenous women experience and embark on an equally unrelated and unreliable solution to that violence. In the end, the power or powerful people we sought were found in the processes that pervade the system. We found that when practitioners acted on "cases," they did so with techniques, mechanisms, and procedures, rooted in Westernized concepts that had little to do with women's lived experience. Knowledge about women's lives then rested with disjointed and highly abstracted ways of thinking about Indigenous women, their families, and the violence that they experienced.

Fragmentation and the Specialization of Actions and Workers' Jobs

We begin by looking at the how the U.S. legal system isolates an incident from people's lives, defines it, and divides its response to that incident into a series of precise and distinct steps, each of which has its own specialists, and none of whom has an overview of the whole case.

Institutional specializations divide the broad reality of a woman's everyday life into distinct, institutionally defined problems. Different agencies and administrative processes are in place to intervene in aspects of her situation as if they were unrelated to each other. To the "system," she may be a medical case, a police case, a divorce case, a civil protection order case, a child protection case, a chemical dependency case, a welfare case, a mental health case. She might be simultaneously drawn into a number of agencies subjecting her to different case management procedures. So there could be eight different agencies operating in a woman's life, each having its own case management process itself divided up into series of fragmented interchanges. Each interchange is assigned a specialist, which leaves a woman with many different people charged to ensure that a step in the process is carried out in a prescribed institutional manner. That alone is a maze not easily navigated. Add to that a process that is coordinated, not by a person, but by a file—a collection of texts that acts almost as an active person in the process. One life, eighteen practitioners, seventy-six interchanges, and eight different agencies, later, all working towards their own goals oftentimes working at cross-purposes to one another, and not one practitioner knowing the totality of the circumstances. For example, in one case a woman's situation was being processed as a divorce case, and the abuser was granted joint legal custody of their children, with visitation every other weekend. He was told by the court to work out the details with her to pick up the children. At the same time, in protection order court, he was ordered to have no contact with her or the children. In his court-ordered alcohol treatment program, she was asked to come in for family therapy. Domestic violence advocates offered her groups separate from her abuser and did not allow the provision of counseling that she could attend with him.

In our analysis, we found that this kind of fragmented approach to complex situations created many limitations in protecting Indigenous women. Fragmented methods of intervention in the private lives of community members is so integral to the social landscape in modern Westernized states that it is rarely the focus of critique. Rather it is accepted as an inevitable feature of human social interaction. In our investigation it became the first observable gap between the reality of Indigenous women seeking protection from abuse and the state's intervention designed to provide that protection.

In addition, the specialization of job functions contributed significantly to what we saw as victim-blaming attitudes by practitioners in the system. When her interests and the institutional task did not coincide, the woman was "uncooperative." Her lack of "cooperation" might make perfect sense if one were to know her entire life, but this frequently became neither relevant nor apparent to the practitioner. Disjunctures of this kind are interpreted by practitioners in the system as the victim's problem rather than a problem stemming from case-processing.

We observed countless examples of missed opportunities to "get the whole picture," resulting from the specialization of practitioners' work, including 911 operators who rarely anticipated information needs beyond the responding police and police officers who stopped their investigations at the point of getting sufficient evidence to make an arrest. We found many examples of practitioners who did not have enough information or resources to perform their duties. For example, probation officers charged with monitoring offenders' compliance with probation agreements were not aware of orders in civil protection order court, family court, or juvenile court, yet their clients were obligated as part of their probation to comply with those orders. We found dozens of examples of how this fragmented system makes adequate protection of battered women improbable.

Institutional Use of Categories

We observed how the work of institutional practitioners in the U.S. legal system is regulated through devices such as rules, regulations, guidelines, officially authorized definitions, matrices, forms, protocols, and directives that are standardized across particular jurisdictions and work settings. These devices ensure that workers operating in different locations, agencies, and time frames are coordinated in their actions. It is a distinctly Westernized way of pulling highly individualized situations or events into clearly delineated categories to organize how their practitioners perceive, discuss, and handle institutional business. The categories operate in selective fashions that don't necessarily represent what had actually occurred, but what was of institutional concern. The information selected by the practitioner at the intersection of an institution and people's everyday lives was put into a category as an expression of a given rule or procedure. Hence, the institutional order in the U.S. legal system puts together a picture of an event that is very different from the way it was actually lived. No one calls 911 to report, "I'm the *victim* of an *in progress misdemeanor, physical no weapon, violation of a protection order.*" Most of the time, neither the categories nor the action that follows make sense in terms of what was going on in people's lives. For example, one case began with a 911 operator and later the responding officer having to determine if a man who had just thrown his child off the front porch, terrorized his wife, and then threatened to kill himself was going to be treated as a child abuser, as a wife abuser, or as a person attempting to commit suicide. (Case was reported in Research Team Meeting, December 2000.) The case was treated as a suicide attempt, and the abuse aspects of the situation disappeared from the institutional radar screen.

Practitioners at the front line are required to categorize but not to describe actualities. Perhaps the most striking example was the use of the institutional term *domestic violence* to group all acts (and at times this meant illegal acts, while other times it seemed to encompass legal acts of self-defense) of violence committed by one intimate partner against another. In one case this term categorized acts of a man beating his partner by kicking her, stomping on her back while she lay facedown in a mud puddle, and dragging her down a gravel path by her hair into the same grouping as her kicking him in the back of his legs as he walked away from her.

In our investigation, we identified a number of ways in which institutional categories were either unsuccessful in achieving the protection of women who were abused or resulted in situations in which it was the abused rather than the abuser who was punished. During our study, we noted that at each point of intervention (i.e., police investigation, prosecution, and sentencing), although practitioners may proceed entirely properly within institutional rules or guidelines, the categories used to define the relevance to the institutional mandate may obstruct rather than promote the protection of victims of ongoing abuse.

One example was the case of Flora and John James (Community E, Police report 59). John has been physically abusing Flora for many years. One particular night, John attempted to strangle Flora and hit her head several times against a wall. She then stabbed him four times in the chest. John was taken to the hospital, and police treated the case as an "attempted homicide." The categorization of the incident in this manner prompted very specific ways of collecting statements and evidence. Because Flora used what is institutionally defined as "deadly force" with a weapon, her account of how John choked her, struck her repeatedly in the head, and threatened to kill her became an explanation for her motive to use deadly force rather than the evidence for an assault case against John. Her status as a victim was legally compromised when she stabbed him a final time after he had dropped to the floor.

When we, as Indigenous women, reviewed this and similar cases, we tried to understand the actions of practitioners, specifically, how their actions are institutionally organized. In the institutional process, Flora and John's experiences were reduced to a criminal case. Yet they were so much more. The case was rooted in both Flora and John's poverty, their use of alcohol, in how their lives were marginalized within their own community and the larger society, and in the experiences that brought John to the point of beating Flora over and over again. We asked, as members of the Indigenous community: What about this woman who was living a nightmare? Who was trying to help her? Who is there to help him? Who is now in danger?

In criminal cases, the goal of successful prosecution shapes how law enforcement officers activate institutional categories. Flora James was the suspect, not the victim. Once the categories had been determined, the lines of investigation and the reports written by the police became the primary resource of information in later stages of the processing of the case. A framework in institutional terms is transmitted forward, controlling what happens next and how the case is pursued. The documentation is organized in the early stages by the possibility of a homicide, and then, when John is recovering, with the felony assault charge that is brought against Flora. Other possibilities disappear from view. If Flora's husband had also been charged with assault, it would be easier for her to convince a jury that she acted in self-defense. However, backtracking was not possible once the case had been structured around Flora's assault; the information needed to support Flora's claim that she was in need of protection from John, or to even prosecute John for assaulting Flora, was simply not there.

In the full report we document a number of ways in which the U.S. legal system's reliance on the use of categories to standardize how individual workers act thwarted the goal of public safety and in fact appeared to increase the likelihood of future violence. We find and document a use of categories that consistently failed to attend to the complexities of the situations of Indigenous women and men.

Institutional versus Lived Time

Institutions manage everyday world occurrences in a time zone decidedly different from how we as members of a community live. As we observed the institutional responses to, and the processing of domestic violence cases, we became aware of how "institutional time" is imposed on and overlays lived time.

Domestic violence erupts in the world we live in. It arises in relationships that are ongoing and part of a reality that we experience through touch, sight, sound, and feeling. But the institutional process is not responsive to how we actually live our experiences of fear and insecurity. We know that a domestic dispute can escalate into serious and life-threatening violence, sometimes ending in death. The eruption of violence in lived time can be fast—within minutes something can escalate from verbal to the point of putting a woman's life in danger. Once the police have arrived institutional time kicks in: the man is arrested; three days later he is out of jail; weeks later he is arraigned; seven months later the woman is subpoenaed; nine months later, the day his trial is to begin, he pleads guilty. Lived and institutional times intersect in some institutionally defined events; but once the institutional process begins, institutional "efficiency" takes priority over victims' needs. In our report we show how institutional categories and reporting practices that are integral to case management lift events out of an individual's everyday setting and enter them into a time zone controlled, organized, and coordinated by processes that are negotiated by practitioners in the system.

Our scrutiny of more than a hundred criminal cases led us to conclude that the only occasions on which institutional and lived time coincide are in the early hours following an assault. In that time, dispatchers and, for the most part, the responding officers seem responsive to the lived time of the victims and offenders involved. However, after the initial 911 call and police response to the emergency, the case proceeds through a maze of administrative steps, completely unresponsive to what might be happening in the victim's life. When practitioners talk about a case, it is almost exclusively about the administrative process; what is happening between actual people has no other relevance.

Institutional time in the U.S. legal system is organized in fixed sequences of steps. In addition, specific scheduling practices are adopted in the interests of efficiency. For example, "bunches"[3] of cases involving one specific institutional response such as arraignments, bail hearings, pretrials, etc., are heard on the same day. Dozens of cases are "bunched" so that a large number of each are acted upon at the same time. This also means that cases are treated in rapid-fire fashion. In the pretrial hearings that we observed, most cases were disposed of in a matter of three to five minutes. More hotly contested situations would take an extra ten minutes at the most. The push was on moving cases along without holding up the flow of the assembly line. There was pressure on everyone not to crowd up an already overloaded court calendar. Yet in the cases we observed (Community E, Case Follow-up 3, 4, 5, 10, 13, 14, and 17), when we tried to estimate the time someone actually worked on the case, we conservatively guessed that most cases take fewer than ten hours of actual work but months to accomplish.

Texts in the U.S. Legal System

In the early stages of our meetings we had the opportunity to spend days with Dorothy Smith. She provided a way for us to think about how to observe and interview and, of course, to read the texts we would be gathering and seeing in case management processes. We ended our two days with a little phrase: "if we're going to use Smith, we're going to do texts." We tried to follow her many tips on reading and seeing texts in action in all of our observations and interviews: "see what the text is doing," "it is not inert," "don't read a report as a factual account of what happened," and "find the institutional account of a course of action taken by a worker in the system."

In all of our observations, interviews, and court record reviews, we sought to expose the role that texts played in defining the ways that practitioners thought about and acted on cases. To better understand how the legal system intervenes in the lives of Indigenous women who are abused, we paid attention to how the case file organizes the relationship between the state (or its representative worker) and the woman. A case record or file is a key organizational element in taking action—it is the institution's representation of the "incident" (here, the incident is an assault on a woman) that precipitated the opening of the case—so it necessarily reflects the concerns of the institution. Professionals in the legal system are trained to translate what they see and hear from the everyday world into prearranged terms and concepts specific to their field. As practitioners document what they see, hear, and observe in cases through administrative forms, computer screens, narrative reports, and case notes, the reality of the Indigenous woman who has been abused is transformed into an institutional representation of a domestic abuse case. All of these texts act as filters; they select what is relevant and make other aspects, determined not to be of institutional relevance, hard to see.

We saw documents, papers, and computers organize the sequencing of all practitioners' work. For example, a computer screen prompted dispatchers to consider certain information when coding a call. The code they used informed officers how quickly they should respond. It was paperwork that created links between the practitioners who were working in different agencies and performing different tasks, all of which had consequences for the woman. For example, police reports from domestic calls in which children were involved were automatically routed to a child protection agency. That simple paper routing routine had devastating effects for several women and their children. It was in place presumably to protect children. At every point of intervention we observed the use of standardizing texts like a child protection worker's parent/child interaction checklist, a police officer report-writing format, or risk assessment guides used by probation officers recommending bail.

In order to understand what we were seeing in relation to our questions we spent several meetings analyzing in depth three types of texts: a parenting assessment form, a police format for writing investigative reports, and a form used by the court to facilitate a request by a petitioner to drop the protection order. We found that like many of the texts we were seeing in action, each of these texts organized workers to act in ways that transformed women's experiences into something institutionally actionable. But these texts so distorted the reality of the situation that there was little relationship left between what the woman needed and what the institution had produced as her *case.*

By observing and interviewing workers using and producing texts we were able to locate the conceptual framework that told the worker what to note, how to transform what was observed into institutional categories in her or his report, and finally how to link this report (text) to a subsequent step in the process. What we could not find was a way to retain the voices and stories of what had been going on in the lives of the people who were the subjects of these reports or entries into a case file.

We documented a number of ways that texts shape case management in the U.S. legal system. While practitioners admittedly leave their own imprints on these cases—shaped by biases, personalities, and level of knowledge about domestic violence—what they produce fits institutional ways of thinking about cases embedded in forms, rules, regulations, matrices, and so forth that provide the overarching method and structure for managing cases. Regardless of the personal beliefs and work habits of individual practitioners in the system, a general outcome is achieved through the use of standardized forms and formats for documentation.

The Institution Is Deaf to Women's Stories

As Indigenous People, we are storytellers. When we tell stories, what kind of stories we tell, who tells stories, and how they are told are all part of our traditions and cultural customary ways of doing things. In our report, we examine the extent to which the institutional processing of domestic abuse cases under U.S. law is open to hearing women's stories. We started our inquiry on this topic by asking the following: (1) when is a woman allowed to talk to the people acting on her case; (2) how is her knowledge of the situation incorporated into the state's determinations of public safety, truth, and justice; and (3) what restrains women from speaking in this process?

In the end, we found that virtually no part of the process allowed a woman to tell her story as she experienced it. Every interchange had its constraining features. The use of institutional language, relevancies, processes, and ideological frameworks was so overpowering that women's lived experiences were virtually written out of the final story that formed the basis of the state's actions.

As we reviewed our conversations and interviews, three patterns came into focus that shaped the talk between practitioner and battered Indigenous women. The first is a phenomenon we called *communication without dialogue.* Institutions provide formulaic procedures that operate in many settings to restrict how practitioners relate to those involved in their cases. We found only a very few instances in which a practitioner and an Indigenous woman engaged in a truly respectful, open, and free discussion about what was happening to her and what she needed to be safe. The second was the use of *administrative forms* and procedures that prevented the full account of women's experiences from coming forward. As discussed earlier, these forms created a boundary around what could be known about the case. The third was the *intimidation of women* in court processes by the abuser. For example we received a 911 transcript (Community H, 911 Transcript) in which the woman was afraid that her husband would hurt her brother. Because he lived eighty miles away and outside of the 911 district, none the information she gave the 911 operator was communicated to the responding officers. These types of exchanges struck a fundamental chord of dissonance in us, yet they were routine.

Procedures for gathering information for a form or report were a significant point where women's stories got lost. Forms are integral to the institutional process and to organizing sequences of institutional action. We analyzed a number of forms and the respective processes by which they are completed in order to understand how these institutional tools produce an eventual account of the case. In all the forms we reviewed we saw only vague attempts to document an account of events and interpretation of the situation from the woman's perspective. Police report formats, bail-setting interviews, pretrial consultation formats, and presentence investigation processes all treated women as data points eliciting very specific information and rarely calling on the practitioner to flesh out women's accounts. Even when a form did allow a practitioner to draw out a woman's account of events, we found practitioners almost universally failed to use it that way.

The civil court forms for eliciting women's account of events and their desires for state intervention are markedly different from those used in the criminal court process. In civil court, the woman initiates the action and, in her own words, tells the court why she needs protection. However, the judge was not likely to hear the woman's story in her own words in either criminal or civil court due to court procedures. In both the civil and the criminal court, shortcuts avoid proceeding to full trial on these matters. In criminal court, prosecutors and defense attorneys reach plea agreements, thus eliminating the probability that the judge will be exposed to the details of the case and thus learn about the defendant who is about to be sentenced. In civil court, the petitioner is encouraged to negotiate a settlement with the respondent to avoid a lengthy hearing about the facts of the case.

Perhaps the most disturbing practices we observed and uncovered in our examination of women's ability to tell their stories was the use of intimidation by practitioners and, occasionally, by abusers. While we observed a number of overt and covert methods of intimidation, we also discovered a number of recent efforts to reduce the use of those methods. Women, advocates, and some practitioners use the term *revictimization* of women to describe the practices discussed in this section.

We were able to fully document five aspects of that process: (a) the threat of arrest or charges against women who refuse to cooperate with practitioners; (b) the threat of removal of children; (c) the use of force or overt hostility by practitioners against a victim or her family members; (d) turning of a call for help into an unrelated enforcement opportunity for police; (e) the failure of practitioners to curb abusers' intimidation; and (f) the impact of the adversarial structure of the system on the ability of women to provide a full account.

We saw many ways in which institutional processes inhibit women who are victims of domestic abuse from telling their stories. This prevents the judicial process from hearing their account of violence and hence responding appropriately to their needs. These effects are intensified by the institutional distrust built into the U.S. legal system of offender and victim. The nature of the adversarial process lends itself to cover-ups, lies, misrepresentations, obfuscation, and distortions of events.

Our inquiry helped us to see how Indigenous battered women's experiences are stripped of their context when the legal system develops its account of events, which considers each incident to be a discrete act. Often, community observers and the women who experience institutional actions viewed the processes that were taken for granted by practitioners as "odd."

At first we wondered about the humanity and ethics of the people responding to these cases, but we gradually shifted our thinking, recognizing that the problem was less one of the individual practitioners than of the routine institutional processes for dealing with this widespread social phenomenon. Often, what seemed like a callous response from a dispatcher, prosecutor, or jailer was due to institutional frameworks that transformed actual events into institutionally actionable items. Criminal codes, Supreme Court rulings on probable cause and self-defense, legislative definitions of assault and abuse, and liability considerations have defined the parameters of data selected by practitioners as they process cases.

Sidetracking Violence

Our research exposed how legal processes inhibit victims of domestic violence from expressing to the police and the courts the extent, nature, and persistence of the violence they experience. It follows, then, that because the police and courts do not know the extent of the harm being done, there is a gap in how women's experiences of violence can be taken into account in the processing of a case. Institutional practitioners work in an institutional manner; their work engages them with the abuse but not with the abused.

Notification of Release—Arraignment

Following routines and moving cases are institutional objectives seen as pivotal to case-processing; making sure that women are safe is not. Perhaps the clearest example we saw was the application of the law that requires correctional facilities to make "reasonable attempts" to notify the victims of violent offenders prior to the offender's release. Team members observed the following steps of release: (1) immediately after a suspect was arraigned, he was returned to the county correctional facility for release; (2) the suspect changed into his street clothes while the correctional officer completed his release paperwork; and (3) if the victim's name and telephone number had been recorded on the original booking sheet completed by the arresting officer, the correctional officer made phone calls to notify her of the offender's imminent release. Most releases occurred in the midafternoon, and the process took approximately thirty minutes. In all three instances of notification observed, the victims were not available to answer the phone call by the correctional officer.

We were able to observe the documentation of the cases we were present for, as well as an additional five files on domestic-abuse-related releases. In the first case we observed, the file showed that the correctional officer had called the victim three times: 1:06 p.m., no answer; 1:08 p.m., no answer; and again at 1:16 p.m., still no answer. According to departmental policy, three attempts to contact the victim are considered as expending reasonable efforts to notify the victim. Three other files showed a similar pattern of three attempts to contact the victim by telephone within a fifteen-minute period. The correctional officer explained this rapid cluster of calls by stating that once the judge releases a suspect, he does not have the authority to hold him in order to locate the victim for notification. Thus, he makes three calls to comply with the requirement of "reasonable attempt" and allows the suspect to go. Notification becomes especially difficult in practice when, as is often the case, the booking sheet that the officer relies on shows only one and sometimes no number. In Indigenous communities, it is not uncommon for people to have no phone at home. The scheduling of the release may also be a problem as many people are at work during the day. As a backup in each case, a form letter is filled out and mailed to the victim on the day of the suspect's release.[4]

This is an example of how institutions can technically meet regulations introduced to protect the interests of victims, without affording any of the protections its advocates had hoped for. We found the system's accountability mechanisms to be extremely weak, with almost no active engagement by practitioners to notice the failure to protect victims of domestic abuse and promote their change.

Our Conclusions

> My family gathers sweetgrass today. We travel to the site where we have always picked. A truck and other conveniences make the trip and preparations much easier now than it was for my father as a child, or for his parents before him, but this short trip, taken over and over again by my family and ancestors, and the ceremony within which we gather the sweetgrass, seem otherwise unchanged. We know all the eagle nests along the way, notice each new patch of wildflowers, observe the water level of a handful of rivers and creeks, and see that young partridges have already gathered along the road to pick at the glacial gravels.
>
> When we arrive at the spot, we know how to scuttle through the muskeg ditch along a path so that none of us will slip and disappear into the muddy quicksand of the bog. My mom and I gather our first twelve green strands of the grass, braid it, and hand it to my dad. My dad offers some tobacco and recites a Cree prayer, then hangs the braid gently on a tree. This I will do someday, as will my nieces and nephews after me.
>
> We each find a spot in the grass and start picking. Each individual piece is pulled gently from the earth and cleaned off until twelve strands can be tied together with one more piece. This time we tie the strands together with red yarn. These braids will be for my giveaway.

> Sitting on the ground, I smell the sweetness of the grass and watch as the slender blades brush, bend, and twist together in the slightest breeze. Bear musk hangs over the heavy scent of the earth. Little bugs march around and over my body as though I am no more and no less than the landscape they are traversing. For that brief time, we all exist in perfect harmony.
>
> We place the sweetgrass strands on a sheet and soon have gathered enough. We lovingly wrap up the large bundle and start the journey home. We will lay the strands out to dry at home and braid them a few days from now. I will take care of the braids until it is time to give them to friends and other family members.

In Cree and Ojibwe communities, sweetgrass is a sacred plant and medicine that connects us physically, spiritually, emotionally, and cognitively to our present, past, and future. When our ancestors died, they returned to the earth to become part of the soil in which sweetgrass grows. Our ancestors are substantiated in each blade of sweetgrass. When we light and burn a braid in ceremony, our relations are released to us. We are connected, protected, calmed, and reflective.

In sweetgrass ceremonies, we and all living creatures are drawn more closely together, both within the limited physicality of here and now and across the limitless extent of time. This sense of place simultaneously empowers and humbles us. Our ceremonies honor relationship and remind us that we not only are connected but also are accountable to each other. In burning sweetgrass, we invite our ancestors to be our witnesses.

Connection and its correlate, accountability, are fundamental ethics of Indigenous cultures. We learn that all that we do is done for, to, and with others, including our family and community. Our connectedness and the accountability that goes with it are not just a set of behaviors—they are who we are. When we gather sweetgrass, we draw on the knowledge our ancestors accumulated, follow the paths they cleared for us, share the gifts they reserved for us, then watch over and prepare the next generation to continue this task. Each of us brings our share to the group. Braided together, the single strands of sweetgrass become a powerful whole, an expression and substantiation of our relationships.

These traditional values, however, are difficult to preserve in the legal response to violence against Indigenous women. Throughout these legal processes, assaults against women are treated as the actions of individual offenders against individual victims, or of single offenders against the state. Offenders and, in many cases, their victims are separated from their families and communities and isolated in treatment centers and prisons. From the initial contact of a 911 call through the resolution of cases in civil and criminal courts, many of the legal system's practices value opposition and isolation and seek justice in ways that undermine relationships, sever connections, and abandon accountability between people.

We found that the processes and practices of the U.S. legal system ignore the familial and social cohesion that is a vital part of Indigenous cultures. For Indigenous People, women, children, and men are not subjects separate from their relatives, clan, and tribe. They cannot be plucked out of their relations and treated as separate entities. We are tied to our ancestors, our future generations, and our clans in ways that are ignored in every aspect of the U.S. legal system.

The U.S. legal system privileges professional knowledge over the knowledge of laypeople, thus making women powerless to work with intervening practitioners to rid their lives of the violence. The U.S. legal system produces a workforce of practitioners working in each case in limited roles. The institutional structuring of their work means that they may not even be aware of what happens down the line, still less of the outcome of a case. Many of the people we interviewed were aware of the ineffectiveness of their interventions and cared about the people with whom they worked, but once the case passed through their hands, they were unlikely to learn about the outcome of a case.

The system creates a myriad of mechanisms by which institutions elicit conformity from its workforce. These mechanisms include the use of forms, institutional categories, matrices, guidelines, specifically crafted definitions, risk assessments, scoring devices, and so forth. But, at the same time, the mechanisms are not designed to account for the severe social disruption brought about by the colonization of the Indigenous People. Homelessness, alcoholism, and despair are seen as personal dysfunctions rather than normal consequences of the experience of colonization and all of its imprints marking the present-day lives of Indigenous People.

The U.S. legal system produces a series of processes that range from answering a call for help to conducting a trial by jury. For Indigenous women and men, no identities other than victims and offenders are possible. It is inevitable that when context is stripped from an experience, the resulting account cannot be an accurate reflection of what actually happened. The system is designed to understand what generally "goes on" in these "cases" as opposed to what is actually going on in "this case." We noticed, for example, that the institutional framework for reporting cases removed the motivational context from people's narratives; their actions are not readily understandable.

There is no requirement that any one practitioner comprehensively understands what is going on in a "case" from beginning to end. In fact, workers are discouraged from being caught up in the stories, pain, and fears of battered women. They are institutionally and professionally directed to focus only on the efficiency of their particular act of intervention. It is a workforce that, whatever as individuals they may think, can only, in institutional settings, write and talk one-dimensionally about the violence in the lives of Indigenous women and about domestic violence generally. Institutional procedures produce a perspective that locks practitioners responding to Indigenous women into culturally universalizing mechanisms, regardless of the individual worker's personal beliefs about Indigenous People. This results in a continuing process of cultural imposition.

We found ample evidence that the system replicates many of the characteristics of a battered woman's relationship with her abuser: (a) it threatens her with harm if she doesn't cooperate, (b) it threatens her with the removal of her children if she doesn't do something, (c) it tells her when and how she can speak, and (d) it labels her as sick or uncooperative.

We found that the system organized workers to prioritize actions that maintain the function of the institution over those effective in preventing crime and providing public safety. Many of the system's interventions are entrenched in values, customs, beliefs, and philosophical premises that are antithetical to Indigenous values and beliefs.

A Vision of Integrity

The concept of the "sacred circle" is a part of most Indigenous North American cultures. Representations of the sacred circle vary from community to community, but however it may be represented, the fundamental understanding expressed by the sacred circle is common across the communities—that is, that healthy and whole individuals, communities, and Nations are constituted by physical, emotional, cognitive, and spiritual elements. A corollary to this understanding is that individuals, communities, and Nations are at peace only when these elements are in balance and harmony. The philosophy expressed by the sacred circle has been put into action by Indigenous People since the beginning of our time and affected by a commitment to integrity in our everyday language, action, and ceremony. Indigenous People, as individuals and communities, who value and strive for harmony and balance, understand that they are responsible to one another and to their communities and that their communities are accountable to community members.

Systems such as the U.S. legal and justice system, which are structured as hierarchies, stand in sharp contrast to societies structured around a sacred circle. While structural features of the U.S. legal and justice system do not in and of themselves necessarily preclude an individual's choice to act with (or without) integrity, the structure of the system *in its entirety* prevents the state from intervening effectively in domestic abuse cases involving Indigenous women.

During the course of our research, we have attempted to view the U.S. legal system from the standpoint of Indigenous women who have been and are being abused and who have been and are seeking protection from the system. This position led us to envision a system that embraces the Indigenous values of respect for women, holism, and honoring relations—that is, an Indigenous system that operates with integrity. In this section we propose some of the foundational pieces of a system that protects women who are abused and holds offenders accountable to the women (and children) they have abused and to their community of relations.

Towards an Indigenous Criminal and Civil System

An effective intervention in domestic violence against Indigenous women will occur only in a system that enables those who intervene in domestic violence to engage with all aspects of a woman's experience. For a system such as this to operate with integrity, it must incorporate the following understandings:

1. The processes and case management strategies currently employed in the U.S. legal and judicial systems typically are more attentive to institutional needs than to the simultaneous and interrelated needs of Indigenous women who are the victims of domestic abuse. A system that operates with integrity will prioritize and be built around victims' needs for safety, rather than the management needs of the institutional structure.
2. The U.S. legal and judicial system currently deals with domestic abuse involving Indigenous women by focusing on and isolating specific incidents of abuse. A community intervention that approaches domestic abuse with integrity will deal with the entirety of a woman's experience. This means that the intervention will not focus exclusively on an act of violence a woman has experienced but rather will consider and engage with the full range of her needs, be they emotional, physical, economic, cognitive, or spiritual. Just as this incident of violence is only a piece of all of the violence she is experiencing, so is the violence only a piece of her loss of autonomy and a part of her complex life. Those who intervene in domestic violence need to pay attention to all the aspects of violence in a woman's life and all the aspects of her life itself.
3. Practitioners in the current U.S. legal and judicial system currently are held accountable primarily for the specific institutional tasks assigned to them as part of the system's intervention in domestic violence involving Indigenous women rather than for the overall safety of the women who are the victims of violence. In a system that operates with integrity, individuals intervening in domestic abuse are accountable to each other,

collectively accountable to their group and their community and ultimately accountable for the safety of the woman who is the victim of the violence. People who intervene in domestic abuse need to see themselves in relation to the woman they seek to protect and be connected to her in a way that is rooted in her vitality and importance to the community.

4. The gap between the real time in which Indigenous women experience domestic violence and the institutional time in which the U.S. legal system intervenes in that violence endangers women. In a system that operates with integrity, this gap will, wherever possible, be drawn close or bridged. The schedules within which community interventions operate will prioritize the immediate needs of victims. If a woman's need for physical protection is acute, then the community's interventions will proceed with corresponding urgency.
5. In the U.S. legal system's current response to domestic violence involving Indigenous women, a woman's knowledge and understanding of her experiences are displaced by institutionally fabricated abstract representations of her experience. A system that operates with integrity will ensure that a woman who has been the victim of violence is in dialogue with those who are intervening in the abuse. The story she offers, one that is told from the context of her whole life, must be validated and returned to her. She must not be rendered as the representation of an abstract idea, in portrayals of women as victimized, battered, battering, alcoholic, homeless, depressed, dysfunctional, and colonized and/or "native" or not to some legally measurable degree. The system must create opportunities for each woman to voice her knowledge, then listen carefully and incorporate what she knows and what she wants to happen into the community's intervention.
6. In the U.S. legal and judicial system's current response to domestic violence against Indigenous women, responsibility for the protection of women who are abused is taken from the community and discharged to isolated agencies (including tribal agencies) and arms of the government. In a system that operates with integrity, agencies that are given responsibility for the protection of women will share that responsibility with the community at large.
7. In the U.S. legal and judicial system's current response to domestic violence against Indigenous women, practitioners take part only in limited segments of the intervention and are rarely able to see many of the outcomes of their actions. In a system that operates with integrity, people who intervene in domestic violence will be able to maintain their involvement throughout and beyond the formal processes of the intervention.

8. The U.S. legal and judicial system's current response to domestic violence against Indigenous women is prescribed by rigid protocols, procedures, and priorities. A system that operates with integrity must be dynamic, vital, self-reflective, and consequently able to respond to the particular and personal needs of the women it seeks to protect.
9. In the U.S. legal and judicial system's current response to domestic violence against Indigenous women, concern, regard, and respect for a victim of violence are frequently displaced by more immediate concern for the completion of institutional tasks. A system that operates with integrity will consistently treat women with respect and, in that way, provide a model to others, including (most notably) the men who have abused them.
10. In the current response to domestic violence against Indigenous women, crippling limitations are placed on the resources and jurisdiction of tribal legal and judicial systems. In a system that operates with integrity, adequate tribal resources and energy will be devoted to all aspects of the intervention in domestic violence, from prevention to healing. It recognizes that we cannot replace one aspect of the intervention with another. On an individual level, this means that a man cannot start on the healing process before he has stopped committing acts of violence. On the tribal level, this means that we cannot alter one aspect of the intervention system without altering all aspects of our ways of helping our families. The features of the U.S. legal system that became so starkly present for us are replicated in all of our agencies and institutions of social management. We cannot change one and expect results if all the other related interventions are rooted in this same problematic ways of knowing and acting.

The quest for integrity is not easily realized, but the path to it is clear. As Indigenous People work toward restoring or rebuilding our unique ways of creating justice and protecting women and children, we must inquire of each process, each rule, each assumption: Does it honor all our relationships? Is it holistic? Does it promote respect for women?

Notes

1. The chart, figure 11.1, was adapted from a chart given the team by Ellen Pence based on her research with probation and police processes in domestic abuse cases. She also provided a framework for interviews to keep researchers and community members focused on processes rather than individual attitudes of ways of doing things.

2. In addition to organizing our data to show how these features of the system produce problematic outcomes for Indigenous women, we wrote extensively on four aspects of the U.S. legal system not summarized here, including (a) a section analyzing sixteen felony presentence investigations involving men who assaulted Indigenous women, (b) a summary of how we saw the two processes of the civil and criminal system taking up the harm that violence had done to the relationship of women to their children, (c) a piece describing the history of the federal government's restrictions on tribal government's sovereignty in the area of creating systems of social control within tribal nations, and (d) a description of six cases in which serious harm had come to an Indigenous woman and all of the problematic features described in this report were present. For all these see Mending the Sacred Hoop (Peacock et al. 2000).

3. We debated the use of the term *bunching* but decided to leave it in because it was an observation of one of our community members when she reported back on her observation of arraignment court: "they bunched up the oddest things and acted like they were all the same."

4. Recently two law enforcement agencies, Communities E and H, have rewritten their documentation guidelines to require arresting officers to obtain the phone numbers of at least two relatives or friends that can always find the victim. This procedure is being implemented to enhance the ability of the system to keep victims informed of all case status changes, including release from jail (Report to X Bench on the Status of the Civil and Criminal Processing of Domestic Violence Cases, February 2001).

References

ABCNews.com. (Friday, January 24, 2003, 11:05 PM AEDT). Depression twice as high among single-parent kids: study. ABCNEWS.com (Retrieved from http://fact.on.ca/news/news0301/abc030124.htm).

Alarcon, N. 1994. The theoretical subject(s) of this bridge called my back and Anglo-American feminism. In *The postmodern turn*, ed. S. Seidman, 140–152. Cambridge, UK: Cambridge University Press.

Anderson, Gary R. 1984. Children and AIDS: Implications for child welfare. *Child Welfare* 63(1) January: 62–72.

Andre Bechely, L. N. 2005. *To know otherwise: Parents and the inequities of public school choice.* New York: Routledge.

Armstrong, J. 2004. DNA test identifies B. C. man's missing sister. *Globe and Mail*, January 17: A9.

Atkinson, J. M. 1978 *Discovering suicide: Studies in the social organization use of sudden death.* London: Macmillan Press.

Bakhtin, M. M. 1981. *The dialogic imagination: Four essays.* Ed. Michael Holquist. Trans. Caryl Emerson. Austin: University of Texas Press.

———. 1986. *Speech genres and other late essays.* Ed. C. Emerson et al. Austin: University of Texas Press.

Bar On, B. 1993. Marginality and epistemic privilege. In *Feminist epistemologies*, ed. L. Alcoff and E. Potter, 83–100. New York and London: Routledge.

Berger, P. L., and T. Luckmann. 1966. *The social construction of reality: A treatise in the sociology of knowledge.* New York: Anchor Books.

Black, David. 1985. *The plague years: A chronicle of AIDS, the epidemic of our times.* New York: Simon and Schuster.

Bodnar, A., and M. Reimer. 1979. The organization of social services and its implications for the mental health of immigrant women. Report prepared for the Secretary of State in conjunction with the Working Women Community Centre in Toronto.

Bogen, D., and M. Lynch. 1989. Taking account of the hostile native: Plausible deniability and the production of conventional history in the Iran-Contra hearings. *Social Problems* 36(3): 197–224.

Boland, M. G., et al. Children with HIV infection: Collaborative responsibilities of the child welfare communities. *Social Work* 33(6).

Bourdieu, P., and J. C. Passeron. 1977. *Reproduction in education, society and culture.* Trans. R. Nice. London: Sage.

Bourgon, M., and G. Renaud. 1989. AIDS and social work: A fruitful juncture for thought. *The Social Worker/Le Travailleur social* 57(1) Spring: 48–52.

Bresalier, M., L. Gillis, C. McClure, L. McCoy, E. Mykhalovskiy, D. Taylor, and M. Webber. 2002. *Making care visible: Antiretroviral therapy and the health work of people living with HIV/AIDS.* Toronto: Making Care Visible Working Group.

Burton, F., and P. Carlen 1979. *Official discourse: On discourse analysis, government publications ideology and the state.* London: Routledge and Kegan Paul.

Calnan, M., and S. J. Williams. 1996. Lay evaluation of scientific medicine and medical care. In *Modern medicine: Lay perspectives and experiences,* 26–46. London: UCL Press.

Campbell, M. L. 1984. Information systems and management of hospital nursing: A study in social organization of knowledge. PhD dissertation, University of Toronto.

———. 1988. Management as 'ruling': A class phenomenon in nursing. *Studies in Political Economy* 27: 29–51.

———. 1992a. Administering child protection: A feminist analysis of conceptual practices of organization. *Canadian Public Administration,* 34(4): 501–518.

———. 1992b. Nurses' professionalism: A labour process analysis. *International Journal of Health Services* 12: 751–765.

———. 1995. Teaching accountability: What counts as nursing education? In *Knowledge, experience, and ruling relations studies in the social organization of knowledge,* ed. M. Campbell and A. Manicom, 221–233. Toronto: University of Toronto Press.

———. 1998a. Institutional ethnography and experience as data. *Qualitative Sociology* 21(1): 55–73.

———. 1998b. Research on health care experiences of people with disabilities: exploring the everyday problematic of service delivery. Paper presented at the conference "Exploring the Restructuring and Transformation of Institutional Processes: Applications of Institutional Ethnography," October, York University, Toronto.

———. 1999. Home support: What we've learned about continuity and client choice. Discussion paper, Project Inter-Seed: Learning from the health care experiences of people with disabilities. University of Victoria and South Vancouver Island Resource Centre for Independent Living, Victoria, BC.

———. 2001. Textual accounts, ruling action: The intersection of knowledge and power in the routine conduct of community nursing work. *Studies in Cultures, Organizations, and Societies* 7(2): 231–250

Campbell, M. L., B. Copeland, and B. Tate. 1998. Taking the standpoint of people with disabilities in research: Experiences with participation. *Canadian Journal of Rehabilitation* 12(2): 95–104.

Campbell, M. L., and F. Gregor. 2002. *Mapping social relations: A primer in institutional ethnography.* Toronto: Garamond.

Campbell, M. L., and N. Jackson. 1992. Learning to nurse: Plans, accounts and action. *Qualitative Health Research* 2: 475–496.

Campbell, M. L., and A. Manicom, eds. 1995. *Knowledge, experience, and ruling relations: Studies in the social organization of knowledge.* Toronto: University of Toronto Press.

Canadian Association of Schools of Social Work. 1988. *AIDS and social work training in Canada,* Report, Ottawa: Federal Centre for AIDS.

Canning, K. 1994. Feminist history after the linguistic turn: Historicizing discourse and experience. *Signs,* 19(2): 368–414.

Cassin, M. A., and A. I. Griffith. 1981. Class and ethnicity: Producing the difference that counts. *Canadian Ethnic Studies/Etudes Ethniques au Canada* 13(1): 109–129.

Cecchi, Robert Lee. 1986. Health care advocacy for AIDS patients. *Quality Review Bulletin* 12(8) August: 297–303.

Central Toronto Youth Services AIDS Project. 1989. *HIV Infection and AIDS: A policy development framework for children and youth social service agencies.* Toronto: Ontario Ministry of Community and Social Services.

Chamboredon, J. C., and J. Prevot. 1975. Changes in the social definition of early childhood and the new forms of symbolic violence. *Theory and Society* 2(3): 331–350.

Child Welfare League of America. 1990. *Serving HIV-infected children youth, and their families—A guide for residential group care providers.* Washington, DC: Child Welfare League of America Inc.

Christ, G. H., et al. 1986. Psychosocial issues in AIDS. *Psychiatric Annals* 16(3) March: 173–179.

Chua. B. 1979a. Describing a national crisis. *Human Studies* 2: 47–62.

———. 1979b. Democracy as textual accomplishment. *Sociological Quarterly* 20: 541–549.

Church, K. 2005. *Forbidden narratives: Political autobiography as social science.* New York: Routledge.

Clark, E., et al. 1989. An assessment of the psychosocial needs of the HIV antibody positive population using the Montreal health and social service network, Abstracts: V International Conference on AIDS: Tile Scientific and Social Challenge, June 4–9, in Montreal, Quebec, Canada. Ottawa: International Development Research Centre.

Clausson, N. I. 1989. AIDS: The community-based response. *Canadian Journal of Public Health* 80 (Supplement 1) May/June: 18–20.

Clough, P. 1993. On the brink of deconstructing sociology: Critical reading of Dorothy Smith's standpoint epistemology. *Sociological Quarterly,* 34(1): 169–182.

Code, L. 1991. *What can she know?* Ithaca, NY: Cornell University Press.

Currie, D. H., and A. Wickramasinghe. 1998. Engendering development theory from the standpoint of women. In *Learning to write: Women's studies in development,* ed. D. H. Currie, N. Gayle, and P. Gurstein, 175–192. Vancouver: Collective Presss.

Darville, R. 1995. Literacy, experience, power. In *Knowledge, experience and ruling relations: Studies in the social organization of knowledge,* ed. M. Campbell and A. Manicom, 249–261. Toronto: University of Toronto Press.

de Montigny. G. A. J. 1989. Accomplishing professional reality: An ethnography of social workers' practice. PhD dissertation, University of Toronto.

———. 1995a. *Social working: An ethnography of front-line practice.* Toronto: University of Toronto Press.

———. 1995b. The power of being professional. In *Knowledge, experience, and ruling relations: Studies in the social organization of knowledge,* ed. M. Campbell and A. Manicom, 209–220. Toronto: University of Toronto Press.

Deen, Thalif. 2005. World's celebrated paper factory tries to save trees. *Asian Tribune* May 20.

DeVault, M. L. 1991. *Feeding the family: The social organization of caring as gendered work.* Chicago: University of Chicago Press.

———. 1999. *Liberating method: feminism and social research.* Philadelphia: Temple University Press.

De Vault, Marjorie, and Liza McCoy. 2002. Institutional ethnography: Using interviews to investigate ruling relations. In *Handbook of interviewing research: Context and method,* ed. J. F. Gubrium and J. A. Holstein, 751–775. Thousand Oaks, CA: Sage Publications.

Dhooper, S. S., David D. Royse, and Thanh V. Tran. 1987/1988. Social work practitioners' attitudes towards AIDS victims. *Journal of Applied Social Sciences* 121, Fall/Winter: 108–123.

Diamond, T. 1992. *Making gray gold: Narratives of nursing home care.* Chicago: University of Chicago Press.

Direction Générale de la Santé France.1989. Compte rendu et évaluation d'une expérience de formation des travaileurs sociaux sur la SIDA. Abstracts: Le Conférence Internationale sur le SIDA: Le défi scientifique et social, 4–9 juin, Montréal, Québec. Ottawa: le Centre de recherches pour le dévelopment international.

Dobson, S., and D. E. Smith, eds. 2001. *Institutional ethnography,* special edition. *Studies in Cultures, Organizations, and Societies* 7(2).

Eastwood, L. 2000. Textual mediation in the international forest policy negotiation process. Paper presented at the conference "Making Links: New Research in Institutional Ethnography," May, Ontario Institute for Studies in Education, Toronto.

Eastwood, Lauren E. 2005. *The social organization of policy: An institutional ethnography of UN forest deliberations.* New York: Routledge.

Emerson, R., R. Fretz, and L. Shaw. 1995. *Writing ethnographic field notes.* Chicago: University of Chicago Press.

Evenson, B. 2003. Children of single parents suffer poorer health: Study. Eight years of research. *National Post* (Retrieved Friday, January 24, 2003, from http://fact.on.ca/news/news0301/np030124.htm).

Fietz, Margaret. 1989. Children with AIDS in need of care and protection. *The Social Worker/Le Travailleur social* 57(1) Spring.

Fisher, S., and A. D. Todd. 1983. *The social organization of doctor-patient communication.* Washington, DC: The Center for Applied Linguistics.

Fraser, Andy. 1987. Dealing with AIDS in the community . . . Avoiding the plague mentality. *Family Service Canada/Services a la famille-Canada* 6(4) December: 1–3.

Furstenberg, A. L., and M. Meltzer Olson. 1984. Social work and AIDS. *Social Work in Health Care* 9(4) Summer: 45–62.

Garfinkel, H. 1967. *Studies in ethnomethodology,* Englewood Cliffs, NJ: Prentice Hall.

Golombok, S. 2000. *What really counts?* London: Routledge.

Goulden, Peter Todd, et al. 1984. AIDS and community supportive services: Understanding and management of psychological needs. *Medical Journal of Australia* 141(9) October: 582–586.

Grahame, K. M. 1998. Asian women, job training, and the social organization of immigrant labor markets. *Qualitative Sociology* 21: 75–90.

———. 1999. State, community and Asian immigrant women's work: A study in labor market organization. PhD dissertation, University of Toronto.

Grahame, P. R. 1998. Ethnography, institutions, and the social organization of knowledge. *Human Studies* 21: 347–360.

———. 1999. Doing qualitative research: Three problematics. *Discourse of Sociological Practice* 2(1): 4–10.

Graveline, F. J. 1998. *Circle works: Transforming eurocentric consciousness.* Halifax, NS: Fernwood.

Green, B. 1983. *Knowing the poor: A study in textual reality construction.* London: Routledge and Kegan Paul.

Griffith, A. I. 1984. Ideology, education, and single parent families: The normative ordering of families through schooling. PhD dissertation, University of Toronto.

———. 1992. Educational policy as text and action. *Educational Policy* 6: 415–428.

———. 1995. Mothering, schooling and children's development. In *Knowledge, experience, and ruling relations: Studies in the social organization of knowledge*, ed. M. Campbell and A. Manicom. Toronto: University of Toronto Press.

———. 1998. Educational restructuring in Ontario. Paper presented at the conference "Exploring the Restructuring and Transformation of Institutional Processes: Applications of Institutional Ethnography," October, York University, Toronto.

Griffith, A. I., and D. E. Smith. 1987. Constructing cultural knowledge: Mothering as discourse. *Women and education: A Canadian perspective*, ed. J. Gaskell and A. McLaren. Calgary, AB: Detselig.

———. 2005. *Mothering for schooling.* New York: Routledge.

Gubrium, Jaber, and James Holstein. 1997. *The new language of qualitative method.* Oxford: Oxford University Press.

Handelman, D., and E. Leyton. 1978. *Bureaucracy and worldview: Studies in the logic of official interpretation.* Institute of Social and Economic Research, Memorial University of Newfoundand.

Hanohano, P. 2001. Restoring the circle: Education for culturally responsible native families. PhD dissertation, University of Alberta, Edmonton.

Hanson, S. 1995. *Single parent families: Diversity, myths and realities.* New York: Haworth Press

Hardey, M., and G. Crow, eds. 1992. *Lone parenthood: Coping with constraints and making opportunities.* Toronto: University of Toronto Press.

Harvey, David. 1996. *Justice, nature and the geography of difference.* Oxford: Blackwell Publishers Ltd.

Hassen, P. 1993. *Rx for hospitals: New hope for Medicare.* Toronto: Stoddart.

Heatherington, E. M., G. Clingempeel, and E. R. Anderson. 1992. *Coping with marital transitions: A family systems perspective.* Chicago: University of Chicago Press.

Hick, S. F. 1991. An ethnography of an Ontario welfare office: The reproduction of labour market relations. PhD dissertation, University of Toronto.

Hudson, J. 1993. *Single parent families: Perspectives on research and policy.* Toronto: Thompson Educational Publishing.

Humphreys, David. 1996. *Forest politics: The evolution of international cooperation.* London: Earthscan Publications.

IAITPTF. 2005. *Expert meeting: Traditional forest-related knowledge and the implementation of related international commitments: Summary report.* International Alliance of Indigenous and Tribal People of the Tropical Forests.

Ibrahim, S. 2004. Science writing and science writers: An ethnographic examination into the creative practice of writing science for the public. Unpublished paper. Toronto: York University

Isaacs, Gordon. 1985. Crisis psychotherapy with persons experiencing the AIDS related complex. *Crisis Intervention* 14(4): 115–121.

Jackson, N. 1995. These things just happen: Talk, text, and curriculum reform. In *Knowledge, experience, and ruling relations: Studies in the social organization of knowledge*, ed. M. Campbell and A. Manicom, 164–180. Toronto: University of Toronto Press.

Jensen, A., and L. McKee, eds. 2003. *Children and the changing family: Between transformation and negotiation.* New York: Routledge Falmer.

Kaetz, D. 1989. Living with HIV. *The social worker/Le Travailleur social* 57(1) Spring: 65–68.

Kelly, Jeffrey A. 1989. *The AIDS crisis: psychological and social intervention.* New York: Plenum Press.

Khayatt, D. 1995. Compulsory heterosexuality: Schools and lesbian students. In *Knowledge, experience, and ruling relations: Studies in the social organization of knowledge*, ed. M. Campbell and A. Manicom, 149–163. Toronto: University of Toronto Press.

King, Alan J. C., et al. 1988. *Canada youth and AIDS study*, Kingston, ON: Queen's University (Social Program Evaluation Group).

Kinsman, G. 1989. Official discourse as sexual regulation: The social organization of the sexual policing of gay men. PhD dissertation, University of Toronto.

———. 1996. *The Regulation of desire: Homo and hetero sexualities.* Montreal: Black Rose.

Kinsman, G., and P. Gentile. 1998. In the interests of the slate: The anti-gay, anti-lesbian national security campaign in Canada. Preliminary research report, Laurentian University, Sudbury, ON.

Lane, S. R., and R. N. Levine. 1990. Caring for homeless people with HIV disease. *Focus: A Guide to AIDS Research and Counselling* 5(5) April: 1–2.

Lareau, A. 1989. *Home advantage: Social class and parental intervention in elementary education.* London and New York: Falmer Press.

———. 2003. *Unequal childhoods: Class, race and family life.* Berkeley: University of California Press.

Lee, J., et al. 1988. *Counselling and education for the prevention of AIDS: A training course for health and social service workers.* New York: City University of New York (Center for Community Action to Prevent AIDS).

Lewis, L. 1988. Housing people with HIV dementia: No specialized programs, but communities are coping. *AIDS Patient Care* June: 35–37.

Lofland, J., and L. H. Lofland. 1995. *Analyzing social settings: A guide to qualitative observation and analysis*, 3rd edition. Belmont, CA: Wadsworth.

Lopez. D. J., and G. Getzel. 1984. Helping gay AIDS patients in crisis. *Social Casework: The Journal of Contemporary Social Work* 65(9) September: 387–394.

Luken, P. C., and S. Vaughan. 1991. Elderly women living alone: Theoretical and methodological considerations from a feminist perspective. *Housing and Society* 18: 37–48.

———. 1996. Narratives of living alone: Elderly women's experiences and the textual discourse on housing. Paper presented at the annual meeting of the Society for the Study of Social Problems, New York.

———. 1998. Talk about race and housing. Paper presented at the annual meeting of the Society for the Study of Social Problems, San Francisco.

———. 2003. Living alone in old age: Institutionalized discourse and women's knowledge. *Sociological Quarterly* 44: 109–131.

———. (Forthcoming). . . . to be a genuine home maker *in your own home:* Gender and familial relations in state housing practices. *Social Forces,* 17–22.

Lynch, M. 1983. Discipline and the material forms of images: An analysis of scientific visibility. Paper presented at the Canadian Sociology and Anthropology annual meeting, Vancouver, BC.

Lynch, M., and D. Bogen. 1996. *The spectacle of history: Speech, text, and memory at the Iran-Contra hearings.* Durham, NC: Duke University Press.

Makoul, G., P. Arntson, and T. Schofield. 1995. Health promotion in primary care: Physician–patient communication and decision making about prescription medications. *Social Science & Medicine* 41(9): 1241–1254.

Manicom, A. 1995. What's health got to do with it! Class, gender, and teachers' work. In *Knowledge, experience, and ruling relations: Studies in the social organization of knowledge,* ed. M. Campbell and A. Manicom, 135–148. Toronto: University of Toronto Press,

Marx, K., and F. Engels. 1976. *The German ideology,* Moscow: Progress Publishers.

Mathews, F., J. Radford, and D. Weatherbee. 1991. *HIV+ Youth: A needs assessment study.* Toronto: Central Toronto Youth Services.

McAlary, D. 2003. Swedish study: Kids of single parents more likely to suffer mental health problems. *Voice of America News,* (January 24, 2003, 05:20 UTC) Washington, DC. (Retrieved from http://fact.on.ca/news/news0301/voa030124.htm)

McCoy, L. 1987. Looking at wedding pictures: A study in the social organization of knowledge. MA thesis, University of Toronto.

———. 1995. Activating the photographic text. In *Knowledge, experience, and ruling relatioms: Studies in the social organization of knowledge,* ed. M. Campbell and A. Manicom, 181–192. Toronto: University of Toronto Press.

———. 1998. Producing 'what the deans know': Cost accounting and the restructuring of post-secondary education. *Human Studies* 21: 395–418.

———. 1999. Accounting discourse and textual practices of ruling: A study of institutional transformation and restructuring in higher education. PhD dissertation, University of Toronto.

———. 2005. HIV+ patients and the doctor-patient relationship: Perspectives from the margins. *Qualitative Health Research* 15(6): 791–806.

McKendy, J. 1999. Bringing stories back in: Agency and responsibility of men incarcerated for violent offences. Unpublished manuscript, St. Thomas University, NB.

Mead, G. H. 1962. *Mind, self and society from the perspective of a behaviorist.* Chicago: University of Chicago Press.

Mending the Sacred Hoop. 2002. *Community based analysis of the U.S. legal system's interventions in domestic abuse cases,* Final Report to the National Institute of Justice, Duluth, MN: Minnesota Program Devlopment, Inc.

Meyer, M. 1998. *Native Hawaiian epistemology: Contemporary narratives*, PhD dissertation, Harvard Graduate School of Education.

Montour-Agnus, P. 1995. *Thunder in my soul: A Mohawk woman speaks.* Halifax, NS: Fernwood Press.

Mueller, A. 1995. Beginning in the standpoint of women: An investigation of the gap between *Cholas* and "Women of Peru." In *Knowledge, experience, and ruling relations: Studies in the social organization of knowledge,* ed. M. Campbell and A. Manicom, 96–107. Toronto: University of Toronto Press.

Mulkay, M. 1981. Action and belief, or scientific discourse: A possible way of ending intellectual vassalage in social studies of science. *Philosophy of the Social Sciences* 11: 163–171.

Mykhalovskiy, E. 2000. Knowing health care/governing health care: Exploring health services research as social practice. PhD dissertation, York University.

———. 2004. Rethinking decision making: Contributions from research on the health-work of people living with HIV. Paper presented at American Sociological Association annual meeting, San Francisco.

Mykhalovskiy, Eric, and Kathryn Church. (Forthcoming). Of t-shirts and ontologies: Celebrating George Smith's pedagogical legacies. In *Sociology for changing the world,* ed. Gary Kinsman.

Mykhalovskiy, E., and L. McCoy. 2002. Troubling ruling discourses of health: Using institutional ethnography in community-based research. *Critical Public Health* 12: 17–37.

Mykhalovskiy, E., L. McCoy, and M. Bresalier, 2004. Compliance/adherence, HIV, and the critique of medical power. *Social Theory and Health* 2(4): 315–340.

Mykhalovskiy, E., and G. W. Smith. 1994. *Getting hooked up: A report on the barriers people living with HIV/AIDS pace accessing social services.* Toronto: Ontario Institute for Studies in Education.

Naples, N. 1997. Contested needs: Shifting the standpoint on rural economic development. *Feminist Economics* 3: 63–98.

———. 1998. Bringing everyday life to policy analysis: The case of white rural women negotiating college and welfare. *Journal of Poverty* 2: 23–53.

———. 2002 Negotiating the politics of experiential learning in women's studies: Lessons from the community action project. In *Women's studies on its own,* ed. Robyn Wiegman. Durham, NC: Duke University Press.

National Lawyers Guild AIDS Network. 1990. Housing and the AIDS epidemic. *The Exchange* 12, April: 1–8.

New York State Department of Social Services. 1989a. DSS EXploring AIDS housing alternatives for homelesss adults. *AIDS Update* 2(3) Spring: 11–12.

———. 1989b. Living at Home: The preferred option. *AIDS Update* 2(3) Spring: 8–9.

———. 1989c. Toward AIDS awareness in housing. *AIDS Update* 2(3) Spring: 1,3.

Ng, R. 1981. Constituting ethnic phenomenon: An account from the perspective of immigrant women. *Canadian Ethnic Studies/Etudes Ethniques au Canada* 13(1): 97–108

———. 1995. Multiculturalism as ideology: A textual analysis. In *knowledge, experience, and ruling relations: Studies in the social organization of knowledge*, ed. M. Campbell and A. Manicom, 35–48. Toronto: University of Toronto Press.

———. 1996. *The politics of community services: Immigrant women, class and state.* Halifax, NS: Fernwood.

———. 1999. Homeworking: Dream realized or freedom constrained? The globalized reality of immigrant garment workers. *Canadian Woman Studies* 19(3): 110–114.

Nicholson, L. 1990. *Feminism/postmodernism.* New York: Routledge.

Offord, D. R., N. Abrams, N. Allen, and M. Poushinsky. 1979. Broken homes, parental psychiatric illness and female delinquency. *American Journal of Orthopsychiatry,* 49(2): 252–264.

O'Neil, B., and Josephine Naidoo. 1990. Social services to lesbian and gay men in Ontario: Unrecognized needs. *The Social Worker/Le Travailleur social* 58(3) Fall: 101–104.

———. n. d. Social services to homosexuals in Ontario: Major issues and annotated bibliography (available from B. O'Neil. Faculty of Social Work, Wilfrid Laurier University, 75 University Ave. W., Waterloo, ON N2L 3C5).

Parada, H. 1998. Restructuring families and children in the child welfare bureaucracy. Paper presented at the conference "Exploring the Restructuring and Transformation of Institutional Processes: Applications of Institutional Ethnography," October, York University, Toronto.

———. 2002. The restructuring of the child welfare system in Ontario: A study in the social organization of knowledge. PhD dissertation, University of Toronto.

Peacock, T., L. George, A. Wilson, A. Bergstrom, E. Pence, and associated contributors. 2000. *Community based analysis of the U.S. legal system's intervention in domestic abuse cases involving Indigenous women*, Duluth, MN: Mending the Sacred Hoop/Minnesota Program Development Inc.

Pence, E. 1996. Safety for battered women in a textually mediated legal system. PhD dissertation, University of Toronto.

———. 2001. Safety for battered women in a textually mediated legal system. *Studies in Cultures, Organizations, and Societies* 7(2): 199–229

Pence, E. and K. Lizdas. 1998. *The Duluth safety and accountability audit: A guide to assessing responses to domestic violence*, Duluth, MN: Domestic Abuse Intervention Project.

Pence, E., and M. Paymer. 1993. *Education groups for men who batter: The Duluth model.* New York: Springer Publishing Company.

Pence E., and M. Shepard. 1999. *Coordinating community responses to domestic violence: Lessons from Duluth.* Thousand Oaks, CA: Sage.

Popay, J., L. Rimmer, and C. Rossiter. 1983. Lone parents and their children. In *One parent families: Parents, children and public policy*. London: Study Commission on the Family.

Price, J. 1994. Lean production at Suzuki and Toyota: A historical perspective. *Studies in Political Economy* 45, Fall: 66–99.

Price, M. E. 1989. *Shattered mirrors: Our search for identity and community*. Cambridge, MA: Harvard University Press.

Radford, J., et al. 1989. *Street youth and AIDS*. Kingston, ON: Queen's University (Social Program Evaluation Group).

Rae-Grant, Q. 1976. New family structures and the latency child. *Canadian Psychological Association Journal* 21(4): 197–198.

Rankin, J. H. 1983. The family context of delinquency. *Social Problems*, 30(4): 466–476.

Rankin, J. M. 1998. Health care reform and the restructuring of nursing in British Columbia. Paper presented at the conference "Exploring the Restructuring and Transformation of Institutional Processes: Applications of Institutional Ethnography," October, York University, Toronto.

———. 2003. "Patient satisfaction: Knowledge for ruling hospital reform—An institutional ethnography." *Nursing Inquiry* 10(1): 57–65.

———. 2004. How nurses practice health care reform: An institutional ethnography. PhD dissertation, University of Victoria.

Rankin, J. M. and M. L. Campbell. 2006. *Managing to nurse: Inside Canada's health care reform*. Toronto: University of Toronto Press.

Reimer, M. 1995. Downgrading clerical work in a textually mediated labour process. In *Knowledge, experience, and ruling relations: Studies in the social organization of knowledge*, ed. M. Campbell and A. Manicom, 193–208. Toronto: University of Toronto Press.

Richardson, T. R. 1989. *The century of the child: The mental hygiene movement and social policy in the United States and Canada*. Albany, NY: SUNY Press.

Ridzi, Frank. 2003. Processing private lives in public: An institutional ethnography of front-line welfare intake staff post welfare reform. PhD dissertation, Maxwell School of Citizenship and Public Affairs, Syracuse University, NY.

Ross, E. 2003. One-parent children at higher risk, study finds. *Toronto Star* (January 24) (Retrieved from http://fact.on.ca/news/news0301-ts030124).

Rowlingson, K., and McKay, N. 2002. *Lone parent families: Gender, class and state*. New York: Prentice Hall.

Rukszto, K. 1994. Grade appeals procedures as co-ordinating courses of action, unpublished paper. Department of Sociology, York University.

Ryan, W. J. 1989. AIDS: The community response. *The Social Worker/Le Travailleur social* 57(1) Spring: 53–56.

Schmazi, R. F., and A. J. Nahmias, eds. 1988. *AIDS in children adolescents and heterosexual adults*. New York: Elsevier Science Publishing Co.

Schutz, A. 1964. *Collected papers II: Studies in social theory*. Ed. A. Brodersen. The Hague, Netherlands: Martinus Nijhoff.

Schwartzman, H. B. 1993. *Ethnography in organizations*. Newbury Park, CA: Sage Publications.

Scott, J. 1991. The evidence of experience. *Critical Inquiry* 17(3): 773–797.

Silverman, D., and J. Jones. 1976. *Organization work: The language of grading and the grading of language.* London: Collier Macmillan.

Smart, C., B. Neale, and A. Wade, eds. 2001. *The changing experience of childhood: Families and divorce.* Malden, MA: Blackwell.

Smith, D. E. 1973. The social construction of documentary reality. *Sociological Inquiry* 44: 257–268.

———. 1974. The ideological practice of sociology. *Catalyst,* no. 5: 39–54.

———. 1974b. Women's perspective as a radical critique of sociology. *Sociological Inquiry* 44: 7–13.

———. 1977. *Feminism and Marxism: A place to begin, a way to go.* Vancouver: New Star Books.

———. 1979. A sociology for women. In *The prism of sex,* ed. J. Sherman and E. T. Beck. Madison: University of Wisconsin Press.

———. 1981. The active text: A textual analysis of the relations of public textual discourse. Paper presented at the World Congress of Sociology, Mexico.

———. 1983. No one commits suicide: Textual analysis of ideological practices. *Human Studies* 6: 309–359.

———. 1984. Textually-mediated social organization. *International Social Science Journal* 36(1): 59–75.

———. 1987. *The everyday world as problematic: A feminist sociology.* Boston: Northeastern University Press.

———. 1990a. *The conceptual practices of power: A feminist sociology of knowledge.* Boston: Northeastern University Press.

———. 1990b. *Texts, facts, and femininity: Exploring the relations of Ruling.* London: Routledge.

———. 1990c. No one commits suicide. In *The conceptual practices of power: A feminist sociology of knowledge.* Toronto: University of Toronto Press.

———. 1992. Sociology from women's experience: A reaffirmation. *Journal of Sociological Theory* 10(1): 88–98

———. 1993a. The standard North American family: SNAF as an ideological code. *Journal of Family Issues. (Special issue: Rethinking family as a social form,* ed. Jay Gubrium), 14(2): 50–65.

———. 1993b. High noon in textland: A critique of Clough. *The Sociological Quarterly* 34:183–192.

———. 1996a. The relations of ruling: A feminist inquiry. *Studies in Cultures, Organizations and Societies* 2: 171–90.

———. 1996b. Telling the truth after postmodernism. *Symbolic Interaction* 19(3): 171–202.

———. 1998. The underside of schooling: restructuring, privatization, and women's unpaid work. *Journal for a Just and Caring Education (Special issue: Mothering, educating and schooling,* ed. A. Griffith and S. Schecter) 4(1): 11–29.

———. 1999. *Writing the social: Theory, critique, investigations.* Toronto: University of Toronto Press.

———. 2000. Report: Analyzing court psychologists' evaluations of women in relation to custody cases, Duluth, MN: Praxis International, Inc.

———. 2002. Report: Analyzing court psychologists' evaluations of women in relation to custody cases, Duluth, MN: Praxis International.

———. 2001. Texts and the ontology of institutions and organizations. *Studies in Cultures, Organizations, and Societies* 7(2): 159–198.

———. 2002. Institutional ethnography. In *Qualitative research in action*, ed. T. May, 17–52. London: Sage.

———. 2005. *Institutional Ethnography: A sociology for people.* Lanham, MD: AltaMira Press.

Smith, D. E., and A. I. Griffith. 1990. Coordinating the uncoordinated: Mothering, schooling, and social class. In *Perspectives on social problems: A research annual*, ed. G. Miller and J. A. Holstein, 25–44. Greenwich, CT: JAL.

———. 2004. *Mothering for schooling.* New York: Routledge.

Smith, D. E., L. McCoy, and P. Bourne. 1995. Girls and schooling: Their own critique. Gender and Schooling Paper No. 2. Centre for Women's Studies in Education, Ontario Institute for Studies in Education.

Smith, D. E., and G. W. Smith. 1990. Re-organizing the jobs skills training relation: From 'human capital' to 'human resources'. In *Education for work, education as work: Canada's changing community colleges*, ed. J. Muller, 171–196. Toronto: Garamond.

Smith, G. W. 1988. Policing the gay community: An inquiry into textually-mediated social relations. *International Journal of the Sociology of Law* 16: 163–83.

———. 1990. Political activist as ethnographer. *Social Problems* 37(4): 629–648.

———. 1995. Assessing Treatments: Managing the AIDS Epidemic in Ontario. In *Knowledge, experience and ruling relations: Studies in the social organization of knowledge*, ed. M. Campbell and A. Manicom, 18-34. Toronto: University of Toronto Press.

———. 1998. The ideology of 'fag': The school experience of gay students. *Sociological Quarterly* 39(2): 309–335.

Snowden. D., and D. F. Cassidy, eds. 1989. *AIDS: A handbook for professionals.* Carswell: New Book.

Spradley, J. 1979. *The ethnographic interview.* New York: Holt, Rinehart and Winston.

Steinhauer, D. 1997. Native education: A learning journey. MA thesis, University of Alberta.

Stock, A. 2000. An ethnography of assessment in elementary schools. EdD dissertation, University of Toronto.

Suchman, L. A. 1988. Representing practice in cognitive science. *Human Studies* 11(2–3): 305–325.

Swift, Karen. 1995. *Manufacturing bad mothers: A critical perspective.* Toronto: University of Toronto Press.

Townsend, E. A. 1996. Institutional ethnography: A method for analyzing practice. *Occupational Therapy Journal of Research* 16: 179–199.

———. 1998. *Good intentions overruled: A critique of empowerment in the routine organization of mental health services.* Toronto: University of Toronto Press.

Tresse, G. G. 1985. Psychosocial issues related to the diagnosis of AIDS. In *Lesbian and gay issues: A resource manual for social workers*, ed. H. Hidalgo et al. Silver Spring, MD: National Association of Social Workers.

Turner, S. M. 1995. Rendering the site developable: Texts and local government decision making in land use planning. In *Knowledge, experience and ruling relations: Studies in the social organization of knowledge*, ed. M. Campbell and A. Manicom, 234–248. Toronto: University of Toronto Press.

———. 2001. Texts and the institutions of municipal planning government: The power of texts in the public process of land development. *Studies in Cultures, Organizations, and Societies* 7(2): 297–325.

———. 2003. Municipal planning, land development and environmental intervention: An institutional ethnography. PhD dissertation, University of Toronto.

Ueda, Y. 1995. Corporate wives: Gendered education of their children. In *Knowledge, experience, and ruling relations: Studies in the social organization of knowledge*, ed. M. Campbell and A. Manicom, 122–134. Toronto: University of Toronto Press.

United Nations. 1989. *Resolution adopted by the United Nations General Assembly: United Nations conference on environment and development.* (A/RES/44/228).

———. 1992. *Non-legally binding authoritative statement of principles for a global consensus on the management, conservation and sustainable development of all types of forests.* (A/CONF.151/26 Vol.III).

United Nations Consultative Committee on Administrative Questions. 1999. *The continuing process of management and administrative reform in the UN system of organizations.* Document prepared for the United Nations Office of Inter-Agency Affairs.

U.S. Department of Justice [USDOJ]. 2000. *Full report of the prevalence, incidence, and consequences of violence against women: Findings from the national violence against women survey.* NCJ 183781 Available: http://www.ncjrs.org/pdffiles1/nij/183781.pdf.

Vaughan, S., and P. C. Luken. 1997. Here and there/now and then: The social organization of women's moving experiences. Paper presented at the annual meeting of the Pacific Sociological Association, San Diego, CA.

Visvanathan, Shiv. 1991. Mrs. Brundtland's disenchanted cosmos. *Alternatives* 16: 377–384.

Volosinov, V. I. 1973. *Marxism and the philosophy of language.* Trans. I. R. Titunik. New York: Academic Press.

Vo-Quang, Edouard. 1998. L is academically prepared: A textual analysis of the 'Assessment Report' on an applicant to graduate studies. Unpublished paper, University of Victoria.

Waitzkin, H. 1991. *The politics of medical encounters: How patients and doctors deal with social problems.* New Haven, CT, and London: Yale University Press.

Walker, G. A. 1990. *Family violence and the women's movement: The conceptual politics of struggle.* Toronto: University of Toronto Press.

Walker, Gillian. 1995. Violence and the relations of ruling: Lessons from the battered women's movement. In *Knowledge, experience, and ruling relations: Studies in the social organization of knowledge*, ed. M. Campbell and A. Manicom, 65–79. Toronto: University of Toronto Press.

Walkerdine, V. 1984. Developmental psychology and the child centred pedagogy. In *Changing the subject: Psychology, social regulation and subjectivity*, ed. J. Henriques, W. Holloway, C. Urwin, C. Venn, and V. Walkerdine. London: Methuen.

Walters, J., and L. H. Walters. 1980. Parent-child relationship: A review 1970–79. *Journal of Marriage and the Family* 142(4): 807–822.

Weber, M. 1978. *Economy and society.* Ed. Guenther Roth and Claus Wittich. Trans. E. Fishoff et al. New York: Bedminster Press. Reissued at Berkeley: University of California Press.

Weitoft, G. R., A. Hjern, B. Haglund, and M. Rosén. 2003. Mortality, severe morbidity, and injury in children living with single parents in Sweden: A population-based study. *The Lancet* 361, 9354, p. 289.

Wilson, A. 1997. Research dreams and nightmares. Unpublished paper, Harvard Graduate School of Education.

———. 1998. How our stories are told. *Canadian Journal of Native Education* 22(2): 274–278.

———. 2001. Dashing berdache—the two-spirit race. Qualifying paper, Harvard Graduate School of Education.

———. 2004. *Living well: Aboriginal women, cultural identity and wellness.* Winnipeg, MB: Manitoba Aboriginal Women's Health Community Committee and the Prairie Women's Health Centre of Excellence.

Wilson, S., and P. Wilson. 1998. Relational accountability to all our relations. *Canadian Journal of Native Education* 22(2): 155–158.

———. 1999. Taking responsibility: What follows relational accountability? *Canadian Journal of Native Education* 23(2): 137–139.

Zimmerman, D. H. 1974. Fact as a practical accomplishment. In *Ethnomethodology,* ed. Roy Turner. Harmondsworth, UK: Penguin Books.

Index

Page numbers appearing in *italics* refer to figures.

About the Editor and Contributors

Dorothy E. Smith is professor emerita in the Department of Sociology and Equity Studies in Education of the University of Toronto and adjunct professor, Department of Sociology, University of Victoria (Victoria, British Columbia). She has been preoccupied for the past thirty or so years with developing the implications of women's standpoint for sociology, problematizing the objectified forms of organization and social relations characteristic of contemporary society, and focusing more recently on the significance of texts for the organization of power. Her published books are *Women Look at Psychiatry: I'm Not Mad, I'm Angry* with Sara David, editor; *Feminism and Marxism: A Place to Begin, a Way to Go*; *Women and the Canadian Labour Force* with Naomi Hersom, editor; *El Mundo Silenciado de las Mujeres*; *The Everyday World as Problematic: A Feminist Sociology*; *The Conceptual Practices of Power: A Feminist Sociology of Knowledge*; *Texts, Facts, and Femininity: Exploring the Relations of Ruling*; *Eine Soziologie für Frauen*; *Writing the Social: Critique, Theory and Investigations*; *Mothering for Schooling* with Alison Griffith; and *Institutional Ethnography: A Sociology for People.*

Marie L. Campbell, whose academic career followed a number of years in the nursing profession, studied with Dorothy E. Smith, first at UBC, then at OISE/University of Toronto. Her PhD research was an ethnographic-based study of changes in the management of hospital nursing in the early 1980s—focusing specifically on technologies being introduced then for determining objectively how much work (in units of time) is represented in an assignment of patients. From 1990 until retirement in 2002, she taught at the University of Victoria where she was a founding faculty member of an interdisciplinary graduate program for nurses, social workers, and child and youth care professionals. She is currently professor emerita of the Faculty of Human Studies and Development at the University of Victoria.

Her research has been focused primarily on organizational analysis—studying how work in the human services is socially organized, conducted, and managed. Unlike most organizational analyses, these studies address issues "from the standpoint" of those who know the work experientially—either from doing it or having it done to them. Publications include studies arising in child protection agencies, nursing homes, hospitals, and community health agencies and include a book that explains how she taught institutional ethnography to graduate students: *Mapping Social Relations: A Primer in Doing Institutional Ethnography* with F. Gregor; an edited collection *Knowledge, Experience and Social Relations: Studies in the Social Organization of Knowledge* with A. Manicom; and articles of which "Textual Accounts, Ruling Action: The Intersection of Knowledge and Power in the Routine Conduct of Community Nursing Work" in *Studies in Cultures, Organizations and Societies*, is an example. A new book with coauthor Janet Rankin, *Managing to Nurse: Inside Canada's Health Reform*, was published in early 2006.

Marjorie L. DeVault is professor of sociology and a member of the Women's Studies Program at Syracuse University. Her research has explored the "invisible work" in women's household and family lives and in the historically female field of dietetics and nutrition education. Trained in the Chicago School fieldwork tradition and deeply influenced by the feminism of the 1970s, she has written broadly on qualitative and feminist methodologies. Since the 1980s she has been learning about institutional ethnography (IE) from Dorothy Smith and others in the "IE network," and she works with graduate students on IE projects and maintains an IE website at http://faculty.maxwell.syr.edu/mdevault. She is the author of *Feeding the Family: The Social Organization of Caring as Gendered Work* and *Liberating Method: Feminism and Social Research.*

Timothy Diamond is a research associate at the School of Disability Studies, Ryerson University in Toronto. He received his PhD in sociology from Ohio State University. His best-known work is *Making Gray Gold: Narratives of Nursing Home Care.* The book, on which the article in this volume (chapter 3) is based, received the Humanist Sociology Annual Book Award, and the American Sociological Association's Gerontology Section Book Award, and was a finalist for the C. Wright Mills Award from the Society for the Study of Social Problems.

Currently, Diamond's research concerns the coordination of activities, local and translocal, between personal support workers and persons with disabilities. The research is framed as an institutional ethnography. It is funded by Social Development Canada.

Lauren E. Eastwood is currently an assistant professor of sociology at the State University of New York, Plattsburgh, where she teaches courses in environmental sociology, gender, and social theory. Her area of expertise is in sociology of the environment, with an emphasis on international environmental policy. She recently published *The Social Organization of Policy: An Institutional Ethnography of UN Forest Policy Deliberations*, in which she analyzes nongovernmental participation in the negotiation of forest policy through the UN. She is currently continuing this research, as well as beginning to investigate UN-based policymaking related to Indigenous Peoples, and the social responses to current energy policies in the Western United States.

Alison I. Griffith is a professor in the Faculty of Education at York University, Toronto. She is the chair of the institutional ethnography division of the Society for the Study of Social Problems (2005–2007) and the graduate program director (2006–2009) in the Faculty of Education at York University. She has published extensively in scholarly journals in the areas of institutional ethnography in education, mothering work for schooling, and the family-school relation. Her books include *Families and Schools: A Chorus of Voices in Education* with E. St. John and L. Allen-Haynes; *Education, Equity and Globalisation* with C. Reynolds; and *Mothering for Schooling* with D. E. Smith.

Liza McCoy is assistant professor of sociology at the University of Calgary. She did her MA and PhD with Dorothy Smith at the Ontario Institute for Studies in Education. Her broad area of interest is the social organization of knowledge, which she has been exploring through institutional ethnographic studies in the fields of photographic representation, education, health, and employment. Recent research has examined restructuring in higher education and the health work of living with HIV/AIDS (with Eric Mykhalovskiy). Her current research, funded by the Social Sciences and Humanities Research Council of Canada, is investigating employment services for new immigrants with backgrounds in nonregulated professional occupations.

Eric Mykhalovskiy is an assistant professor in the Department of Sociology, York University. His primary research interest is the social organization of health knowledges. His recent research includes studies of formal discourses of health knowledge, in particular health services research and evidence-based medicine, published in such journals as *Social Science & Medicine* and *Health*, as well as studies of the interface of biomedical and experiential knowledges in the context of HIV/AIDS, published in *Critical Public Health*, *Social Theory & Health*, and elsewhere. He is currently principal investigator of a study funded by the Social Sciences and Humanities Research Council of Canada on the gap between lay and biomedical knowledge in HIV/AIDS. He is also engaged in collaborative research projects on interspecies health and on global public health surveillance.

Ellen Pence is the director of Praxis International, an education and research organization focusing on issues of violence against women and children. Using institutional ethnography, Ellen has developed an interagency method of analyzing problematic practices in institutional responses to victims of abuse. The process she has developed, called the Praxis Safety and Accountability Audit, was significantly influenced by the research project she and Wilson describe in chapter 11. Ellen is the author with Michael Paymer of *Education Groups for Men Who Batter: The Duluth Mode*; and, with Melanie Shepard, of *Coordinating Community Responses to Domestic Violence: Lessons from Duluth*. Ellen was a student of Dorothy Smith and received her PhD in 1996 from the University of Toronto.

George W. Smith took his master's degree at the University of Michigan with a thesis on Charles S. Peirce's pragmatism. He taught for many years after that at both the high school and university levels. He turned to sociology in 1977. While in the doctoral program in sociology at the Ontario Institute for Studies in Education (OISE), he was appointed a research associate working with Dorothy Smith on a number of projects, a position he held until shortly before his death from AIDS in 1994.

George was active in gay politics in Toronto, where he wrote for gay publications and helped found several gay community organizations. He was committed to connecting sociology to political action in the gay community and political activism to sociology, a project he described in one of his best known sociological publications, "Political Activist as Ethnographer" (Smith 1990). He also published other fine analysis focused on gay issues, including "Policing the Gay Community: An Inquiry into Textually Mediated Relations," "Accessing Treatments: Managing the AIDS Epidemic in Ontario," and "The Ideology of Fag" (published posthumously). In sociology at OISE he was a founding and very influential member of the group that originally developed what later came to be known as institutional ethnography.

Susan Marie Turner is a research program coordinator at the Centre for Families, Work & Well-Being, and a part-time lecturer in the sociology and anthropology department at the University of Guelph. She studied with Dorothy Smith at the Ontario Institute for Studies in Education/University of Toronto and her dissertation, *Municipal Planning, Land Development and Environmental Intervention: An Institutional Ethnography*, won the 2004 OISE/UT Outstanding Thesis of the Year Award. Currently, she is developing applications of her mapping method of analyzing policy processes and discourse practices in a five-year program of community-based research. The Rural Women Making Change Community University Research Alliance, which is using the institutional ethnography approach, is funded by the Social Sciences and Humanities Research Council of Canada. Susan is a partner in Turner Reid Associates in Guelph, Ontario, consulting on communications and organizational change to a range of organizations, government departments, educational institutions, and businesses.

At the time of preparing the research proposal included in this volume, **Doug Weatherbee** was a graduate student at the Ontario Institute for Studies in Education where he later received a master's degree in sociology in education. During this time he was also involved in the community-based response to HIV and AIDS. The research proposal he, George Smith, and Eric Mykhalovskiy prepared as an institutional ethnography was, for Doug, an attempt to link his academic and community work.

Doug has also worked as a program analyst in the Ontario Ministry of Health as a policy advisor for the Ontario Minister of Health and coordinated research in Nova Scotia for the Federal New Democratic Party.

Alex Wilson is a member of the Opaskwayak Cree Nation. Among other publications, she is author of "Research Dreams and Nightmares," "How Our Stories Are Told"; "Dashing Berdache—The Two-Spirit Race," and *Living Well: Aboriginal Women, Cultural Identity and Wellness.* As a member of Mending the Sacred Hoop (comprising Indigenous staff at Minnesota Program Development, Inc.), she was consultant to the Mending the Sacred Hoop project with the National Institute of Justice and coauthored and coordinated the writing of the final research report, *Community Based Analysis of the U.S. Legal System's Intervention in Domestic Abuse Cases Involving Indigenous Women* (see Peacock et al.). She is currently pursuing doctoral studies in education at Harvard University.

Made in the USA
Lexington, KY
26 September 2014